Praise for *LLMs and Generative AI for Healthcare*

A comprehensive view of the potential of AI in the healthcare space, explained in a simple yet powerful way.

—*Ram Viswanathan, CTO-AI, Rackspace Technology*

The authors have undertaken a tour de force exploration of healthcare's future and how the latest AI developments will shape our well-being, diagnoses, and treatments in the coming decades. This book is mandatory reading for anyone interested in how generative AI will change our health—with both opportunities and warnings for the path ahead.

—*Rick Hamilton, CTO, Focused Ultrasound Foundation*

LLMs and Generative AI
for Healthcare
The Next Frontier

Kerrie Holley and Manish Mathur

Beijing · Boston · Farnham · Sebastopol · Tokyo

LLMs and Generative AI for Healthcare

by Kerrie Holley and Manish Mathur

Published by O'Reilly Media, Inc., 1005 Gravenstein Highway North, Sebastopol, CA 95472.

O'Reilly books may be purchased for educational, business, or sales promotional use. Online editions are also available for most titles (*http://oreilly.com*). For more information, contact our corporate/institutional sales department: 800-998-9938 or *corporate@oreilly.com*.

Acquisition Editor: Michelle Smith	**Indexer:** Sue Klefstad
Development Editor: Angela Rufino	**Interior Designer:** David Futato
Production Editor: Aleeya Rahman	**Cover Designer:** Karen Montgomery
Copyeditor: nSight, Inc.	**Illustrator:** Irul (@mwkhoirul)
Proofreader: Helena Stirling	

August 2024:　　　First Edition

Revision History for the First Edition

2024-08-19:　First Release

See *http://oreilly.com/catalog/errata.csp?isbn=9781098160920* for release details.

978-1-098-16092-0

[LSI]

Table of Contents

Introduction

Why We Wrote This Book

In a new era of technologies that will change society and human life, the new synergy between AI and healthcare gradually emerges with new possibilities. *LLMs and Generative AI for Healthcare: The Next Frontier* explores what the future of healthcare may look like with the public awareness and breakthrough capabilities of AI large language models (LLMs) and generative AI.

We understand that a lot of promises have been made on the future of AI in healthcare[1] that have not been kept. Challenges remain to truly make AI transformational for healthcare, but there is no denying the positive impacts of AI in healthcare.[2] As authors and software engineers, we have built and seen the application of various aspects of AI in healthcare, which include machine learning, deep learning, computer vision, and natural language processing. This book is about a future we believe will fully come to fruition in a five- to seven-year time period, with transformational impacts to healthcare.

This is not a technical whitepaper but rather a nontechnical primer or vision guide about what is possible using the capabilities of LLMs. It describes several healthcare use cases that are possible but not yet developed. LLMs enable many challenging and time-consuming healthcare tasks to be easier, faster, and even automatic. The allure of the future for LLMs is not to further automate most of the trivial tasks but eventually address big challenges to make healthcare work for everyone and to make healthcare more efficient, more personalized, and simply better. This is a vision of

---

1 Liz Szabo, "Are Health Care Claims Overblown about Artificial Intelligence?" PBS News, December 30, 2019, *https://www.pbs.org/newshour/health/are-health-care-claims-overblown-about-artificial-intelligence*.

2 "Revolutionizing Healthcare: How Is AI Being Used in the Healthcare Industry?" Lost Angeles Pacific University, December 21, 2023, *https://www.lapu.edu/ai-health-care-industry*.

what is possible in healthcare using AI and LLMs, but it is not a guide on how to build these future LLM solutions.

There are no recipes for LLM development here. This is a guidebook for healthcare companies, organizations, entrepreneurs, and health professionals on understanding and applying LLMs through the depiction of multiple use cases. The healthcare world of data is the most complicated type of problem for data science. Queries are very hard, expertise is required for many unique use cases, critical information can be easily missed, or searches for patient medical data can be like finding a needle in a haystack.

Medical-specific language models like Med-PaLM and general-purpose language models will likely evolve significantly in the next two years, potentially transforming their capabilities and applications in clinical settings. Now is the time to understand and begin to build LLM-based apps and applications for patients, consumers, and clinicians. This journey is not easy! There are several challenges and also significant ethical issues. Should LLMs interfere with the sacred patient-physician relationship, or should they enhance communication and outcomes?

If we solve these challenges, millions of lives can be saved with the utilization of medical LLM apps, transforming healthcare globally. We need better, finely tuned LLM apps for healthcare, with search and conversation modalities that are extensively quality controlled in the real world with real clinical usage. The potential of LLMs in healthcare is boundless. They provide a once-a-century opportunity to finally improve human health and usher in a new era of healthcare delivery. We invite you to join us in imagining what actual AI products and solutions are going to look like in the near future.

There are many stories that inspired this book. One such story is about a young family having their first baby, and like all such families, they were excited. Their obstetrician was quite experienced but unknown to the young couple. The baby's abdomen was swollen from a congenital condition called hydrops. It was a potential birthing disaster. The baby was predictably stuck in the birth canal. We were told this story from the lawyer representing the family and pursuing a case against the obstetrician and her employer, a large healthcare provider.

The provider's obstetrician knew or should have known that a cesarean section would be an infinitely safer option, but went forward with a vaginal delivery. The obstetrician failed to provide the parents with the options or notify them of the risks. At time of delivery, the obstetrician presented a life and death situation for both the mother and the baby. Seconds mattered. The obstetrician removed the baby from the birth canal using forceps by the head, consequently breaking the baby's neck, shoulder, and her arms. The baby was left as a partial quadriplegic with brain damage. A lawsuit was brought describing a litany of medical errors and wrongful conduct by both the provider and its obstetrician.

The provider who employed the obstetrician was accused of not fostering a culture of patient-centered care, one that promotes communication and respects patient's ideas about their treatment options. This is not an isolated story in healthcare, and we can do better.

There are many ways a chatbot powered by an LLM could have assisted the parents. The hypothetical Medical Swiss Army Knife LLM chatbot previewed in Chapter 1 could be trained to scour physician review sites such as Healthgrades, Vitals, and RateMDs, as well as social media sites like Yelp, and then could retrieve and process reviews containing the name of the targeted obstetrician. Scraping and paraphrasing existing bad posts written by upset former patients would be quick and easy.

The LLM could use a sentiment analysis method to automatically assign the reviewed cases to positive, negative, or neutral. Giving the parents a measure of the parental satisfaction with the obstetrician would enable them to use their own judgment when choosing a specialized care provider. The LLM could listen in on conversations between the parents and the obstetrician, and it could inform the parents when clinical guidelines were not being followed. The Medical Sherpa app, a chatbot, would operate as a companion to the parents to both listen to their concerns and make recommendations. These would not be clinical recommendations but would make sure the parents were asking the right questions and being listened to by the obstetrician.

One more story. Gerry, short for Geraldine, is an African American woman who celebrated her 93rd birthday in 2024. She has high blood pressure and type 2 diabetes. Gerry takes two pills every morning: one is an extended-release formula of Metformin (MXR), prescribed for those with diabetes, and the second is for her chronic high blood pressure. Gerry trusts her primary care physician but feels that her doctor does not really know her. She doesn't believe his treatment plan for her accounts for how she is responding.

One weekend, she's talking to her cousin who is a tech guy (not an MD, but he has experience with AI). Gerry explains how she missed taking a dose of one of the medications and noticed the swelling she has been experiencing has subsided. She wonders if one of the medications is causing swelling and if she should stop or change the dosage. Her cousin gently responds to her: "Now, Gerry, as you know, I'm not a physician of any kind and thus my recommendation to you at this time is to check with your primary care doctor before making any changes to your treatment plan."

However, Gerry's cousin realizes that her question isn't a good fit for a typical search-engine query that Gerry might use, and wonders if an LLM chatbot could have been useful in this scenario. Using this conversational medical-centric chatbot might have been able to provide Gerry with a more personalized and context-appropriate answer to her questions about medication adherence. For example, an LLM could provide general information on the importance of adherence to prescribed regimens and the potential risks of discontinuing medications without medical supervision. Such a chatbot could also help Gerry craft questions to ask her doctor at her next appointment, and help Gerry advocate for her health needs. Of course, an LLM chatbot should never replace the care and expertise that a physician provides to Gerry, but it could act as a supplement to that expert care, providing her with a supportive tool to help her engage with health questions.

Patients and consumers need help in navigating healthcare for a number of reasons. We preview several use cases of LLMs in Chapters 3, 4, and 5 that will make healthcare more personalized and be an aid to both clinicians, patients, and consumers. This book hopes to get professionals in the healthcare business to think about the art of what is possible using AI and LLMs.

Who This Book Is For

This book targets a diverse audience yearning to unlock the potential of AI in healthcare. Its pages offer insights for the following:

Doctors and clinicians
> Learn how AI-powered diagnostics illuminate hidden patterns, enabling early interventions and personalized treatment plans. Discover how generative AI helps you craft patient-specific therapies and empowers deeper collaboration with AI colleagues.

Chief medical officers
> Understand the unique capabilities of LLMs and generative AI for healthcare. Delve into various use cases for patient care and clinician decision making and business process automation.

Chief technology officers
> There are myriad compounding challenges facing healthcare and life science companies, making it essential for the CTO to adopt technology to meet patient needs and ultimately transform care delivery.

Clinical leaders
> Learn about LLMs' present and future capabilities and learn about generative AI. Understand how LLMs will transform healthcare for clinicians, patients, and healthcare organizations.

Medical researchers
> Dive into the LLMs and generative AI world to fuel your research with an understanding of emerging use cases. Explore the ethical considerations of AI deployment in clinical trials.

Ethicists
> Navigate the complex ethical landscape of AI in healthcare, and grapple with data privacy issues, algorithmic fairness, and potential biases. Contribute to frameworks and guidelines for responsible development and deployment of AI tools.

Students
> This book is your portal to the future of healthcare. Gain a solid foundation in LLM and generative AI principles and explore their potential to revolutionize diagnosis, treatment, and research. Be inspired by diverse career paths at the intersection of medicine and technology.

Whether you are a seasoned practitioner or a curious student, this book offers a compelling journey into the future of healthcare, where human expertise and AI intelligence converge to heal, empower, and transform.

How This Book Is Organized

The content of this book is structured in seven chapters and is organized as follows—reflecting the distinct characteristics of LLMs and other generative AI models in healthcare and their potential as well as their challenges and applications.

Chapter 1: Doctor's Black Bag

This chapter explores the potential of LLMs and generative AI in healthcare, offering an overview of the promise of LLMs and their use in healthcare. In addition to describing future possibilities of LLMs, this chapter introduces challenges with using LLMs in healthcare.

Chapter 2: Peeking Inside the AI Black Box

Here, readers will learn about the anatomy of an LLM and how LLMs work. Instead of amorphization of LLMs, this chapter helps the reader understand the architecture and basic workings of how LLMs work and generate content.

Chapter 3: Beyond White Coats

This chapter examines how LLMs and generative AI can be used to automate more tasks in healthcare. It examines areas where this technology can be applied to improve operations and patient care.

Chapter 4: LLM and Generative AI's Patient and Clinical Potential

In this chapter, we explore how generative AI can elevate the patient experience and impact clinical decision making: health bot concierges; doctors' notes and doctor visits; health plan wizards; application for common health concerns such as black maternal health; medication reminders; and even oral health. Beyond common health concerns, we'll explore clinical decision support tools, clinical insight bots, and AI curbside physicians. We also can't forget about remote patient monitoring, digital twins, fully automated doctor letters, and the role of generative AI in health equity.

Chapter 5: LLMs in Pharmaceutical R&D, Public Health, and Beyond

This chapter presents the utilization of LLMs in drug discovery, clinical trial design and analysis, and genomic research. Specifically, we discuss the diverse applications of LLMs in pharmaceutical research and development as well as public health and genomics, and we further explore their benefits and potentials.

Chapter 6: Steering the Helm for Ethical Use of LLMs

This chapter focuses on the question of how LLMs used in healthcare can be developed in a responsible manner and designed to maximize positive impact. It begins with a discussion of what we mean by a "positive AI imaginary" and goes on to describe the ethical considerations surrounding LLMs, including bias, privacy, and the risk of illicit uses. It also discusses some strategies for dealing with these issues (e.g., monitoring LLM behavior, securing and protecting privacy, policies to enable ethical uses of LLMs, etc.). It discusses "AI and the Paperclip Problem" (i.e., alignment), which states that we must make sure that the goals of AI are aligned with human goals.

Chapter 7: Objects Are Closer Than They Appear

The final chapter provides a peek into the future of LLMs, including a discussion of the singularity and the potential for AGI to evolve. The final section is titled "Whispers of Tomorrow," which provides five predictions of future LLMs and how they could affect our healthcare and society. Through this diverse collection of cases, the book provides a holistic view of the present reality and the future opportunities of LLMs and generative AI in healthcare, arming the reader with required knowledge and insights to navigate the ethical, technical, and social implications of these rapidly emerging technologies. After reading these seven chapters, readers will understand the possibility, problems, and the ethics of using LLMs and generative AI in healthcare. It is hoped that the sequencing across chapters will guide the reader to grasp a detailed understanding of how these tools, if used intelligently, can transform healthcare delivery and enhance patient outcomes.

O'Reilly Online Learning

 For more than 40 years, *O'Reilly Media* has provided technology and business training, knowledge, and insight to help companies succeed.

Our unique network of experts and innovators share their knowledge and expertise through books, articles, and our online learning platform. O'Reilly's online learning platform gives you on-demand access to live training courses, in-depth learning paths, interactive coding environments, and a vast collection of text and video from O'Reilly and 200+ other publishers. For more information, visit *https://oreilly.com*.

How to Contact Us

Please address comments and questions concerning this book to the publisher:

O'Reilly Media, Inc.
1005 Gravenstein Highway North
Sebastopol, CA 95472
800-889-8969 (in the United States or Canada)
707-827-7019 (international or local)
707-829-0104 (fax)
support@oreilly.com
https://www.oreilly.com/about/contact.html

We have a web page for this book, where we list errata, examples, and any additional information. You can access this page at *https://oreil.ly/llms-gen-ai-healthcare*.

For news and information about our books and courses, visit *https://oreilly.com*.

Find us on LinkedIn: *https://linkedin.com/company/oreilly-media*.

Watch us on YouTube: *https://youtube.com/oreillymedia*.

Acknowledgments

We would like to express our profound gratitude to the numerous colleagues and mentors who have shaped our understanding and perspectives on healthcare and AI throughout our careers. Our experiences at Google, IBM, Optum, and Johnson & Johnson have been invaluable, providing us with diverse insights and opportunities for growth. The collective wisdom and innovative spirit of these organizations and the individuals within them have been instrumental in forming the ideas presented in this work.

Kerrie Holley

First and foremost, I would like to express my deepest gratitude to my beloved wife, Melodie Holley. Your unwavering support, love, and encouragement have been the bedrock of my life and career. Your patience and understanding during the long hours spent researching and writing this book have been invaluable. I am truly fortunate to have you by my side.

Kier and Hugo, you are the living embodiment of all the traits I could have ever imagined and wished for in my sons. Your presence in my life is an unparalleled gift, and I am forever grateful for the joy, love, and inspiration you bring into my world every single day.

Reece, as a proud father and as you stand on the precipice of your senior year, I find myself filled with an overwhelming sense of pride and admiration for the young man you have become. I am excited to witness the incredible journey that lies ahead of you.

Aliya, my favorite daughter, you bring me joy and happiness every single day and in the moments we share. I love our daily bedtime activities and your old soul, intellect, kindred spirit, and sweet nature.

I am deeply grateful to Julie Zhu of UnitedHealth Group for her invaluable guidance in applying machine learning to healthcare, which has profoundly shaped my thinking. Her expertise opened my eyes to the transformative potential of deep learning and AI in medicine. I extend my heartfelt thanks to Dominik Dahlem, PhD, for challenging my perspectives and broadening my horizons in AI, particularly in MLOps. His insights on treating machine learning as a software discipline, integrating best practices of ML and software engineering, have been instrumental in tackling complex healthcare challenges. I appreciate the thoughtful review by Rackspace AI CTO, Ram Viswanathan. I also thank Rick Hamilton, an incredible inventor and technology executive, for his insightful review of the manuscript.

Manish Mathur

I would like to express my heartfelt gratitude to my parents, Dr. P. B. Mathur and Mrs. Asha Mathur, whose unwavering inspiration and guidance have been the driving force behind my pursuit of excellence. My father, Dr. P. B. Mathur, who now rests in the heavenly abode, has bestowed his blessings upon this endeavor, and I am confident that he continues to watch over me with pride. My mother, Ms. Asha Mathur, remains a constant source of blessings and wisdom, guiding me through life's journey with her unique and invaluable ways.

Furthermore, I extend my deepest appreciation to the lights of my life, my sons Abhyuday and Kush, whose charming aspirations continuously motivate me to strive for greater heights each day. Their presence is a constant reminder to embody the values of perseverance and dedication, inspiring me to be a better person for their sake and for the betterment of society.

Kerrie and Manish

We would also like to thank the colleagues, mentors, and friends who have supported us throughout this journey. Your insights, feedback, and collaboration have been invaluable in shaping the ideas and concepts presented in this book.

We'd like to thank Angela Rufino, the O'Reilly content development editor, for shepherding us through the author process and for her insightful comments and edits. We also thank Adam Lawrence for his exceptional copyediting.

Finally, thank you, the reader, for taking the time to engage with the ideas and perspectives presented in this book. It is our sincere hope that the knowledge and insights shared within these pages will contribute to the ongoing conversation about the role of LLMs and generative AI in healthcare and beyond.

CHAPTER 1

Doctor's Black Bag

In C. M. Kornbluth's short story "The Little Black Bag,"[1] Dr. Full, a struggling physician, discovers a mysterious doctor's bag from the future filled with advanced medical devices and medicines. This futuristic equipment enhances his abilities as a doctor, allowing him to diagnose and treat patients with unprecedented efficiency. As he explores the bag's contents, Dr. Full finds himself marveling at the potential of future medical innovations, feeling as though he's standing on the cusp of a healthcare revolution.

However, Kornbluth's tale is not simply a celebration of medical progress. As the story unfolds, it becomes clear that such powerful technology, in the wrong hands, can be exploited for personal gain rather than the greater good. The narrative serves as a reminder that while future medical advancements may seem magical in their capabilities, they also come with significant ethical responsibilities and potential for misuse. This fictional account prompts us to consider both the exciting possibilities and the ethical challenges that lie ahead as medical technology and AI (LLMs and generative AI) continue to advance rapidly, often in interconnected ways.

AI and LLMs have the potential to enhance clinical care, especially in those areas that augment clinicians' decision-making processes, enhance patient-doctor interactions, streamline administrative tasks, improve patient education and engagement, and ultimately lead to better health outcomes. By leveraging the capabilities of multimodal LLMs, healthcare institutions have the potential to develop sophisticated virtual medical assistants that can proactively monitor patient health and aid in diagnosis,

---

1 C. M. Kornbluth, "The Little Black Bag," in *The Best of C. M. Kornbluth*, ed. Frederik Pohl (Garden City, NY: Nelson Doubleday, 1976), 42–69.

according to a senior medical executive at NewYork-Presbyterian, a prominent hospital network in New York.[2]

Just as the traditional black bag equipped physicians with essential tools to provide quality care, AI is poised to become an indispensable asset empowering clinicians to deliver more personalized, efficient, and evidence-based care to their patients. This chapter explores the possibilities for improved patient care using LLMs—especially where they might improve healthcare where clinicians and patients benefit the most.

LLMs are natural language processing (NLP) machine learning models that can seemingly understand[3] and generate human language text. LLMs are a type of artificial intelligence (AI) that comprehends and manipulates human language with remarkable proficiency. They are called "large" because they are trained on vast amounts of text data, often billions of words, which enables them to learn the nuances of human language.

For clinicians, LLMs can be thought of as advanced language processing tools that can assist with a variety of administrative tasks involving healthcare data (structured like electronic health records [EHRs] or unstructured doctor notes). Just as stethoscopes and X-ray machines extend a clinician's abilities to assess a patient's health, LLMs can enhance a clinician's capacity to analyze and interpret large amounts of research data, email threads with embedded videos, a patient's historical health records, clinical notes, discharge summaries, and more.

Generative AI is a subset or type of AI, just as LLMs and machine learning are types of AI. Generative AI is focused on creating new content such as text, images, video, or audio often in response to a user's questions. The generated outputs often resemble human created content in terms of style and structure.

When we use phrases such as LLMs or generative AI in this book, we do so as catch-all terms that encompass a wide range of AI systems, even if they have different attributes or employ different machine learning algorithms. These catch-all terms include but are not limited to LLMs, small language models, multimodal models, and generative AI.

Think of these models as having been trained on lots of our written information (e.g., books, articles, and websites) and on tons of subjects in the world. This allows them

---

2 Matt Marshall, "NY Hospital Exec: Multimodal LLM Assistants Will Create a 'Paradigm Shift' in Patient Care," VentureBeat, March 6, 2024, *https://venturebeat.com/ai/ny-hospital-exec-multimodal-llm-assistants-will-create-a-paradigm-shift-in-patient-care*.

3 LLMs may seem to understand human language, but they are sophisticated statistical models. These models recognize patterns, translate between languages, predict likely words, and generate coherent text. However, they don't truly comprehend meaning in the way humans do. See "Risks of Large Language Models (LLM)," IBM Technology, April 14, 2023, YouTube video, 8:25, *https://www.youtube.com/watch?v=r4kButl DLUc&t=278s*.

to understand something about the relationships among words in sentences and paragraphs, the meanings that accumulate upon chapters, the overall progressions exhibited by narrative arcs, and so on.

When OpenAI released its language model ChatGPT in 2022, it transformed conversational AI and liberated NLP, opening up human-sounding conversation and question-answering for the masses with an easy web interface. This LLM gained worldwide popularity for its ability to hold human-like conversations, answer questions, ghostwriting essays and perform a wide range of tasks. It sparked interest from CEOs with technology companies about the technology impact on business and everyday life. But let's remind ourselves of how we should think about using LLMs.

A 2023 blog[4] discusses ChatGPT experiments providing insights on how we should think about and use LLMS. If we treat LLMs as summarization tools and treat their prompts not as commands to another sentient being but as anchors for that process where summarization is attuned to something in the real world, we can use these tools effectively in healthcare. We did something similar with the laconic constraints of keyword search: we learned and are still learning how to "steer" search toward anything we want. Since the advent of search some decades ago, we have learned how to formulate questions in linguistic anchors that are likely to lead their search toward what they want. We can do the same for LLM prompts, treating them as anchors for summarization in preference to specifications and thereby focusing it well. Once we treat LLM prompts as anchors to summarization, we can steer them more effectively by embedding the summarization task in the model's knowledge base, on the one hand, and in the task scope defined by the prompt, on the other.

As we begin to better understand how LLMs work, the hyperbole needs to be balanced with realistic assessment of how to build and leverage LLMs in healthcare. LLMs are statistical, autoregressive models, a class of machine learning models that predict the next word from the context. For example, let's suppose you are an author writing a story. You have a writing assistant that offers you the next appropriate word based on the words you have already written. This assistant has read many stories, of all different types, so it knows approximately how words follow other words in order to comprise generally useful sentences and more complex narratives. With the story-writing assistant, you keep writing, keep accepting the suggestions, and from word to word, one after the other, your story grows longer. With each step, the next word follows from the words written before. That, in essence, is how an autoregressive model works: it learns from existing data and generates (or predicts) new data, one step at a time, based on the previous sequence of data.

---

4 "ChatGPT Experiments: Autoregressive Large Language Models (AR-LLMs) and the Limits of Reasoning as Structured Summarization," The GDELT Project, February 14, 2023, *https://blog.gdeltproject.org/chatgpt-experiments-autoregressive-large-language-models-ar-llms-and-the-limits-of-reasoning-as-structured-summarization.*

Gemini, ChatGPT, Claude.AI, and other autoregressive LLMs provide the illusion of reasoning the way people do, providing amazing responses to nuanced or complicated prompts. They even seem to act like people providing seemingly emotional reactions and empathetic understanding. These illusions are made more believable because of our cognitive biases, that is, our tendency to anthropomorphize. The next chapter, Chapter 2, discusses the workings of LLMs more specifically, including in explicit details the tokens, parameters, etc.

Potential of LLMs and Generative AI

While existing medical LLMs are already impressive and useful in some ways, development is in the early stages, and these innovations have achieved only a fraction of the potential to transform how we deliver healthcare. Current developments emphasize reducing clinician burden and documentation—but this is still only the beginning of LLM impacts on healthcare delivery. There are already entire medical-specific versions published, but they're not yet making a splash in how clinical care gets delivered for a variety of reasons.

Data availability and quality
> LLMs are trained on huge datasets, and their performance will depend on the quality of the data used to train them. In medicine, data is often distributed across multiple sources, such as EHRs, medical journals, and randomized clinical trials. Moreover, data needs to be complete, accurate, and consistent; data of lower quality can impact how LLMs perform.

Bias and fairness
> LLMs learn from biased data, meaning they are trained on data that reflects the biases of the world. This can lead to transferring and reinforcing already potent biases in how we deliver care to certain patient groups. For example, an LLM that's trained on a biased dataset of medical records (e.g., datasets that contain low numbers of specific racial or ethnic groups) can also generate biased recommendations. When discussing bias, the focus is on the system working properly as intended. Mitigating bias is often critical to system functionality and successful usage.

Interpretability and explainability
> Achieving interpretability or explainability has been one of the most significant challenges in AI development. LLMs are often considered "black boxes" due to their complex inner workings, which operate in such an obscure manner that their overall functionality and output are difficult to understand or predict. The lack of interpretability and explainability is problematic in medicine. There will be significant reluctance to adopt LLMs in healthcare if we cannot understand how they arrive at specific recommendations or diagnoses.

Regulatory landscape

A key challenge surrounding AI development in medicine is the regulatory void. There's currently no clear guidelines to define what it means to develop and deploy LLMs in healthcare. This uncertainty effectively dampens enthusiasm in trying to use AI in medically complex and high-stakes contexts since there's little precedent to guide healthcare organizations on how to act under these conditions.

Ethical landscape

In general, concerns about using LLMs in medicine include the potential for misuse, erosion of patient autonomy, and invasion of patient privacy. Ethical concerns must be considered before LLMs can be used in healthcare.

LLMs explicitly model relations between words and meaning over a long stretch of text, resulting in more fluent textual understanding and generation of content. In addition, they differ from more primitive language models, which can only concatenate words into a text pattern due to their scale of data and the parameterization of models. Chapter 2 details how LLMs work, explaining parameters, tokens, and more.

Existing medical and other LLMs are, in many ways, already pretty impressive. We're just in the very early stages of the maturation of these algorithms and models, but the potential for a transformation of healthcare delivery is tremendous. Still, much of the current focus is on decreasing administrative and documentation burdens to clinicians, and that's just the start of how things might change. The current generation of LLMs may soon feel fairly primitive. There will be many more awe-inspiring and transformative applications in the years as LLMs and other kinds of AI grow and improve.

There are several LLMs and other AI platforms that have been specifically created for applications in medicine and healthcare, some of which are research prototypes and others that are more mature and used in real-world applications. Here are a few prominent examples.

PubMedBERT

This LLM[5] and its associated model had pretraining on biomedical text, and the researchers state that it outperforms all prior language models. It's designed to excel in the biomedical domain. It is trained on a large amount of biomedical research papers from the PubMed[6] database. It uses BERT, an NLP model developed by Google. It is designed to help computers better understand and interpret

---

5 Hoifung Poon and Jianfeng Gao, "Domain-Specific Language Model Pretraining for Biomedical Natural Language Processing," *Microsoft Research Blog*, August 31, 2020, *https://www.microsoft.com/en-us/research/blog/domain-specific-language-model-pretraining-for-biomedical-natural-language-processing*.

6 PubMed, accessed June 20, 2024, *https://pubmed.ncbi.nlm.nih.gov*.

human language in a way that considers the context and relationships between words. BERT can understand the meaning of a word based on the words that come before and after it in a sentence or paragraph. BERT has revolutionized the field of NLP and has been widely adopted in various applications, such as search engines, chatbots, and sentiment analysis tools. Its ability to understand and interpret human language has significant implications for improving human-computer interaction and enabling more accurate and efficient processing of large volumes of text data.

BioBERT

This is a specialized language model adapted for biomedical text. It builds upon the original BERT model,[7] which was trained on a general text corpora. BioBERT is further trained on biomedical literature, enhancing its ability to understand and process medical and scientific language. It is pretrained on very large-scale corpora from the biomedical domain—particularly, a combination of PubMed abstracts and PubMed Central (PMC) full-text articles from the US National Library of Medicine.

SciBERT

Designed by the Allen Institute for AI, this BERT-derived model[8] is trained on a large corpus of scientific text from domains, including biomedical and computer science literature, and it has been applied to tasks such as scientific document abstraction.

ClinicalBERT

Designed to learn the domain-specific language of clinical text and its distinctive structure, such as human-sounding paraphrases, ClinicalBERT[9] is a domain-specific LLM based on clinical notes from the MIMIC-III database,[10] and it trains to carry out tasks such as clinical named entity recognition, relation extraction, and sentiment analysis.

---

7 Jinhyuk Lee, et al., "BioBERT: A Pre-trained Biomedical Language Representation Model for Biomedical Text Mining," *Bioinformatics* 36, no. 4 (February 2020): 1234–1240, *https://academic.oup.com/bioinformatics/article/36/4/1234/5566506*.

8 Iz Beltagy, Kyle Lo, and Arman Cohan, "SciBERT: A Pretrained Language Model for Scientific Text," arXiv, September 10, 2019, *https://arxiv.org/abs/1903.10676*.

9 Kexin Huang, Jaan Altosaar, and Rajesh Ranganath, "ClinicalBERT: Modeling Clinical Notes and Predicting Hospital Readmission," CHIL '20 Workshop, April 2–4, 2020, Toronto, ON, *https://arxiv.org/pdf/1904.05342#:~:text=ClinicalBERT%20is%20an%20application%20of,task%20of%20hospital%20readmission%20prediction*.

10 Alistair E. W. Johnson, et al., "MIMIC-III, a Freely Accessible Critical Care Database," *Scientific Data* 3, no. 160035 (2016), *https://www.nature.com/articles/sdata201635*.

Med-PaLM from Google

Google's Pathways Language Model (PaLM) has been fine-tuned on medical knowledge to create Med-PaLM,[11] which scored high on various medical benchmarks, including tasks such as answering medical exam questions and providing clinical decision support. Google also announced Med-PaLM2,[12] which reached human expert level on answering U.S. Medical Licensing Examination (USMLE) type questions.

Whether using the domain-specific examples of LLMs previously mentioned or coupling multiple core models such as GPT-4 (OpenAI), Claude 3 family (Anthropic), Gemini (Google), or LLaMA 2 (Meta) coupled with a company's proprietary data, LLMs will change the healthcare industry for the better. These AI models make navigating, finding, and understanding content on a health plan or payer's website easier. The models accelerate medical research by analyzing large datasets from EHRs, clinical trials, and scientific literature. Recent advances of LLMs offer the ability for a doctor or researcher to have an LLM read a short or lengthy email or set of emails, many of which may include video or audio clips and summaries for the clinician.

Moreover, LLMs are addressing various challenges in healthcare, such as deciphering and cleaning up medical notes. They also bridge patient-provider communication gaps through conversational AI, ensure thorough understanding of patient histories before treatment, and analyze healthcare data from various sources to gain better patient insights. As LLMs continue to evolve and integrate into the healthcare system, their impact is expected to be transformative, shaping the future of patient care, research, and communication.

They still have much ground to cover to consistently surpass the most skilled medical professionals' expertise. Still, there is enormous potential for integrating LLMs as a third element in the doctor-patient relationship. LLMs could be useful for assisting in diagnosis, documentation, and patient communication.

Every clinical and administrative healthcare process that requires humans to create original work with the data extracted from medical coding, patient education, diagnosis, patient intake, treatment planning, medication management, etc., is up for reinvention.

---

11 "Med-PaLM," Google Research, accessed June 20, 2024, *https://sites.research.google/med-palm*.

12 Karan Singhal, et al., "Towards Expert-Level Medical Question Answering with Large Language Models," arXiv, May 16, 2023, *https://arxiv.org/pdf/2305.09617*.

LLM and generative AI applications or apps are starting to take off, thanks to the maturation of the platform layer, the continuous improvement of models, and the increasing availability of free and open source models. This gives developers, startups, and enterprises the tools they need to build innovative applications. As mobile devices spawned new types of applications with new capabilities like sensors, cameras, and on-the-go connectivity, LLMs are poised to usher in a new wave of generative AI applications and devices for healthcare.

For instance, Perplexity AI demonstrates how LLMs can be leveraged to create powerful, user-friendly interfaces for information retrieval and analysis. Perplexity is a popular AI-powered search and chat platform that utilizes existing LLMs (such as GPT-3.5 and GPT-4) rather than being a distinct LLM itself. As an AI application or interface built on top of these models, Perplexity showcases how developers can create innovative tools by harnessing the capabilities of advanced LLMs. While not specifically focused on healthcare, such applications illustrate the potential for LLM-driven tools to revolutionize information access and decision support across various fields, including medicine.

These days, there is no shortage of healthcare gadgets to help us optimize our lives. A search of the internet shows a vast array of wearable medical devices used in healthcare[13]—including blood pressure monitors, glucose meters, ECG monitors, fitness trackers, and more. We like to attach these devices to ourselves to make our lives healthier and our working conditions easier. These devices will become more useful as health LLMs advance. For example, LLMs could integrate data from multiple sources—such as your Fitbit, diet app, exercise app, fasting app, and sleep tracker—to provide a more holistic view of your health. They could then analyze this combined data to identify patterns and trends that might not be evident when looking at each data source in isolation.

Making internet searches remains a common research method for self-diagnosis. Researching one's symptoms in this manner is often colloquially referred to as "consulting Dr. Google." However, the evidence is clear that internet searches correlate to small increases in diagnostic accuracy and almost none in triage accuracy.[14] LLMs will change this equation as internet search and LLMs integrate over the next few years. The question-and-answer interaction model of leading LLMs directs you to a conversation-like exchange with the internet—one that's context-sensitive and generative.

---

13 Amanda Jane Modaragamage, "Top Wearable Medical Devices Used in Healthcare," Healthnews, January 16, 2024, *https://healthnews.com/family-health/healthy-living/wearable-medical-devices-used-in-healthcare*.

14 David M. Levine and Ateev Mehrotra, "Assessment of Diagnosis and Triage in Validated Case Vignettes Among Nonphysicians Before and After Internet Search," *JAMA Network Open* 4, no. 3 (2021): e213287, *https://jamanetwork.com/journals/jamanetworkopen/fullarticle/2777835*.

Let's explore the current differences between, say, a Google search and leading LLMs question-and-answer prompt.

Interaction style

A Google search is an initiating-response style, whereas leading LLMs employ a question-and-answer style, where you ask it questions in natural language and it responds with a specific answer. A Google search typically returns many responses to your search terms and phrases. It is a relatively flexible system because it returns all matching results while ranking them. A Google search also cites sources.

Information sources

When you do a search on Google, the system taps into the internet's humongous index of web pages and other content in order to find what may match your search request and load it. In contrast, leading LLMs tap into information sources that it was trained on, comprising a corpus of text data leading up to a specific date, which often has a lag between that date and the current date of the user's prompt.

Specificity of answers

When you search on Google, you will likely see a range of web pages, articles, and other resources you need to browse and scroll through in order to find the specific information you are looking for. Leading LLMs attempt to provide you with specific answers—directly relevant to what you are looking for—without requiring you to do all the searching. This of course may also result in *hallucinations*, which is another way of saying AI is generating nonsensical outputs, or simply providing factually wrong information. We should remind the reader that by saying AI or leading LLMs hallucinates, we anthropomorphize AI. As a nonhuman object which lacks many human qualities, an AI is not capable of experiencing literal hallucinations.

Making new things

A Google search is a method of finding information on the web that has already been made. An LLM can not only find that information but also analyze, make new text, and explain or argue some conclusion.

LLM-powered chatbots will answer our questions about our health, and LLM-powered diagnostic tools will help doctors diagnose diseases more accurately. Clinicians will engage medical LLMs to develop personalized treatment plans and monitor patients' progress.

LLMs will revolutionize how consumers and patients navigate their health and healthcare systems. By providing personalized insights, recommendations, and support, LLMs can enable patients and consumers to assume greater responsibility for their well-being and make well-informed choices regarding their healthcare.

LLMs could revolutionize healthcare in several ways:

Personalized health education

LLMs provide consumers and patients with customized education about their health conditions, treatment options, and prevention strategies. Generative AI can be used to create personalized educational videos allowing clinicians to tailor the education to the individual's specific needs, language, and preferences.

Medical decision support

Consumers and patients using an LLM chatbot app can assist in helping with educated choices concerning their healthcare. The chatbot can perform product or plan comparisons of various treatment alternatives, and explain the advantages and disadvantages of each option using a variety of modalities like video. This would occur with dispensing medical advice or clinical advice as the chatbot would only organize and summarize data and content already readily available and provided to the patient. The chatbot operates as a tool for understanding the content.

Navigation assistance

LLMs help consumers and patients navigate the complex healthcare system to find qualified providers, schedule appointments, and understand insurance coverage. Using a chatbot to scour the internet (e.g., *ratemds.com*, *vitals.com*, *healthgrades.com*, or Yelp) to find and summarize patient reviews of a provider or specific clinician could be critical to one's health. Although these reviews are subjective, a tool like a chatbot, which summarizes such data, allows a consumer to make a more informed choice.

Emotional support

LLMs support the emotional health of consumers and patients. LLMs can listen to concerns, offer encouragement, and connect patients with others facing similar challenges. The conversational nature promoted by LLMs offer an opportunity for a dialogue that supports and empowers consumers and patients.

LLMs will change the current personalization landscape that patients and consumers face, leading to increased personalization of healthcare. This will include coaching support, providing more individualized information and recommendations. LLMs could empower patients and consumers to be more responsible for their own health and well-being by making well-informed decisions about their health.

The choice of an LLM-powered chatbot lies in the power of conversational AI enabled by LLMs.[15] A few examples of LLM-powered chatbots in practice might include any of the following:

- A person with chronic health conditions might use a chatbot with LLM-powered capability to track and document symptoms, help manage prescriptions, and provide tailored information on living well.

- A terminally ill patient facing a choice—to have surgery or not—might use an LLM chatbot to quantify the risks and benefits of each option and get advice tailored to her own level of risk aversion as input to a conversation with her doctor.

- A caregiver for a patient with a chronic health condition, for example, might use an LLM-powered chatbot to coordinate appointments and care among several providers, provide explanations and context for what providers have said, and help navigate decisions.

In each of these examples, an LLM-powered chatbot offers certain benefits over a generic machine learning approach.

Natural language understanding

We've already mentioned how adept LLMs are at natural language understanding, which in turn empowers human-sounding natural language input (e.g., asking questions about symptoms in our own words), which is more intuitive and accessible compared with filling out a structured form or keyword-based search.

Contextual awareness

LLMs can hold context during the course of a conversation and understand how pieces of information relate to each other, allowing the chatbot to provide more informative and less repetitive or meandering answers to the patient's questions. The bot can then track how its answers have changed over the course of its interaction with the patient, based on the context from the patient's initial statements describing their symptoms, prescribed medications, and lifestyle factors.

Personalized support

By having a dialogue with the user and learning about their specific situations and problems, an LLM-powered chatbot could offer helpful advice and suggestions tailored to an individual's health condition as well as their treatment plan and their lifestyles, which could be more meaningful and useful.

---

15 "What's Next in Store for Conversational AI in Enterprise Apps?" Koru, June 11, 2024, *https://www.kor uux.com/blog/conversational-ai-in-enterprise-apps*.

Prognostic support

LLMs can derive signals from the stream of information a user provides over time, and synthesize these insights into what trends have occurred in the patient's records. Armed with all this data, the chatbot could, for example, flag an issue to the user or automatically refer them to helpful resources or preventive care that the algorithm thinks they could benefit from, with the goal of ultimately enhancing health outcomes.

Emotionally intelligent support

LLMs can be trained to communicate in an understanding, supportive voice. Individuals who struggle with the daily challenges of chronic illness can benefit from having a supportive conversational partner to keep them motivated and maintain their mental health.

Scalability

Most ML models require explicit training in the nuances of each new task or capability that you want them to perform. However, because LLMs can effectively adapt their already general knowledge of language to support even quite different kinds of tasks on quite different topic domains, it becomes easier to scale and adapt the chatbot to handle more diverse user needs and to expand the breadth and depth of its knowledge base over time.

Alternatively, a bespoke ML model could draw on less structured data inputs and simpler logic, and could not offer much support or broader context. This, in turn, might mean less customization for the user, a shallower and narrower scope for support, and more work over time to build and maintain.

For example, an LLM-driven bot does not require a definition of mental pain or a functional classification. This suggests that LLMs can operate without rigid, predefined categories or definitions, allowing for more flexible and nuanced interactions. However, it would nonetheless bring to bear its own capabilities—including some of the advantages of natural-language interaction, contextual understanding, and "deep" knowledge integration—to deliver a type of broad, tailored support that seems promising in helping people with chronic health conditions.

LLMs will help to equalize access to healthcare. Patients and consumers will be able to seek and access higher-quality health information and advice. Healthcare professionals and the broader health system will be better able to help realize patients' potential for wellness.

The point is not simply that LLMs can do things for us. We can use LLMs and generative AI to enable us to be healthier and happier. In the next section, we will sketch some of these future apps or applications.

Promise and Possibilities of LLMs in Healthcare

Eight million people are dying every year worldwide who would have lived if they had better access to healthcare.[16] Medicine and healthcare are on the cusp of a tsunami of change as LLMs and generative AI fundamentally transform medicine. LLMs trained on large healthcare and medical data linked to cutting-edge breakthroughs in artificial intelligence will facilitate a personalized form of healthcare.

Coupling the knowledge captured in their training corpus with data from a patient's chart has the potential to dramatically advance clinical decision support systems, and ultimately improve care and outcomes for patients. LLMs can help physicians make more precise diagnoses, identify the best treatment, and even predict patient prognosis.

In a future where LLMs have been embedded in clinical decision support systems, doctors might have access to an almost inexhaustible supply of medical knowledge at the point of care. With such tools, physicians might be able to reduce medical mistakes. LLMs created to help clinicians who might themselves hover on the verge of a mistake get steered away from danger.

LLMs could provide clinicians with a degree of real-time care that has never existed before, by tracking medical notes in EHRs, data from home-based devices, and patient-entered information on digital platforms. This approach could create an early-warning system of symptoms, signs, and laboratory test results suggesting worsening illness. By identifying health problems early on, LLMs offer a great opportunity in helping to prevent the onset of chronic diseases, which can adversely affect patients' health-related quality of life and often lead to a high financial burden for the healthcare system.

Beyond that, LLM-derived insights can inform precision health approaches, aiming to optimize primary, secondary, and tertiary prevention, as well as treatment interventions according to each individual patient's genetic, environmental, and lifestyle characteristics. As a result, precision healthcare could be crafted to optimize treatment responses, increase patient engagement and regimens adherence, and improve health outcomes, as much for individuals as for populations.

Given the rapid progress of LLMs, as well as their inevitable integration into other disruptive technologies in the future, the potential of AI to develop a truly predictive, preemptive, and individualized system of healthcare is multiplied. Big data for healthcare and AI/LLM holds the promise of making preventive and preemptive medicine the new normal.

---

16 Margaret E, Kruk, et al., "Mortality Due to Low-Quality Health Systems in the Universal Health Coverage Era: A Systematic Analysis of Amenable Deaths in 137 Countries," *Lancet* 392, no. 10160 (November 17, 2018): 2203–2212, *https://www.ncbi.nlm.nih.gov/pmc/articles/PMC6238021.*

As new AI features such as agentic reasoning, retrieval-augmented generation, and bigger prompts are introduced into LLMs, the value of LLMs increases. They can handle more pointed and more nuanced queries based on more medical and other domain-specific "data"; reason about hypothetical scenarios; and reply to questions with replies that seem context-aware and personalized. Today, clinicians may use one of several apps for medical questions, like the UpToDate app.[17] The adoption of LLMs can improve the functionality of such apps in areas of search, summarization, user interface, and more.

Imagine two healthcare scenarios, each harnessing the power of apps driven by LLMs and generative AI. These AI cutting-edge apps seamlessly integrate conversational AI, advanced search functionality, and intelligent summarization capabilities, revolutionizing the way patients and consumers interact with technology and access information. Let's delve into these hypothetical scenarios and explore the potential impact of these AI-powered apps in healthcare.

In the first scenario, a Medical Swiss Army Knife is the name of a consumer app focused on helping patients and consumers as they engage and navigate the healthcare system. In the second scenario, a Medical Sherpa, is the name of a clinician app designed to be a companion or virtual assistant to a clinician. In both scenarios, the LLMs are trained or augmented with trusted knowledge sources, clinical data, pharmacy data, EHR data, and more.

Medical Swiss Army Knife App for Consumers

An AI startup company introduces a novel chatbot, built using a medical-specific LLM. The chatbot is a healthcare app called Medical Swiss Army Knife, which orchestrates multifunctional capabilities for consumers or patients in healthcare contexts such as scheduling doctor appointments, summarizing a patient's history, and listening to doctor and patient dialogue in order to provide plain and intelligible summarization of doctor instructions. Medical Swiss Army Knife also offers provider steerage to help users navigate and identify the probable optimal provider for their medical condition.

David, a 75-year-old man, is in love with his Fitbit wearable. Over several weeks, he repeatedly receives a signal detecting atrial fibrillation (AFib) and contacts his doctor, who refers him to a cardiologist. David takes medication for high blood pressure and statins to control his cholesterol. David recently had a calcium scoring test showing him in a high-risk category. His cardiologist recommends and performs an AFib ablation, but it does not fix the problem. David is rechecked into the hospital to give

---

17 "UpToDate: Trusted, Evidence-Based Solutions for Modern Healthcare," Wolters Kluwer, accessed June 20, 2024, *https://www.wolterskluwer.com/en/solutions/uptodate*.

his heart a controlled electric shock and cardioversion to restore a normal rhythm, but to no avail.

David wonders if there is an alternative to the AFib ablation that he should consider. He talks with his doctor, who advises him that the AFib has good results and they should try again, as this hospital specializes in this procedure to treat AFib. David has the Medical Swiss Army Knife app on his iPhone, a recommended download from his wife Ann, and decides to use it to research his question on AFib ablation alternatives. The Medical Swiss Army Knife app uses a medical-specific LLM, a foundational LLM like Google Gemini, combined with data from David's medical records, medical history, and health information. The app informs David of another procedure, a catheter ablation. Showing David verified videos of a preeminent research hospital and physician specializing in this procedure. David is intrigued and consults with his physician, who advises him that this is an alternative treatment that he cannot provide and that David should contact the research hospital to learn more.

The app starts a conversation with David about his calcium scoring test showing him at high risk. It informs David that a cardiac computed tomography (CT) scan would most likely be performed at the research center before the catheter ablation to help his attending physician anticipate potential difficulties during the procedure.

David uses the Medical Swiss Army Knife app to contact the hospital and make the initial phone appointment to learn more. David enjoys the conversation and finds himself enlightened, deciding to pursue treatment at this research hospital. The app makes the appointment, flight, and hotel reservations. David engages in a conversation with the Medical Swiss Army Knife app to better understand what questions he should be asking. The app suggests that David ask the following:

- What is the best treatment plan for me, given my circumstances?
- What are the different treatment options available, and what are the risks and benefits of each?
- How does my AFib affect my heart?
- What is my risk of stroke?
- What should I do if I have an AFib episode?
- What are the long-term implications of living with AFib?

The app development, by a reputable company, employs state-of-the-art security measures to protect patient privacy. The app design attempts to avoid misinterpretation of the conversation or providing inaccurate information by:

Using a large and diverse dataset to train the LLM
   This dataset includes medical conversations. This helps the LLM learn the nuances of medical language and avoid making mistakes.

Using state-of-the-art NLP techniques

These NLP methods are used to comprehend the conversation effectively. This, in turn, assists the LLM in pinpointing the essential aspects of the discourse and refraining from drawing unsupported inferences.

Incorporating feedback from doctors and patients

This app improves the accuracy of the LLM. The app's continuous feedback loop helps identify areas where the LLM is struggling and make necessary adjustments.

Providing transparency to users

The app allows users to find out about how it works, and it uses their data to help users understand the app's limitations and use it responsibly.

The LLM Medical Swiss Army Knife app reminds David that it is not a doctor and cannot provide clinical advice or diagnoses. It informs David that he should seek medical advice from his AFib doctor before making decisions about his care. David and his wife fly 2,000 miles and check in to the recommended hotel adjacent to the hospital. Both are immediately impressed as the cardiologist phones and asks if he can stop by and say hello. This personal service is beyond their expectations. Before the doctor's meeting, David opens the Medical Swiss Army Knife app to check on the questions he wants to ask. The app prompts David if he would like the app to listen in on the conversation. David informs the doctor he is using an app that will listen to their conversation and help David better understand the conversation afterward. The doctor smiles and says of course, and reminds David that he would be happy to answer any questions he has any time before or after the surgery.

It is now Monday and time for a pre-procedure CT scan in preparation for the Isolator Synergy ablation clamp to treat David's AFib. The CT scan shows severe blockage in his main arteries, and the cardiologist cautions David that he is at high risk of a heart attack, so much so that he needs immediate open heart surgery because of the blockage.

David begins conversing with his Medical Swiss Army Knife app, asking if his local doctors should have discovered this blockage. The app informs David that further tests may not have warranted it because he had no reported symptoms. It also advises him to ask his treating cardiologist and local doctor this when time permits.

Without using the Medical Swiss Army Knife app, David would have remained solely engaged with his local cardiologist, unaware of his high risk of a heart attack. Although perhaps just fortuitous, David would never have undergone the CT scan showing severe blockage but for seeking a catheter ablation.

David entered what was expected to be a three- to four-hour surgery but was instead six hours. The doctor completes the surgery and tells David's wife, Ann, what occurred. He says the reason that David's surgery took longer is that he had a physical abnormality, causing blood to go from his lungs to his heart in a way that the doctor had never seen or that anyone he knows had ever experienced.

The doctor emphasizes he has been doing this for decades, even working with babies with congenital heart disease and birth abnormalities, and has never seen anything like it. It took them time to try to get to the bottom of it, and instead of using one pump to recycle the blood, they had three of them working, which wasn't enough.

We would be remiss not to mention why Ann had such confidence in the Medical Swiss Army Knife LLM medical app. She was diagnosed with CLL leukemia four years earlier. She had an appointment with an oncologist on a Monday and received a call from her daughter the previous Thursday. Her daughter was an active user of the Medical Swiss Army Knife app. The app suggested her mother would receive the best outcome at a cancer research hospital versus the local hospital she had planned for treatment. Her mother was not too keen on rescheduling her appointment as she liked her oncologist, and the local hospital was a short drive away compared to the research hospital. But she relented, canceled her appointment, and made an appointment to see an oncologist at the research hospital.

The research hospital had a slightly different treatment plan, which included a recently available FDA drug, IMBRUVICA®. Ann was quite pleased with the results and currently finds her cancer in remission. She credits her daughter and the app directing her to a care facility that produced better CLL leukemia outcomes. Ann understood that clinical outcomes could differ drastically based on the provider, and she was delighted that she got her husband, David, connected to an expert in treating AFib. She firmly believes it saved her husband's life. It's no secret that medical facilities that released research findings achieved elevated patient satisfaction scores and exhibited reduced patient mortality rates across a variety of medical conditions and procedures.[18]

By leveraging expansive data on providers' clinical outcomes, the Medical Swiss Army Knife app, powered by an LLM, can match individual patients with the physicians statistically poised to provide the most effective treatment for the patient's particular condition profile and risk factors.

Medical Sherpa App for Clinicians

Dr. Davis had been a primary care physician for over 20 years and had seen it all. But when his patient, John, came in for a routine physical checkup, Dr. Davis noticed something that made him pause. John had a small lump on the side of his throat.

---

18 Michael Morrison, "Do Hospitals That Conduct Research Provide Better Care for Patients?" Massachusetts General Hospital, press release, February 28, 2022, *https://www.massgeneral.org/news/press-release/do-research-hospitals-provide-better-care-for-patients*.

"John," Dr. Davis said. "I'd like to have a closer look at that lump on your throat." John nodded, so Dr. Davis palpated the lump with his relaxed fingers and furrowed his brow. The lump was firm and fixed, and it did not move under gentle finger pressure. "I am worried," Dr. Davis said, "that this lump could be cancer." He continued: "It would be my recommendation to follow up with a specialist immediately to be on the safe side." John looked fretful. "But I do not feel ill," he said. "I do not have any symptoms."

"Cancer can often be asymptomatic early on," Dr. Davis added. Reluctantly, John agreed to see a specialist. Dr. Davis consulted his Medical Sherpa, an LLM diagnostic app that could sift through mountainous factual knowledge.

Dr. Davis described the lump to his Medical Sherpa. The app bounced back with several suggestions, including asking for a fine needle aspiration (FNA) biopsy—a minimally invasive way to extract a cell sample from the lump—and directing John to an otolaryngologist, the right specialist for diagnosing and treating ear, nose, and throat conditions.

Following the guidance of the Medical Sherpa, Dr. Davis ordered an FNA biopsy for John. He also referred John to an otolaryngologist. Several days later, the results of the FNA biopsy came back positive for cancer. Dr. Davis called John, delivering an asymmetric shock of information: "I'm sorry to say that you have cancer, but we caught it early, and you can still receive therapy. Would it be OK," Dr. Davis asked John, "if my Medical Sherpa helped you schedule an appointment with the otolaryngologist to discuss your treatment options?"

Medical Sherpa is a clinician-facing LLM app that is typically used by physicians seeking a consultation. A somewhat common practice in medicine is hallway, elevator, or curbside consultations. A Medical Sherpa app is in essence a consultation, albeit brief and informal, between a clinician and an LLM. The use of the name "sherpa" is apt because, similar to the guides who assist climbers ascending Mount Everest, the Medical Sherpa will assist clinicians in navigating through complex medical terrain. LLMs are envisioned to act as virtual assistants practicing beside physicians, offering insights and completing tasks. However, an essential component of the human in medicine is the guiding hand of clinical judgment.

There are both general reasons for medical sherpas to facilitate better and safer care as well as specific benefits to clinicians. For instance, when physicians work with their sherpas, they obtain proximate knowledge that is not afforded when relying upon data and analytics from afar. Similarly, the sherpa of nurses, being at the bedside, is better able to provide real-time support and advice via ubiquitous communication, enabling the nurse to make more informed decisions.

Furthermore, medical sherpas can assist providers in increasing productivity by saving them time. With fast and easy access to consultation and support, doctors and nurses can use the time saved to focus attention on other critical aspects of their job, which could help improve healthcare outcomes.

In addition, by reducing provider burnout, which has become recognized as a serious problem in healthcare, medical sherpas allow clinicians to spend more time caring for patients and less time training new learners for each case. Having someone with ongoing experience in this form of care can make a huge difference in the experience and confidence levels of clinicians here at home. Together, these benefits can lead to better quality of care for patients and a more sustainable system for the future.

LLMs' Emerging Features

LLM-powered applications occupy an interesting space between a tantalizing vision for the future and a daunting series of obstacles to overcome. We're very close to a future where LLM-based systems can tackle increasingly complex tasks, free humankind's creative impulses in new directions, and fundamentally change how we interact with the world around us. But first, we must progress on technical frontiers involving data, performance, stability, and security.

There's a human side to this other than technological infrastructure. There are matters related to privacy concerns around data-hungry LLMs. Bias, baked into the training data, creates the need for continuous monitoring and proactive mitigation strategies to prevent the reproduction of biases and harm in healthcare settings.

This means that while we haven't reached our destination yet and while technology by itself won't get us there, we are inching our way forward. Social, ethical, and conceptual thinking will be vital to scaling up responsible design approaches, making LLMs tools for improving physicians efficiency and effectiveness and patient-doctor interactions while preventing them from becoming tools of exclusion and harm.

The current form factors of LLM-based apps capabilities offer broad utility for healthcare, with the potential to provide assistive convenience into consumer lifestyles and healthcare operations. From our smartphones' symptom checkers to clinical decision support in the back office, LLM use cases amplify the potential for better healthcare at numerous points along the spectrum of patient-doctor interactions.

Even though true game-changing innovation remains just beyond the horizon, we can see today that AI is already reshaping clinical spaces and consumer health tech to improve workflow efficiency and patient care. The book *AI-First Healthcare*[19]

---

19 Kerrie Holley and Siupo Becker, *AI-First Healthcare: AI Applications in the Business and Clinical Management of Health* (O'Reilly Media, 2021), *https://learning.oreilly.com/library/view/ai-first-healthcare/9781492063148.*

documented numerous examples of how AI makes healthcare better. LLMs take AI another step forward, and automated note-taking, conversational chatbots, and summarization tasks are just the beginning.

More than any other emerging technology, LLMs promise an ongoing increase in social benefit—making existing systems aware of holes in nurses' care, redirecting decision trees, and maximizing outcomes for every patient through both provider and purchaser empowerment. The here and now of this optimistic treatment of our shared future is occasioned by the arrival of consumer and business LLMs into our lives.

There are exciting changes ahead in the near future for LLMs, which include expanding prompt windows or what is called *context windows*. The window size continues to expand, and researchers are working on a prompt that allows for functionally infinite size.

Infinite Context Prompts

LLMs with extensive or unlimited context windows can now process text, audio, and video data simultaneously. This advancement opens new and enhanced possibilities for healthcare providers, health plans, and payers. This is interesting for clinicians because it could strengthen patient consultations by analyzing diverse data types in real time. Here are some of the ways this AI improvement might transform healthcare:

- LLMs with access to medical literature, clinical notes, and guidelines can offer clinicians point-of-care, evidence-based recommendations for diagnosis, treatment, and care planning in real time. However, as with humans, there may be a pause (i.e., latency) in the reply, depending on the complexity of the prompt. By evaluating patient data alongside the medical literature and clinical best practices, LLMs might assist clinicians in reducing medical errors and enhance decision making to improve patient outcomes.

- Models that can understand and generate natural-sounding text, audio, and video can enable more meaningful interactions between patients and clinicians that span across language barriers. LLMs could help transform complex medical information to versatile natural-sounding text that can be understood by a wider variety of patients, answer common queries, offer nuanced patient education that can be personalized to meet individual needs, and encourage early intervention. These interactions could then enhance patient engagement, adherence, and satisfaction with care.

- Different LLMs could help automate paperwork and clinical documentation, including coding and billing, streamlining healthcare processes and liberating providers from the burden of administration so they can spend more clinically "face-to-face" with patients. Today, companies like Google offer technology that allows one to use LLMs to summarize an email with embedded video. Imagine what this would be like where the input stream is not bounded by a fixed size.

- Models that can parse audio and video in real time would improve the efficiency and efficacy of telemedicine and remote monitoring services, helping with remote consultations.

- With the capacity to analyze and synthesize massive amounts of biomedical literature and data, including scientific publications, clinical trial data, and patient records, LLMs can expedite medical research and drug discovery. Clinicians could save time with the power of the LLM to summarize clinical trial data or patient notes spanning years.

- LLMs could enable personalized medicine and precision healthcare in delivering tailored care to individual patients based on their unique characteristics (e.g., based on genomic profiling, lifestyle, and medical history data) to identify personalized risk factors, disease trajectory, and therapeutic interventions and treatments. A more personalized approach to care, potentially enabled by LLMs, could increase the effectiveness and efficiency of healthcare delivery by optimizing patient outcomes.

The promise of personalized healthcare would be a big step forward. LLMs with infinite context windows or prompts could process and store large amounts of medical literature, clinical trial data, patient medical history, and clinical data, allowing for a comprehensive and updatable medical knowledge base for a patient or consumer. Chatbots powered by such LLMs would expand to more complex multiturn conversations, creating intuitive and engaging consumer experiences. The former Google CEO, Eric Schmidt, sees the expanding infinite prompt windows occurring within the next five years.[20]

Agentic Reasoning

Agentic reasoning represents another evolution of AI where systems can act autonomously. Andrew Ng, a computer scientist and AI researcher, provides interesting perspectives on the nature of agentic reasoning, and describes four key features or patterns of agentic reasoning that we will explore in this chapter: the patterns of reflection, use of tools, planning, and multiagent interaction.

"Agentic reasoning lies at the heart of creating agents that can take actions aimed at achieving goals," says Andrew Ng,[21] adjunct professor of computer science at Stanford University and cofounder of Coursera, a company that offers massive open online

---

20 "The Future of AI, According to Former Google CEO Eric Schmidt," *Noema Magazine*, May 21, 2024, YouTube video, 20:06, *https://www.youtube.com/watch?v=DgpYiysQjeI*.

courses. As Ng explains, it means an AI system's capability to sense, desire, believe, and act, thereby setting and modifying goals, making decisions under uncertainty, learning from its experiences, and interacting and reasoning with humans and other AI agents in a natural and effective manner. The challenge of achieving agentic reasoning among AI agents, he points out, demands significant advances in multiple areas, such as machine learning, NLP, knowledge representation, and reasoning under uncertainty.

The four patterns of agentic reasoning

The *reflection pattern* in agentic reasoning helps AI improve its performance based on what it has done previously. The reflection pattern allows a healthcare AI system to reflect on its choices, identify ways to improve the outcomes, and continually develop its approach to patient care. For instance, an AI agent designed to provide clinicians with diagnosis and treatment recommendations for a complex disease could adopt the reflection pattern. The agent would have been trained initially on a large diverse dataset of patient records, literature, and clinical guidelines, and it would then make agentic recommendations to the clinician taking into account the prevalent data.

Initial diagnosis and treatment plan

When a new patient case is submitted, the agent will analyze the presenting patient's symptoms, medical background, and test results, then provide an initial diagnosis and treatment plan. The agent will use its training data and apply its agentic reasoning to the situation, as well as modeled data about the modules that make it up, to determine what is likely the true cause of the patient's condition and what the best treatment plan will be.

Reflection on outcomes

Once a patient is put on a treatment plan, the AI agent monitors the patient's course and results as he or she goes along. What the patient achieves will be compared with what the agent would predict for the same patient given its initial recommendations. If the patient improves as the agent expected, it will reinforce itself and grow more confident in similar cases in the future.

But if there is no improvement in the patient's condition or if the outcome is otherwise suboptimal after a certain period, the AI agent would examine why it made the decision it did—by looking at its algorithms, the data it used, and the assumptions it built into it.

---

21 "What's Next for AI Agentic Workflows ft. Andrew Ng of AI Fund," Sequoia Capital, March 26, 2024, YouTube video, 13:39, *https://www.youtube.com/watch?v=sal78ACtGTc&t=524s*.

Adaptation and learning

On the basis of this reflective analysis, the AGI lets the patient's case anchor the adjustment it needs to make to its decision-making mode. For example, the AGI might add a record of the clinical findings to its background knowledge, refine an algorithm to incorporate an empirically known patient-specific nuance, or revise a list of treatment recommendations to reduce the odds of a known complication.

Crucially, this adaptive training process means that the agent is continuously learning to take more actions that improve its behavior in the long run and so ultimately make better recommendations—reducing chances of errors and prompting more appropriate remedies. When it has experienced more patients and engaged in this process of after-action, it can diagnose and treat more complicated medical problems.

Sharing insights and collaborative learning

This knowledge can be shared between AI agents and human experts by means of the reflective insights they acquire, thus enhancing colearning and coknowledge between humans and AI agents. For example, multiple AI agents can work collaboratively to recognize patterns and generate novel treatment strategies and refined patient care on a large scale.

The AI agent can provide feedback to human physicians, pointing out the places where they need to update their clinical practice or need additional research efforts. By engaging in this kind of a human-machine dialogue, we can ultimately enhance the hybrid nature of work between humans and machines.

The reflective structure of agentic reasoning allows AI agents working in healthcare to learn from their experiences, adjust their strategies, and continuously improve their ability to diagnose and treat patients. Through a continual process of reflection and collaborative learning with human experts, AI agents can become a complement to human care, enhancing quality, efficiency, and effectiveness of healthcare delivery. It is imperative that the reflective process is properly directed and informed by robust ethical principles, and that human oversight is always in place in order to prevent the unforeseen negligence and maintain the highest standards of care.

The *tool use* pattern in an agentic reasoning enables AI agents to leverage tools and external resources broadly, moving beyond machine learning, computer vision, or NLP to expand their problem-solving scope and decision-making process by harnessing external resources and knowledge capabilities. For medicine, the tool use pattern can enable AI systems to "borrow" medical resources via incorporating existing medical tools, databases, services, and all other external inputs, such as medical professionals like nurses, doctors, caretakers, and others. These inputs can provide principled and human-centric patient care based on up-to-date clinical know-how and professional decision-making rather than confining AI systems to "black box" decision making that relies exclusively on machine learning examples. Let's look at precision medicine and illustrate how the tool use pattern can be applied.

A healthcare AI agent assists physicians in developing individualized treatment plans for their cancer patients. To do so, the agent uses agentic reasoning to analyze patient data and find optimal treatment options that the patient can follow, and the agent also monitors treatment progress. In order to improve its treatment recommendations further, the agent employs the tool use pattern to access and also combine with external resources and services.

Genomic analysis tools

An AI agent mines the genomic analysis toolbox to collect and make sense of the patient's genetic information. Armed with databases of genomic variants and their known clinical implications, it can identify potential genetic risk factors, suggest likely drug responses, and prescribe a targeted therapy based on the patient's individual molecular profile.

Medical imaging services

The medical imaging services—such as computer vision APIs—that the AI agent relies on analyze patients' scans (MRI, CT, or PET scans) to detect and characterize the presence and shape of tumors, as well as treatment effects and disease progression. This information, combined with insights from other patient data, feeds into the overall assessment of the patient's condition by the AI agent.

Electronic health record (EHR) systems

Utilizing EHR systems for accessing patient's previous diagnoses, treatments, and outcomes will help the AI agent to construct a more accurate approach to the actual treatment. For example, rather than consulting the EHR of that particular patient, it can consult the EHRs of other patients to gain a more comprehensive view of the patient's health status and potentially identify risk factors or comorbidities, which may affect the selection of treatment regimen. With access to data from an integrated system of EHRs and other related hospitals, the AI agent will be able to generate a more personalized care plan and related decisions.

Clinical trial databases

The AI agent searches clinical trial databases for trials relevant to the condition of the patient, and then examines eligibility criteria for trials, data on how to treat participants, and data on outcomes. This enables the AI agent to make a recommendation about trials a patient might benefit from joining or to use trial data for its recommendations on treatment.

Drug interaction checkers

The AI agent uses drug-interaction checkers to assess proposed cancer treatments for potential interactions with the patient's current medications. It then recommends alternative medications or dosing changes based on the outcome as a way of minimizing adverse drug events or contraindications while maximizing efficacy.

Using these tools and services, the AI agent can then offer physicians an integrated approach toward precision medicine by compiling the relevant data from different sources and providing personalized treatment advice vetted by knowledge graphs and probabilistic scoring. This approach is feasible because the agent can journal-crawl, medical-text-mine, download, image-store, and integrate disparate data in a probabilistic manner. It can use patient medical history, genetic data, and imaging data to suggest appropriate therapies, including potential prescriptions, based on lesser-known drug interactions.

Furthermore, because the AI agent is making some of the decisions about new research data, clinical guidelines, and new or untested treatment routes, the agent's tool use profile is largely self-updating—changing with the evolving patterns of discovery in human cancers. The agent will therefore be using the best and most up-to-date knowledge available.

And as the field of agentic reasoning develops in healthcare, this tool use pattern will come to play important roles in building AI systems that can capture, combine, and handle large amounts of diverse medical data needed in precision medicine to provide better patient care—as long as the services used externally to achieve these results respect robust data privacy, security, and ethical rules in order to maintain patients' privacy and integrity of the healthcare system.

The *planning pattern* in agentic reasoning is essential for giving AI agents the ability to craft high-level plans to achieve their goals and optimize processes. This means that, in the healthcare domain, a planning-enabled AI system could be used to work through a detailed patient case, anticipate potential outcomes, and decide upon the best treatment plan before creating it—integrating a wide array of factors and parameters. Consider, for example, the scenario of an AI agent designed to assist physicians in managing patients with chronic diseases, such as diabetes, hypertension, or cardiovascular disease. In this case, the agent is using agentic reasoning to analyze the results of a physical examination, sequence the symptoms that arise, identify factors that place the patient at risk for worse health outcomes, then create strategic and adaptive recommendations for long-term health outcomes.

Goal setting and problem decomposition

The AI agent begins with an abstract objective of optimizing health outcomes and quality of life of the patient, and breaks it down into smaller, more specific subgoals: keep a patient's blood sugar in an optimal range, decrease blood pressure to a safer level, minimize the risk of amputation or renal complications, and so forth. By breaking down the overall problem into distinct subproblems, the agent can formulate and pursue actions that are attuned to each particular aspect of the patient's condition.

Data analysis and situation assessment

Then, the AI agent tries to mirror the entire medical situation of the patient according to its context. It takes into account the patient's medical history, current health condition, and environmental context, as well as his lifestyle background and any identifiable idiosyncrasies. This includes the ability to integrate data from EHRs, wearables, and patient-reported outcomes.

Plan generation and evaluation

Drawing on this situation assessment, the AI agent generates different possible treatment plans that address the defined subgoals. For example, it might include one that involves using a different combination of medication adjustments, lifestyle changes, and referrals to specialists. The agent evaluates each plan by considering predicted effectiveness and side effects, patient preferences and acceptance, available resources, and so forth, using known data and probabilistic predictions before deciding which course of action to recommend.

Plan selection and adaptation

The AI agent would choose the treatment plan with the best value in its opinion, balancing benefits against the risks of treatment. Then it would communicate the selected plan, with supporting justification, to the physician and patient, perhaps also with instructions or support for implementing the recommendations.

Whereas the physician designs the treatment plan, the AI monitors as the plan unfolds and examines the results. If the patient's condition is not following the predicted trajectory, the agent replans. The treatment becomes responsive to new information, such as changing medication dosages or introducing different interventions or lifestyle recommendations.

Continuous monitoring and refinement

The AI agent checks back in later with the patient to see how she has fared and whether the treatment plan is helpful or requires adjustment. It is also on the lookout for risks and adverse events from side effects. Where it can identify patterns in the patient's own data and compare with the trajectory of similar cases, the agent can alter its planning strategies to better guard against emergent health problems.

This planning structure of agentic reasoning can help AI agents in the healthcare context to come up with executive, dynamic strategies of care management in chronic conditions. The AI agent breaks down the complex health problems into meaningful subgoals, runs pattern completion procedures using available patient data, brainstorms feeding and elimination options, provides an analysis of expected consequences, and monitors and self-adjusts its strategy. This way, the AI agent can assist the physician in providing personalized, evidence-based care by balancing short-term costs against long-term health benefits.

It's unlikely that the planning pattern will be the only pattern needed as we progress in the exciting field of agentic reasoning in healthcare. But it will be essential in creating AI systems to help clinicians in the management of chronic diseases that make up a significant portion of the patient population, and it will keep them on the path toward equitable healthcare. We must be protective of the planning process—guiding it with ethical principles, clinical best practices and, patient-centered values to protect individuals from unsafe, ineffective, and unacceptable treatment plans that may emerge as the healthcare caseload continues to add mundane tasks for clinicians.

The *multiagent collaboration pattern* is the means by which the agentic architecture realizes the collaborative work of diverse agents, whether they are conceded agency or not, across different levels of the agentic ontology. Collective event recognition requires two or more agents' awareness and evaluation of an event. In the healthcare domain, the multiagent collaboration pattern is in play when two or more intelligent agents—which can be thought of as AI systems and independent broad-scope healthcare professionals—coordinate their work, share state knowledge or perception, and make decisions and actions based on shared goals or subgoals.

Imagine a patient who has all kinds of long-term conditions—diabetes, hypertension, cardiovascular disease, and so on—and needs advice, monitoring, and treatment from a wide range of health professionals (e.g., a multidisciplinary team of physicians, nurses, dieticians, social workers, and psychologists). In such a situation, a range of different AI agents might be deployed to support the members of the health professional team, for example, to help them optimize medication choices, deliver lifestyle coaching, coordinate care, and so on. These AI agents employ agentic reasoning and the multiagent collaboration pattern to pool skills and working memory to deliver well-targeted, well-informed, coordinated care.

Shared goals and problem understanding
The AI agent and the human expert jointly define the patient's status in terms of health, treatment goals, and potential barriers. Finally, they co-construct a personalized care plan, where the respective strengths of the human and algorithm help provide the best possible treatment for a patient's medical, psychological, and social needs.

Task allocation and coordination

Specific to their assigned tasks, the AI agents allocate some of the work. The medication optimization agent may scan the patient's prescriptions for drug interactions and suggest ways to optimize efficacy and safety. The lifestyle coaching agent can personalize diet, exercise, and stress-management recommendations to complement the patient's self-care regimen.

The care-coordination agent stands at the center, gathering information from the myriad care agents and connecting each of them with the specific information they need. The care-coordination agent also ensures that the other agents and human experts are aware of the patient's current status, change of status, and change of care plan.

Information sharing and knowledge exchange

The AI agents and human experts constantly exchange information and insights that support collective decision making and problem solving. They transmit patient data, treatment recommendations, and clinical insights via encrypted channels and standardized data formats so that each agent and expert can draw upon the collective knowledge of the whole group and update its strategies accordingly. For example, if the medication optimization agent detects a potential adverse drug event, it tells the care coordination agent, which in turn alerts human experts but also other AI agents. The team assesses what's happening and generates an account of the event. They consider whether to remove an offending drug and replace it with a different option. If so, they update the care plan.

Conflict resolution and consensus building

If there are conflicting recommendations or opinions among the AI agents or humans, the multiagent collaboration pattern enables them to engage in argumentation and dialogues, negotiating on trade-offs and reaching a consensus assisted by argumentation, voting, or multicriteria decision analysis methods. This collaboration pattern makes sure the agreed decision is "in the best interests of the patient."

Continuous learning and adaptation

If the patient's condition changes and new data becomes available, the AI agents and human experts learn new strategies for the care coordination process, trading tips (as it were) that help make both their strategies more effective and efficient. The multiple agents interact to learn from each other's successes and failures and develop new approaches in the face of new challenges over time.

This multiagent collaboration pattern from agentic reasoning allows AI agents and human experts in healthcare to work together in a coordinated way to provide holistic and personalized care for patients with complex health needs. Defining a shared goal, allocating tasks, sharing knowledge, resolving conflicts, and learning and adapting are among the components that can help the team to leverage collective intelligence to have a greater impact on optimizing patient outcomes and improving the quality and efficiency of care delivery.

Because agentic reasoning in healthcare is just beginning its evolution, the multiagent collaboration pattern will likely become even more important in the design of AI systems that can work shoulder to shoulder with their human counterparts—and even "learn from them" to complicate the increasingly diverse and interconnected healthcare landscapes. And ethical, profession-standard, and regulatory controls will be necessary to maintain the safety, privacy, and trust of patients and clinicians.

Challenges and future directions

These four different patterns of agentic reasoning provide an opportunity to scale AI to human levels of intelligence in many areas. There are, of course, huge challenges ahead, in determining how to ensure that agentic AI agents interact with humans in a way that is safe, ethical, and aligned. This will involve, for example, developing robust frameworks for value alignment, as well as mechanisms for holding such agents to account and ensuring fairness in their operations.

A second challenge is embedding the four agent-centered patterns of reasoning into unified, flexible, and scalable AI architectures, which could require advances in transfer learning, multitask learning, and open-ended learning to allow AI agents to learn knowledge in one task or situation to help solve another.

Agentic reasoning technologies will likely make significant progress in the long run. What continues to be very interesting about this area of research is that there hasn't been as much work done for researchers to pursue. But it is certainly possible to envision that, over time, we might see AI systems that reflect and perhaps tool, plan, and learn with increasingly complex forms of reasoning and collaboration. Such advances could transform many fields, from healthcare, education, and transportation to manufacturing and beyond.

Context of Use When Using LLMs

Understanding foreseeable use cases of LLM apps recognizes the central importance of "context of use,"[22] a term coined by Margaret Mitchell, when creating healthcare LLM apps. Perhaps Mitchell's thinking lies in a long-standing software engineering practice of human-centered engineering. Because healthcare LLM apps are so open-ended in possible user prompts, they offer interesting use cases for improving the healthcare systems worldwide, yet they also offer challenges in preemptively predicting user interactions.

---

22 Margaret Mitchell, "Ethical AI Isn't to Blame for Google's Gemini Debacle," *Time*, February 29, 2024, *https://time.com/6836153/ethical-ai-google-gemini-debacle*.

Unlike physical objects, which might have a finite number of intended use cases, most software apps are so open-ended in their interactions that we cannot fully predict how end users will ultimately use them. A chair can be used for a finite number of uses (such as sitting), but an app is open-ended. A machine learning model may be developed to predict chronic disease. A disease model may be developed to predict a specific disease, such as heart disease or obesity. Another user or organization may choose to use a specific machine learning model to determine the cost of granting health insurance coverage, while another user may choose to apply the same machine learning model to deny health insurance coverage.

The flexibility of software means users can bend it to their task by using an application in ways that work best with their particular needs, workflows, and users. This productivity app could be designed for task management, but it might be used as a project collaboration tool. The openness of software—made possible through this intrinsic flexibility—means the organizations or companies making that software must also be ready for the ultimate challenge of human exploitation. With respect to the LLM-powered chatbot, the flexibility of natural language interaction means that its prompt openness is difficult to anticipate or restrict in terms of context and potential outcomes. Users might ask questions (or make requests) that are not intended in the scope set for the chatbot. It is possible that users will try to manipulate its responses into causes for harmful or inappropriate outcomes.

For instance, someone seeking a diagnosis might ask a wellness chatbot that was built for general health-related discussion, which could generate off-base or unsafe assumptions. Even the most lighthearted of chatbots is at risk of colliding with hostile or abusive interaction from a customer service bot that becomes unfairly criticized for its errors.

Mitigating these risks will require developers of LLM-powered chatbots to build layers of safety, codes of ethics, and content moderation tools. Examples might include using adversarial forms of testing—where a system is deliberately exposed to the widest range of possible inputs from users to identify holes in its training and specification of representativeness—to ensure that, for example, asking the bot not to be rude doesn't cause it to spout racist comments. Whatever the strategy adopted, developers must make sure boundaries and expectations of impossibilities are clearly set out and communicated to users to reduce the risk of a user trying to force the bot to do the impossible.

Second, as noted previously, chatbots powered by LLMs should be constantly monitored and refined to ensure that they continue to perform as desired. Developers should ground this process by actively seeking the feedback of users regarding their daily experiences with their chatbots. Developers should also examine patterns in interactions. They should subject input and feedback to further analysis, and update knowledge bases and response systems accordingly in order to optimize how the chatbots perform under the new conditions created by their users.

To sum up, the open-ended nature of software applications, including LLM-driven chatbots, can present opportunities and safeguards for anticipating, planning, and addressing users' interactions. The open-ended nature of an LLM-driven chatbot enables creators to foresee novel uses within its framework that can be beneficial to users. The open-endedness of an LLM-driven chatbot can also lead to unforeseen and harmful uses. Nevertheless, by implementing safeguards, morality guides, and continuous monitoring and improvements, creators can enhance users' experience when utilizing LLM-powered chatbots.

Whether it's vetting politically biased search results or catching linguistic markers of dementia, the value of applying context to LLM apps is clear. By designing LLM apps with context in mind, we can build healthcare tools that are more robust, ethical, and beneficial to patients. LLM apps should do the following:

- Encourage responsible use by providing clear interfaces, educational materials for clinicians, and transparency about the limits of the AI.

- Enforce safeguards against identified misuse scenarios (e.g., security controls for data, preventive measures to disable stacking against biased outputs).

- Let AI improve upon itself as it is adaptively deployed in new contexts. Adjustments could occur by monitoring the AI in use in the world (to the extent possible) and tuning the model toward any problems that arise.

Consumer and Business LLMs

Today, we have apps and applications basically divided into two groups, consumer and business. They serve different purposes and target different users. Business apps or applications typically are designed for a company's employees. However, we also have businesses creating apps for their customers to access health plans, understand benefits, make appointments, and more. Perhaps the biggest examples of consumer apps are in areas of social media, entertainment, productivity, gaming, and commerce, to name a few.

In healthcare, we see medical apps designed to make personal health easier. Apps to schedule doctor house calls (e.g., ZocDoc), therapy apps (e.g., Talkspace), telehealth apps (e.g., Doctor on Demand), women's healthcare apps like Maven, and more. We expect to see over time more healthcare LLM-based apps emerge to cover many of the use cases described in Chapters 3, 4, and 5.

Consumer LLMs and Generative AI

This book explores a key hypothesis: the rise of consumer-focused applications powered by LLMs will significantly transform healthcare. These apps, leveraging LLMs' abilities to summarize information and generate content, are expected to:

- Enhance the doctor-patient relationship
- Help individuals better manage their chronic diseases and overall health
- Most importantly, intervene to delay or prevent the onset of chronic diseases

By harnessing LLMs' capabilities, these consumer applications have the potential to revolutionize personal health management and preventive care.

Consumer LLMs are designed for individual users, offering various applications and functionalities tailored to personal needs and interests. These LLMs include models like chatbots, virtual assistants, and content generators. Here are some key characteristics of consumer LLMs:

Conversational assistants
> Consumer LLMs such as virtual assistants (e.g., Siri, Google Assistant) are developed to assist users in setting reminders, answering general knowledge questions, sending messages, and playing music. They are designed for everyday convenience.

Engagement and entertainment
> Consumer LLMs are often designed to provide interactive experiences—such as conversational AI assistants, chatbots, or creative writing tools—that aim to engage and entertain users.

Content generation
> Some consumer LLMs can generate text, which can be helpful for tasks like drafting emails, writing creative content, or even coding assistance. These models focus on enhancing personal productivity and creativity.

Personalization
> Consumer LLMs often prioritize personalization by learning from user interactions to provide tailored recommendations, content, and responses.

Personal assistant
> These LLMs may assist with answering healthcare questions, providing recommendations, writing emails or documents, scheduling appointments with clinicians, and helping with various individual productivity tasks.

Accessibility
> These models are often deployed with user-friendly interfaces, accessible to a broad range of users, and are often available on mobile devices and personal computers.

Business LLMs and Generative AI

Businesses and organizations design their business LLMs and generative AI, both for employee and customer uses, in order to automate tasks, interpret data, and generate things such as text, images, and video. Business LLMs are designed for use in organizations and enterprises, with the following characteristics:

Data integration
> Business LLMs are designed to integrate out of the box with your organization's data sources (e.g., EHRs or other clinical, claims, pharmacy, or eligibility databases). Using all of this health sector data, it can provide you with insights and reports. LLMs allow for analyzing large amounts of business data. For example, an LLM could quickly evaluate the complex and ever-changing prior authorization criteria used by payers and insurance companies.

Business LLMs specific to certain industries
> Developed to benefit a certain industry such as healthcare, industry-specific LLMs can help with tasks ranging from diagnosing an illness to processing claims or making clinical decisions.

Collaboration
> These LLMs often come with features for shared teamwork spaces, document collaboration/sharing, and workflow automation to increase organizational productivity.

Knowledge management
> Business LLMs can help organizations collect and share knowledge by building knowledge bases, summarizing data, and offering contextual suggestions.

Customer service and support
> From commodities trading to buying concert tickets, LLMs can power conversational AI assistants and chatbots to provide customer support and answer queries.

Service guarantees
> Enterprise-level LLMs include service-level agreements and dedicated customer service, making them reliable for business operations.

To summarize, the key difference between consumer and business LLM tools is this: consumer LLMs are mainly geared toward personalized convenience and personal productivity, while business LLMs are built for industry-specific use cases—with custom data integration and enterprise-grade support for operations.

Bridging the Divide

This distinction between the consumer and business LLMs/generative AI is actually an important one because it influences use and its audience. It's important to distinguish between business and consumer LLMs for several reasons:

- Purpose and goals
- Data training
- Regulatory landscape
- Ethics and bias

Purposes and goals

Business LLMs are geared to solving a specific business problem or improving business processes. These range from automating interactions between a health plan member and a customer service employee to creating insights from data that businesses already have.

Consumer LLMs are designed for individual use and educational purposes. They offer services such as language translation and conversational question-answering. Importantly, they can be tailored to individual preferences and needs, providing personalized responses based on a user's past interactions, stated interests, or specific requirements.

Data training

Business LLMs are trained on domain-specific data sets. In this way, we can "tune" the LLM to our business domain so that it's not only addressing content directly but also doing so with knowledge of the business context and jargon.

Consumer LLMs are trained on big, general-purpose corpora (collections of text and code) pulled from diverse public websites. These provide generalist exposure but risk bias and lack specialized knowledge and/or domain expertise. Using the AI framework RAG, the data extends to external data sources just as with a business LLM.

Regulatory landscape

Business LLMs are regulated pursuant to industry-specific rules (for example, the financial sector) or rules regulating data (e.g., medical data protection).

Consumer LLMs are bound by consumer protection statutes and regulations regarding data privacy and ethical AI practices. For example, HIPAA does impose restrictions on how an individual or their designee uses health information consistent with the individual's right of access.

Ethics and bias

Business LLMs: Careful stewardship and mitigation of bias is necessary to avoid discriminatory or otherwise unfair treatment of potential customers, employees, etc.

Consumer LLMs: Bias in consumer LLMs can lead to harmful misinformation, offensive content, or the perpetuation of social inequalities. It's essential that development of these technologies is responsible and that unintended bias is continuously addressed.

In conclusion, while big language models are used by both businesses and consumers, their different, albeit potentially linked, purposes and associated needs for input, control (including security), and ethical considerations should all compel us to think about their development and use differently, according to those different purposes and backgrounds.

Summary

LLMs can open up a world of potential that was once restricted to the domain of science fiction. By delving into the potential of these advanced language models, this chapter explored a range of futuristic promises and applications (two of which—the Medical Swiss Army Knife for consumers and the Medical Sherpa for clinicians—are powered by an LLM). Language models (LLMs)—machines that can read, write, and manipulate human language with remarkable fluency and flexibility—ushered in this new era. LLMs are still evolving rapidly, and their capabilities continue to improve. LLMs promise to transform patient care, research, and medical knowledge across a wide range of health sectors.

But the biggest difference may be what kind of users and use cases are anticipated for an LLM-powered app. Consumer LLM apps (like the Medical Swiss Army Knife) focus on end-user convenience in making educated medical decisions—from small-scale, self-event management and self-diagnosis to broad-based health-promotion, self-care, and family healthcare apps. Business LLM apps (like the Medical Sherpa) will cater to healthcare professionals and organizations populating or searching the ever-growing medical literature, clinicians making diagnosis decisions, and pharmaceutical researchers developing drugs. For consumer LLM apps, convenience and ease of use are key to appeal. For business LLM apps, issues such as data privacy, HIPAA and regulatory compliance, and industry-specific features are the elephants in the room.

But as society moves deeper into LLMs, their solutions and promises will shape a world that will be filled with new tools for health consumers and medical professionals alike, and create a near future diversified by greater access to healthcare and medical knowledge.

CHAPTER 2

Peeking Inside the AI Black Box

As large language models (LLMs) and generative AI tools filter into healthcare applications, they bring along their complex, opaque elements—the inherent "black box" quality that makes the internal workings of these systems seem obscure. This raises natural questions for clinicians and healthcare leaders who are contemplating using LLMs. How exactly do these AI systems develop their clinical competencies? What transpires behind the scenes during their training? Does the black box nature of these emerging tools render LLMs' recommendations and thought processes too inscrutable for serious medical or healthcare use?

Chapter 2 lifts the hood to examine what resides within the AI systems making today's headlines. We discuss how transformers, self-attention mechanisms, neural networks, and other technical elements ingest healthcare knowledge and develop reasoning abilities. While a full accounting of the mathematics behind each component is beyond a typical reader's needs, we provide an accessible explanation of how LLMs work. Peeking inside the black box dispels notions of "magic" while bringing responsible AI adoption within reach, even amid lingering opacity.

LLMs and Generative AI

LLMs use deep learning, a subset of machine learning, and uses layers of algorithms to process data and imitate the human thinking process. The term deep learning and neural network are used interchangeably because all deep learning systems comprise neural networks. The concept of a neural network represents a breakthrough in advancing AI. It's inspired by how biological neurons work in the human brain.[1] In

---

[1] "Brain Basics: The Life and Death of a Neuron," National Institute of Neurological Disorders and Stroke, accessed June 24, 2024, *https://oreil.ly/8iB--*.

an LLM when using deep learning, information is passed through each layer, with the output of the previous layer providing input for the next layer. The first layer in a network is called the input layer, while the last is called an output layer. Each layer is typically a simple algorithm. The underlying technology used by iPhone or Android phones for facial recognition, or for Google search to visually recognize and search for objects, is deep learning. Understanding human speech for tools like Alexa or Siri requires neural networks. Let's take a brief tour of AI history to see how we got here with LLMs and generative AI.

During the 1970s the first AI winter kicked in, explained as a drop in funding and interest in AI, the result of promises that couldn't be kept. The impact of this lack of funding limited both deep learning and AI research. Fortunately, there were individuals who carried on the research without funding. Various overly optimistic individuals and organizations had exaggerated the "immediate" potential of AI.

The next significant evolutionary step for AI and deep learning took place around 1999, when computers started becoming faster at processing data and graphical processing units (GPUs) were introduced and discovered as a way to run deep learning models. Faster processing, with GPUs processing pictures, increased computational speeds, and during this time, neural networks became useful and their use and value rose.

By 2011, the speed of GPUs had increased significantly, and in 2012, Google Brain released the results of a project[2] where a neural network could be given unlabeled data and find recurring patterns. Deep learning has been a field of research for several decades. Its usage and popularity increased rapidly with advancements in computing power, availability of large amounts of data, and algorithm improvements.

In the early days of computing, computers were good at following instructions and sorting information. The early uses of machine learning involved making predictions based on data. Many disease prediction models use machine learning to predict the onset of a disease allowing intervention plans and patient treatment plans to be devised. But deep learning, a subset of machine learning, made them more like sponges, soaking up massive amounts of information and using it to solve problems creatively. Some examples include recognizing different objects in a picture, even if they're blurry or at weird angles, identifying your dog even when covered in mud, or translating languages in real time on your phone app.

---

2 Liat Clark, "Google's Artificial Brain Learns to Find Cat Videos," *Wired*, June 26, 2012, *https://www.wired.com/2012/06/google-x-neural-network*.

But these learning machines didn't stop there. Now, meet the LLMs—the superstars of this story. Imagine them as the top students in the class, trained in even more extensive libraries and special techniques. They can write poems and stories and compose new songs or recombine elements in novel ways to design drugs. That's where things get mind-blowing. We're in the age of generative AI. This means computers don't just copy things; they create them.

In Figure 2-1, we see the progression from hand-crafted rules to machine learning/deep learning to LLMs. In the first cartoon frame, a person manually crafts rules to identify a Chihuahua. This could involve specifying criteria such as size, coat color, ear shape, and other distinctive features. The process is labor-intensive and requires detailed knowledge and expertise in identifying the breed based on predefined rules. Typically, these rules are implemented through coding in a programming language. This process involves creating hand-crafted rules, where programmers manually write specific instructions to guide the system's behavior.

Figure 2-1. Emergence of LLMs

We see a transition to machine learning/deep learning in the second cartoon frame. Instead of explicitly defining rules, the system is trained on a dataset containing labeled images of Chihuahuas and non-Chihuahuas. AI uses machine learning to extract features from the input images and make predictions automatically. Using deep learning where the data can be unlabeled, we can progress further and identify Chihuahuas with a variety of pictures such as when a Chihuahua is pictured alongside objects or in various poses.

The third cartoon frame introduces LLMs. In this frame we are not concerned with identification, but instead the LLM is asked to analyze a vast collection of books, articles, and documents to understand a Chihuahua comprehensively. When presented with an image, the LLM can draw upon its contextual understanding to provide a nuanced evaluation, potentially considering factors beyond visual appearance, such as breed characteristics, behavior, and context.

AI and Machine Learning

One of the core aspects of AI is the use of machine learning, which enables computers to learn patterns and relationships from data without being explicitly programmed. There are several computer scientists who believe the solutions described as AI are nothing more than a machine learning problem being solved. It raises several questions, as depicted in Figure 2-2, where a teacher is discussing AI with his student.[3]

Figure 2-2. What is AI?

AI is a field of research and study in computer science.[4] There are conflicting ideas about how to measure or conceptualize human intelligence, so trying to precisely define AI is equally challenging. Whenever we see machines perform tasks previously

---

3 This drawing is adapted from "AI vs Machine Learning," IBM Technology, April 10, 2023, YouTube video, 5:48, *https://www.youtube.com/watch?v=4RixMPF4xis*.

4 "Artificial Intelligence," Wikipedia, last updated June 24, 2024, *https://en.wikipedia.org/wiki/Artificial_intelligence*.

only seen by humans we see this as machine intelligence. With AI, computer scientists and researchers try to build computer software that exhibits the same qualities of intelligence as humans—that is, AI ≥ a person, as shown in Figure 2-2.

In this diagram, deep learning is shown as a subset of machine learning. Machine learning can be supervised (SUP) where data is labeled to train algorithms and make predictions. Or machine learning can be unsupervised (UNSUP) where machine learning models are given unlabeled data and allowed to discover patterns or insights. For example, when using supervised machine learning to detect diabetes, a person would provide labels for the data that the model should pay attention to such as a patient's A1C—that is, data about blood sugar levels and other factors such as lifestyle. With unsupervised machine learning, the algorithm would work with datasets where the data is not labeled and discover the patterns that denote the likelihood of diabetes.

LLMs use several disciplines of AI, machine learning, deep learning, computer vision, and natural language processing (NLP). For example, Figure 2-2 illustrates AI as a broader concept than machine learning because each of these disciplines is a field of study in their own right but also a subfield in the broader category of AI. A simple definition of AI is that it tries to match the capabilities or intelligence of a human subject.

Before digging into the inner workings of LLMs, let's understand some of the underlying technology used by LLMs.

Detecting a Tumor with Deep Learning

Deep learning is a subset of machine learning, which uses neural networks. Layers are the smallest units of functionality in deep learning, and it's these units that combine to build the neural network. Layers, in cascading order, take their input from the layer below, perform a process upon it, and pass on their output to a layer higher up. If you simply stack enough of these action-packed layers on top of each other, they're capable of learning sophisticated representations of data and performing tasks as diverse as identifying objects in images, understanding language, and more.

Here's a breakdown of the critical points about layers in deep learning:

Input layer
The first layer receives raw data like images, text, or numerical values.

Hidden layers
These pick out features and learn abstract relationships between data points. You can have more than one hidden layer on top of one another—and the depth of that stack is important to what the network is able to learn.

Output layer

This is the final layer that will produce the model's prediction, or output, depending on the task. That output might classify an image as a cat or a dog, translate text from one language into another, or generate new, human-sounding text.

Figure 2-3 illustrates a simple sample neural network with the goal of trying to use a computer to detect whether a tumor is malignant or not malignant.

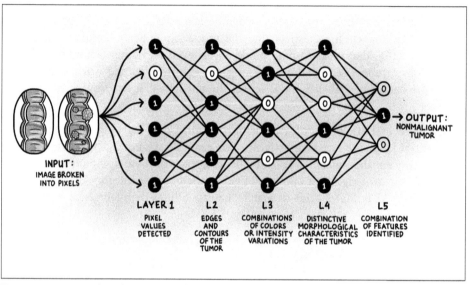

Figure 2-3. Using deep learning to detect cancer in a tumor

In Figure 2-3, each layer in a deep learning neural network designed for tumor classification learns to represent a different level of abstraction from the input image. The image in this case would either be a tumor with cancer or a tumor without. The X-ray of the tumor would be digitized and represented in the computer as pixels. Layer 1 would detect the values of each pixel. This neural network or deep learning model would have been previously trained to know what features of a set of pixels suggest a high probability of cancer. Pixels flow through this network left to right, where each circle represents an artificial neuron, which simply returns a 1 or 0, where 1 represents the signal of possible cancer. As the pixels move to layer 2, the model starts categorizing features in the input image:

- Edges and contours of the tumor
- Basic shapes and patterns within the tumor
- Intensity gradients and texture variations
- Color information (if the input is a color image)

At this point, the neural network is successfully learning an assortment of low-level features, such as edges and blobs, that are connected up into the various components of the image of the tumor, just as the very early stages of the human visual system would perceive them.

By the time the neural network gets to layer 3, it creates a few combinations of the lower level features of layer 2 into higher-level features. Layer 3 might pick up on the following:

- Specific patterns and arrangements of edges and shapes
- Localized texture patterns indicative of tissue types
- Combinations of colors or intensity variations
- Rudimentary representations of tumor subregions or components

In layer 3, patterns are beginning to look more recognizable and more diagnostically relevant to a human specialist viewing the image of the tumor.

In layer 4, the neural network integrates the collections of features from earlier layers into high-level representations of the tumor:

- Distinctive morphological characteristics of the tumor
- Spatial relationships and organization of tumor subregions
- Complex texture patterns associated with specific tumor types
- Learned representations of diagnostically significant features

By this point, the neural network discovers semantically meaningful, high-level concepts that are directly relevant to the classification task: classifying a tumor as malignant or benign. High-level features extracted by a trained network are much closer to what a radiologist or pathologist would spot by hand.

Lastly, in layer 5, the neural network transforms the learned features (high-level features in layer 4) to make the final decision regarding the class of the tumor according to the sample. In this example, the output decision is that of a benign tumor. The network has learned to associate the "learned features" to the known tumor class, leveraging the patterns and characteristics it has seen during learning.

From this representation, and by understanding the hierarchical nature of feature learning in deep neural networks, a clinician can start to understand how (and why) these models can learn locally relevant patterns and features from medical images, and translate those over a hierarchy to enable automatic decision making. Again, this example is solely for illustrative purposes for the reader.

Natural Language Processing and Computer Vision

Natural language processing (NLP) is a field closely linked to LLM development and application. Both involve interaction between computers and human language in some capacity. NLP algorithms are applied to preprocessing and structuring of the textual data used to train LLMs, much like clinicians do when they read a chart—they just do it really quickly. In addition, NLP provides the vocabulary to understand and evaluate the linguistic capacities of LLMs: whether they understand the clinical jargon used by clinicians, their ability to interpret clinician notes, or their capacity to generate explanations to patients that are clear and understandable.

Arguably, LLMs can also derive a visual modality by learning from a complementary source of data modalities, a field known as multimodal learning. In this setting, computer vision comes into play as a form of data analysis that aims to unlock patterns in visual data. In the same way that a radiologist uses medical images, such as X-rays and CT scans, to identify abnormalities and diagnose different conditions, multimodal LLMs can learn to interpret images in conjunction with text in order to provide more nuanced, context-aware responses. For instance, an LLM fine-tuned to medical literature and radiology images might be able to help produce reports or answer questions about clinically relevant imaging findings.

Perhaps, in the field of healthcare, LLMs could support clinicians with clinical decision support (providing evidence-based recommendations and risk assessment based on patient data), with patient communication (generating personalized educational materials, answering basic questions, or providing virtual support), and with medical research (literature reviews, hypothesis generation, and data analysis).

But they're also not coming for your job—they can't. Most patients come to clinicians with complex presentations and symptoms, which might require further investigation or follow-up, or even just someone to chat to. LLMs can become part of a clinician's toolkit to both aid decision making and to assist in the complex work of delivering meaningful and personalized patient care. They could, for example, be the stethoscope of the 21st century.

We will need to consider what ethical implications emerge as we start to use LLMs in clinical practice, including aspects such as data privacy, algorithmic fairness, and the impact of these tools on the doctor-patient relationship. This will require partnerships between clinicians, AI researchers, and ethicists to enable responsible and beneficial deployment in healthcare.

The Anatomy of an LLM

To remind you, the most important constituent of an LLM is a neural network. Recall from the previous mention that your brain is a network of biological neurons, perhaps 100 billion of them! A biological neuron is a cell in the brain that receives input from other neurons, performs some computation on the input, and then sends output to some downstream neurons. That large biological neural network is what allows your brain to be able to process information, make sense of the world, recognize patterns, and behave intelligently.

Artificial neural networks are our best efforts to replicate this process on computers. We create relatively simple mathematical models involving very large numbers of simulated neurons and connections between them. We can train them to recognize such things as images, sounds, and language by feeding it huge amounts of data that exhibit the pattern (e.g., malignant tumor) we want it to detect. And here's the interesting part: these networks work out from the data how the patterns go for themselves, by tweaking connection strengths between neurons through learning. The more layers in the network and the more data we feed it, the more it achieves.

For instance, by presenting an image recognition network with tens of millions of other photos of cats and dogs during training, it learns that certain types of fur textures, ear shapes, and nose shapes offer clues that something probably is or isn't either a cat or a dog. When you show it almost any new photo after training, bang, it now realizes that most likely it's a cat or most likely a dog. The newest neural networks are beginning to ply their way through increasingly impressive algorithmic architecture, including image generation from text, language translation, disease identification from medical scans, and application creation from idea descriptions.

Transformers

Now that we know the mechanics of deep learning, let's peel back the inner workings of the LLM to see what it's actually made of, keeping in mind that the use of a neural network is just one small part of it. An LLM is not a simple algorithm; it's a model that includes both algorithms and architectures such as transformers. Transformers are a key architecture component for NLP tasks, which are a large focus of LLMs. NLP techniques enable LLMs to perform many language specific tasks such as text generation, summarization, and question and answer.

Transformers are a set of neural networks that use an encoder and decoder structure. The encoder converts input text into a numerical representation so the computer can capture its meaning and context, such as taking as input clinical notes that capture a patient's health status. The decoder takes the encoded representation of the input text and generates output text. In the clinical note example, the decoder could generate a summary of the patient's key medical issues.

But here's the clever part: the transformer doesn't just focus on each word individually—it focuses on how that word is related to every other word in the vicinity. It's like a small army of friends are helping you read the story, each of them looking at a different part and reporting back to you. With this transformer architecture, the LLM can read bodies of healthcare data like clinical notes, EHR data, and medical history and do a variety of tasks like summarization or perform question and answer.

The transformer architecture needs one more architectural invention to enable the functionality or what some call magic that we see in LLMs today, an invention that occurred in 2017. Attention is a mechanism allowing the LLM to focus on specific parts of the input when processing and generating text. The attention mechanism allows the LLM to focus on the most relevant parts of a patient's EHR when generating a summary of key medical or health issues.

Tokens

Tokens are the basic units of work that LLMs and transformers work with—either as input or output. Words and characters can be tokens for an LLM. Tokenization is the process of decomposing text into smaller units, called tokens. This process is critical to transformers because it breaks down text into manageable pieces that an LLM can understand and analyze.

With text data, the first thing an LLM does is tokenize the input by splitting it up into smaller successive units (or tokens). Consider this example sentence from the world of healthcare: The patient was diagnosed with hypertension and was given lisinopril.

Using a word-based tokenization method, the 10 tokens (represented in quotes) would be:

["The", "patient", "was", "diagnosed", "with", "hypertension", "and", "prescribed", "lisinopril", "."]

The input tokens are first embedded into vectors that encode their semantic and syntactic information and are then passed through the transformer layers that contain the self-attention mechanisms that learn relations between tokens and produce rich contextual representations.

For example, in a clinical setting, the transformer could determine that the tokens "hypertension" and "lisinopril" are strongly related because lisinopril is the name of a medication used to treat hypertension. This knowledge can be useful for the task of named entity recognition (identifying medical conditions and treatments in text) or relation extraction (identifying the relationships between medical entities).

What an LLM learns during training is how to predict the next token in a sequence given the tokens preceding it. To produce a text, the LLM probabilistic distributions are used to sample—or select—the next token given the immediately preceding tokens. The process is repeated iteratively until some stopping rule is satisfied and the process completes.

In a clinical application, for example, an LLM could generate scribbled notes for the doctor, or summarize the patient's condition, such as this response to the input token sequence "Patient is a 65-year-old male with a history of": Patient is a 65-year-old male with a history of type 2 diabetes, hypertension, and hyperlipidemia, and who presents with complaints of fatigue and polyuria.

With such context and token relationships, LLMs can produce text that's accurate and coherent to read—even when the input is a long medical record for clinical documentation, patient education, or medical research summary.

Attention

Attention, the "secret sauce" of NLP and LLMs, is an innovation by Google in 2017.[5] Imagine giving each word a spotlight. For example, the transformer emphasizes medical details that are related to each other—such as the main diagnosis and key lab results—helping it to filter out noise and focus on what's most relevant for that patient. No order required. Unlike reading a medical record in order, the transformer can hop and skip, consider how a data point early in someone's chart affects a data point later in the chart, and vice versa. Historically challenging cases could be studied in an order similar to how experts sent an email to each other, picking up context along the way. It's similar to how having multiple levels of expertise helps doctors piece together strange medical diagnoses. But the transformer works thanks to dozens of layers of this sort of understanding on top of one another: each new layer gets better at tying together relationships among X-rays, MRIs, symptoms, and health history, until the output is massively insightful.

One of the reasons that LLMs held promise for language modeling was their incorporation of attention. Attention allows a transformer to weigh the degree to which each token is related to other tokens, based on the proximity of the tokens. The transformer ability to identify and weight complex dependencies arguably underpins its ability to produce contextually accurate representations.

In healthcare, attention can shift LLMs' focus to the most clinically pertinent tokens. For example, the patient was found to have chest pain and shortness of breath and was diagnosed to have an acute myocardial infarction (i.e., heart attack). The attention mechanism would enable the model to pinpoint that the tokens "chest pain", "shortness of breath", and "acute myocardial infarction" are semantically clustered together in a way that is especially informative about the meaning of the sentence: they reference the major symptoms of a heart attack. Thus, it would assign higher

---

5 Ashish Vaswani et al., "Attention Is All You Need," 31st Conference on Neural Information Processing Systems (NIPS 2017), Long Beach, CA, *https://proceedings.neurips.cc/paper_files/paper/2017/file/3f5ee243547dee91fbd053c1c4a845aa-Paper.pdf.*

attention weights to these tokens to generate a better representation of the sentence's meaning.

In addition, attention helps LLMs deal with the long-range nature of medical text. For instance, a clinical note could mention the medical history of a patient at the start of the note, but discussing this history at the start of the note can be relevant to what is said about the current condition, observed at the end of the note. With attention, the model can capture this dependency and produce representations that are both more accurate and better suited to the task.

Attention enables the model to assign weights to tokens based on their contextual significance relative to all other tokens in the text, to discover long-term dependencies, and to construct context-sensitive representations. All of these are imperative for healthcare applications, in which the relationships between medical entities and long-distance dependencies play a pivotal role in the text-generation, summarization, and analysis tasks.

LLMs can translate medical jargon to human-sounding text in real time, like a daily on-call medical interpreter; type coherent conversations with patients; establish a convincing medical voice for health education materials that feel like a nurse wrote them; and answer medical questions comprehensively and meaningfully, even when the questions are open-ended and tricky enough that I wouldn't know where to start. This is just one step of where transformers are headed in medicine.

Parameters

Parameters are another critical feature of LLMs. Picture a medical student with a supernaturally good memory. She would be able to read astonishing amounts of information from all the "medical textbooks" of data at her disposal. The more topics in medicine she studied (anatomy, physiology, pharmacology, pathology, etc.), the more she filled her head with knowledge about the topic. All that knowledge would literally be stored in the model's parameters—that is, all the medical facts, concepts, relationships, and context the model picked up and learned from its reading. You can think of parameters as the critical bits of medical knowledge the model picks up and "remembers" from all its reading.

The more parameters, the more medical knowledge is available to the model. A model with 200 billion parameters doesn't just have more history and lines going into it compared with 5 million; it's literally absorbed a whole lot more medical knowledge and connections with other medical information. More parameters means deeper embedded learning of more complicated medical concepts. A model doesn't have to have billions of parameters to be useful in healthcare. Medical students might study entire libraries in one narrow field, but they can still graduate to be decent experts on a narrow spectrum (e.g., cardiology, neurology, or endocrinology). A model of 30 million parameters trained on oncology alone could still answer complex cancer-related questions using the narrow and targeted knowledge it is focused on.

As AI software engineers find new ways to let their models augment what they've learned, such as connecting their LLM to medical models like PubMed, this will allow their LLMs to learn outside of their parameters or to connect models to existing real-world healthcare apps. In the world of medicine, it's as if a medical student was able to plug themselves into the PubMed database or conduct clinical trials as needed.

A common way to think about a healthcare LLM's complexity: the more parameters, the more complicated and capable of learning it becomes. A healthcare LLM consisting of billions of parameters is more powerful than one consisting of millions. Parameters govern many different aspects of an LLM's behavior:

- Identifying patient emotions using tone and content to detect, for example, expressions of pain, hopelessness, or anxiety
- Generating creative medical outputs: combining learned patterns to create new medical text, translating complex medical language into human-sounding text, or writing other creative outputs such as patient education resources

Parameters affect how the LLM understands healthcare text and how it generates text. Parameters can be adjusted to control the quality of generated text and creativity. Adjusting the temperature parameter in an LLM is like turning a precision knob on a complex machine. At the lowest settings, the knob is turned to the left, producing responses that are precise, predictable, and factual. As you gradually rotate the knob clockwise, you introduce more variability and creativity into the system. With each slight turn, you loosen the constraints on the machine's output. As you continue turning to the right toward the highest settings, you give the machine more freedom to explore unusual combinations and less likely outcomes, which may lead to more inaccurate responses. At the far right, with the knob turned to its maximum, the output becomes highly unpredictable and diverse, often producing surprising and sometimes nonsensical results.

Weight is another parameter that influences the importance of connections between words and phrases. For example, an LLM trained and focused on hospital readmissions risks using a patient's medical history, EHR data, medications, and recent lab test results. Let's say that recent EHR data shows a 69-year-old male patient having multiple hospitalizations in the last six months, taking lisinopril and metoprolol with chronic obstructive pulmonary disease (COPD). The LLM would learn weight parameters and may assign higher weights to recent hospitalization history and chronic conditions because they are more predictive of readmission risk.

Temperature and weight are examples of two parameters, but there are many more. More parameters don't necessarily equal better performance in healthcare LLMs. It all depends on how they are designed and trained on the relevant medical data. Smaller LLMs with few parameters can often be trained from scratch and then fine-tuned on small amounts of data for a particular healthcare task at hand. In fact, there have been impressive clinical successes of small LLMs with a handful of parameters.[6] Parameter research is still one of the areas of active development, with continuous efforts being made to find more parsimonious ways to represent and learn medical language.

LLM and Generative AI Potential

With the emergence of AI systems that can learn holistically from raw data, there is no need to have everything structured by humans first. Programming algorithms previously meant that we had to explicitly define all elements structuring a messaging interface, a scientific paper, or code, dedicating time and effort to identify and input representations of concepts, rules, templates, decision trees, and the like that defined the solution space. LLMs digest messaging data, papers, or code in raw form and self-discover relevant forms of representation.

In essence, this implies that LLMs no longer rely on rigid rules and constraints but instead on flexibly stated statistical inferences. In healthcare, this would mean LLMs learning directly from raw, unstructured medical textual notes, research papers, or clinical case notes to attain an intuitive grasp of diseases, treatments, and patient care that would obviate the need for humans to first manually encode medical knowledge.

The difference with this sort of AI, compared with most of the past, is that the noisy, unvarnished messiness of actual life itself gets transmitted more completely into the models via the self-supervised route. Self-supervised learning is a type of machine learning that teaches an LLM without human-generated annotations of the data or labeling of the data itself. For example, an LLM trained on a huge medical literature and case-report database might subsequently pick up on the nuances of disease processes, medical decision making when treating a patient, and patient communication.

Against this background of LLM comprehension, combine generative architectures that can create unbounded novel outputs, and you have systems that go well beyond pattern matching and local optimization. In medicine, this could potentially lead to, say, LLMs developing new disease mechanisms, treatment plans, or even new therapies through creative juxtaposition of insights across the various silos of medicine.

This revolutionary flip to bottom-up self-directed learning (instead of top-down constrained instruction) represents a shift in the basis of AI's paradigm. Principles are emergent from data at scale instead of programmed assumptions or even a tiny fraction of human-scaled knowledge. This provides a path for highly scalable AI that's

---

6 Alex Edwards, "Clinical Translations Better with Smaller Language Models, Research Finds," Slator, December 20, 2023, *https://slator.com/clinical-translations-better-with-smaller-language-models-research-finds*.

much more naturalistic than "narrow" AI. For healthcare, that can mean AI systems that are capable of learning from, and keeping up with, the exponentially growing medical literature and uncovering patterns and insights that might escape the already overworked human experts.

These new LLMs have natural language generation capabilities that are unprecedented in terms of reach and quality. Coupled with emerging agentic AI, new types of applications could become possible. Sophisticated language skills would enable LLMs used to summarize patient notes, history, and instructions into layman's terms for clarity of understanding. An LLM could summarize a lengthy technical medical report on the patient's condition into clear, easy-to-understand layman's terms for the patient. A possible use could be generating personalized patient education such as postoperative care instructions based on the patient's individual procedures and medical conditions.

The LLM could enrich a patient's Electronic Health Record (EHR) through deep linguistic analysis, arriving at an insight concerning a patient's course of treatment that wasn't explicitly stated in the doctor's notes. For example, an LLM might infer from certain tone patterns in two months of notes that this patient is having particular difficulty with medication adherence or perhaps that a patient is hiding unspoken fears about his or her prognosis.

In healthcare, an LLM could help make physician-patient communication less stilted and more natural and effective. A model could translate a patient's informal description of their symptoms from conversational vernacular to precise medical terms, divining the emotional subtext—or the other way around: taking a doctor's explanations of, say, a treatment regimen and rewriting them for easy comprehension and adherence from the patient.

One emerging capacity for LLMs holds the potential to create truly customized and tailor-fit individual experiences: the ability to learn, as well as dynamically evolve and adapt, on a per-person basis to individual-level preferences and needs. By ingesting textual content paired with indicators of subjective human relevance during training, individualized language models can operationalize an understanding of subjective human interests.

As LLMs digest different clinical corpora, they could suggest what type of health intervention approach with the specifics (medication regimen, exercise versus diet, etc.) for the patient's lifestyle factor and comorbidity. Even emotional intelligence as well as empathy modeling that improves patient interaction could be applied.

For example, an LLM might process a patient's electronic health record containing notes from doctors, diagnostic tests, as well as pharmaceutical and recent treatment history to build a profile of that patient's uniqueness. Then it might suggest a patient-centric individualized treatment plan, accounting for medical, behavioral, psychosocial, and environmental parameters impacting the patient's health journeys.

Additionally, LLMs could be used to run empathetic virtual health assistants that can converse with patients in a way that's supportive and encouraging. An LLM-driven chatbot could recognize a patient's own subtle linguistic cues and adjust its own communication style to better align with the patient's needs, inspiring comfort and boosting patients' resilience to stay committed to their treatment plans.

LLMs are still in their infancy today. In the decades ahead, as they learn to process vast amounts of raw data and adjust to circumstances, personalities, and emotionally vulnerable patients, LLMs could truly transform how healthcare is delivered. We'll expand medical decision making, improve patient communication, establish true personalized medication, and improve workplace efficiency. LLMs could be used to imagine interventions that enhance compassionate care while reducing disruptive emotions that hurt patients and disrupt healthcare. We will make better clinical decisions and communicate more effectively with our patients. While such tools can improve clinical care, we will always require the careful attention of committed professionals and humans. AI will not be taking the place of our dedicated doctors. These advancements will augment medical knowledge, hard-won clinical experience, and personal connection to patients.

Art of Building LLMs

We have discussed use cases and the power of LLMs, but in the healthcare and medical domain and perhaps all industries, these LLMs will not provide the desired outcome unless augmented with other data. In the healthcare field, this may include a provider or insurer's website, a company's standard-of-care procedures, electronic health records, clinical data, wearable data, genomic data, and more.

Retrieval Augmented Generation

LLMs sometimes answer with amazing accuracy, and at times they regurgitate facts from their training data that is irrelevant or false. That is, they *hallucinate*. This is because LLMs know how words relate to each other statistically but not what they truly mean. There was a lot of excitement around the concept of emergent capabilities with LLMs when they were introduced to the public at large.

As a result, a number of organizations sought to explore and uncover potential hidden functionalities within these models. They thought LLMs possessed unknown abilities or features that could be harnessed. However, as researchers dug deeper into the concept of emergent capabilities, it became increasingly apparent that the notion was a mirage rather than hidden functionality or feature of LLMs.

Over time, the technical community reached a consensus that the idea of emergent capabilities in LLMs was unfounded. The observed behaviors and outputs of these models could be explained by their extensive training data and the complex patterns they learned during the training process rather than any inherent, undiscovered abilities or functionality.

Instead, LLMs exhibit a strong ability to incorporate and prioritize contextual information provided within the prompts they receive. This characteristic has been consistently demonstrated through research, highlighting the importance of both understanding and optimizing LLMs' known capabilities rather than chasing after the elusive notion of emergent functionalities.

By strategically embedding pertinent information into the prompt, organizations can effectively guide the LLM's output, ensuring that the generated content is more closely aligned with the proper context and desired output. This approach leverages the inherent capability of LLMs to assimilate and apply the knowledge presented to them, resulting in responses that are more accurate, factual, and contextually appropriate.

The inclusion of contextual reference data in prompts has proven to be a highly effective technique for optimizing the performance of LLMs across a wide range of applications. This method enables users to harness the vast potential of these powerful models while maintaining a higher degree of control over the generated content, ultimately leading to more reliable and useful outputs.

The inclusion of contextual reference data or external sources evolved into an AI framework, retrieval-augmented generation (RAG). It is an AI framework designed to improve the quality of LLM-generated responses by grounding the model using external data sources of data, which supplement the LLM's training data.

Without using RAG, a user engaged with a chatbot app using an LLM is depicted in Figure 2-4, which shows a typical user prompt to an LLM.

The first step is the user enters a prompt, like "What can I do to rehab a strain in my hamstring?" The chatbot app or interface receives the prompt and feeds the question to its LLM. The model searches its corpus of data for an answer and returns the answer to the chatbot, which in turns feeds the response to the user. This is a basic example which is not meant to illustrate the workings of any particular chatbot or leading LLMs. Such tools may have more sophisticated methods of incorporating aspects of search or may employ other functionalities to derive a response.

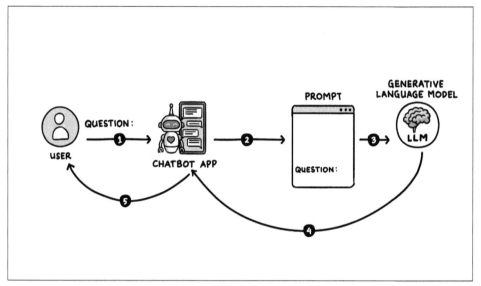

Figure 2-4. User prompt to an LLM

Now let's look at how this picture changes with the use of RAG, illustrated in Figure 2-5.

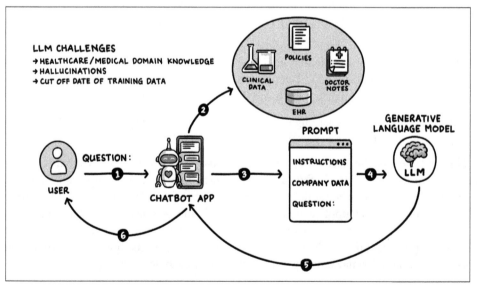

Figure 2-5. Chatbot using RAG

Using RAG solves a few challenges facing LLMs, and in the healthcare or medical domain, a big challenge is the lack of access to healthcare data such as pharmacy, clinical, EHR, policies, doctor notes, and more. Armed with healthcare data and company proprietary information from its own data sources and website, it is less likely the output from the LLM will be inaccurate, making it more likely you can minimize or eliminate hallucinations. More importantly, the LLM may respond with "I don't know."

Returning to Figure 2-5, the user enters a prompt, which is received by the chatbot. Except instead of passing the question on to the LLM, a search (Step 2) is made of the company's data sources. In this example, those sources include policies, doctor notes, clinical data, and EHR data. Other data can be included, such as pharmacy, claims data, or whatever external reference data sources are deemed essential for user queries of the chatbot.

Step 3 has the chatbot providing instructions for the LLM in the prompt. Those instructions may direct the LLM to make the response sound like it's coming from a doctor while using language easily understood by those with a high school reading level. The external data (company data) useful for responding to the prompt is included in addition to the original user question. The LLM armed with these three elements of the prompt will prioritize the company's data or external data sources. The LLM will generate a response and the chatbot will deliver the response to the user.

The benefits of RAG are numerous. Drawing upon the current best-sourced information avoids another problem that afflicts LLMs: they can fall out of date quickly, as their available information reflects their last trained data date. If the model needs to adapt to new information, it must be retrained. Building a content store that can be updated with new material when necessary allows for a quick and dirty adaptation rather than a top-to-bottom revamp.

In addition, the prompt instructions could prod the LLM to demonstrate good behavior, such as acknowledging when it doesn't know the answer to a question. If there isn't sufficient confidence in the content store to answer the user's query, the model can do the right thing and say that it doesn't know rather than provide a plausible but potentially wrong response.

However, the effectiveness of RAG depends on the quality of the retrieval system. If the search doesn't provide the LLMs with the most relevant, high-quality grounding information, the model might not be able to answer any questions—even though the data might be suitable for answering such questions. Hence, the importance of quality healthcare information.

In short, retrieval-augmented generation is a promising new milestone in AI. The best way to improve the performance of LLMs so far is to root them in external, timely, and verifiable data. Supercharging LLMs with a company's proprietary data provides the LLM chatbot reliable information from an external data source allowing more accurate responses. This avoids the issue of the LLM not having the requisite knowledge because it was not included in its training datasets and reduces hallucinations.

Building an LLM is as much an art as it is a science. It involves a creative process that requires imagination, intuition, and a deep understanding of language and human behavior.

The next section describes the art of building an LLM describing six activities:

- Conceptualization
- Data Selection and Curation
- Model Architecture and Design
- Prompt Engineering
- Refinement and Feedback
- Integration with Apps

Conceptualization

Assembling a diverse team often goes a long way in building an LLM that addresses the needs and requirements of its constituent users. Figure 2-6 illustrates a diverse team organized and launched to understand the problem and potential path forward: a conceptualization phase.

Figure 2-6. Conceptualization

The first step in forming an LLM to target a healthcare issue is to crystallize the healthcare problem or task at hand. This would entail landing on a highly specific healthcare domain and use case while describing the desired end game of the LLM. Identifying the healthcare domain may include one or more of the following steps:

1. Specify the medical specialty or niche (radiology, pathology, oncology, etc.) or the enhancement (clinical decision support functions) that is at issue. What kind of data exists for that domain (e.g., medical images, electronic health records, clinical notes, medical literature)?

2. Specify the intended use cases: clearly articulate the purpose and goals of the LLM within the healthcare context. Examples of use cases could include disease diagnosis, risk prediction, treatment recommendation, website navigation, call center assist, and patient communication. Chapters 3, 4, and 5 have a laundry list of use cases. Define the target users of the LLM, such as physicians, nurses, or patients.

3. Determine the desired outcomes or objectives of each use case. Define the relevant measures of performance metrics through which you will assess the success of the LLM. Consider factors such as accuracy, sensitivity, specificity, or other domain-specific evaluation measures. Define any constraints or requirements, such as interpretability, fairness, or regulatory compliance.

4. Evaluate the availability and accessibility of relevant healthcare data needed to train the LLM. Understand the volume, variety, and quality of data, and any potential bias or limitation. Determine if additional data collection or curation efforts are necessary.

5. Engage with domain experts: collaborate with clinicians, researchers, or data scientists who are knowledgeable about the problem domain. Perform user-centered design techniques to create a model that is both needed and usable by the intended users. Ask for their advice to make sure the problem statement stays grounded in clinical realities and helps to address truly important challenges. Enlist them in establishing desired outcomes, choosing relevant data sources, and providing the unique perspective afforded by domain-specific expertise.

Defining the healthcare problem and the use case of the LLM at this stage also focuses both the design team members and the use of data in a specific direction, since they now intuitively understand the context within which the LLM is supposed to be used. They are able to work toward specific performance criteria and have a shared understanding of what the resulting LLM has to "do" or achieve for an actual user.

After it's been clearly and thoroughly defined, here are the typical next steps: data collection/preprocessing, model architecture design, training/optimization, evaluation/validation, deployment/monitoring in a healthcare setting. But all of these would fall apart if the problem definition was compromised.

Data Selection and Curation

In healthcare, where lives or loss of health hangs in the balance, choosing an LLM's training data becomes even more critical. Training data volume matters, but care delivery often requires medical and healthcare LLMs that exhibit extreme precision and nuanced context. Interpreting medical records in a way that's just a bit off the mark could lead to a number of issues, depending on the use case. Figure 2-7 depicts the harried work of data selection and curation where data scientists and sometimes machine learning engineers and AI engineers working on the LLM must understand the external data sources to be used in RAG that will feed the LLM.

Figure 2-7. Data selection and curation

In many healthcare companies, data is siloed and guarded (or "owned") by different data teams. Many companies have no definite policy regarding data governance and access. Getting access to specific datasets is often a challenge. Training data can have gaps that affect the model's resiliency when taken out of the "lab" and applied in clinical settings. For example, training data that is de-identified or has only a certain level of granularity due to HIPAA or GDPR may not reflect "real-world" data, and the model runs into difficulties or does not perform as expected.

Patients' raw medical data will not be released to nonresearchers: that is highly sensitive data and subject to strict rules on privacy as well as ethical issues such as informed consent. Data release policies must balance transparency with patient privacy. Defining how the LLM is to be used (e.g., drug discovery, clinical decision support) will shape what data sources are relevant.

One way to complement both an open source and proprietary foundation model is *retrieval-augmented generation* (RAG), discussed previously. It adds to the model's knowledge so it can extend past what it got a chance to ingest in pretraining; in inference time, it can match contextual documents (for example, website data, patient records, and so on) and condition its outputs on them. It is an easy addition, bolting on domain-specific corpora to the model without touching the fundamentals.

Model Architecture and Design

The specialties of LLMs today run the spectrum from those that use different data types and modes (text only, text and images, text and voice conversations, text and audio streams, text and musical scores, text and programming code, text and video) to those that perform numerous different tasks (summarization, classification, generation, translation, recommendation, and so forth).

An LLM's architecture is its design, specifying how information flows through the model and how the model will process and generate language under that information flow. Architectural design, depicted in Figure 2-8, is an intuitive computational blend of creativity, iteration, and domain knowledge. An early design choice is deciding which deep learning architecture to use for the LLM. There exist different types of neural networks, and deciding which type is the model architecture is an early architecture choice.

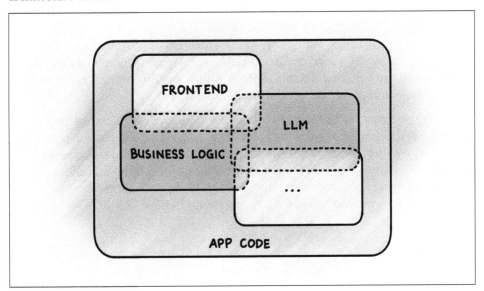

Figure 2-8. Architecture and design

The architecture and design involves not only the LLM model but determining how this model will fit with other components needed to render the model's inferences to users. In other words, is the model frontended with a web application, it is an app like a chatbot, or is it both? Where does the LLM reside in the overall architecture, and how does data flow between the components? These are decisions that can be done and realized, i.e., implemented in parallel with LLM development.

The model must then be built, which is done with deep learning programming libraries. The model must then be fine-tuned and optimized. Fine-tuning an LLM denotes adjusting the values of some model parameters so that the model performs better on certain tasks or on some specific dataset. Since fine-tuning is a heuristic approach, engineers try different methods and make decisions with a mix of experimentation and intuition based on empirical results and on domain knowledge.

Prompt Engineering

Prompt engineering can be an art form, as it involves crafting input prompts or queries to steer the responses of the model. Designing prompts is a skill that requires domain expertise to induce the model to produce answers that the human engineer wants to see. Engineers need to compose prompts that give context, constraints, and cues to the model to hopefully induce it to produce output that is robust (accurate and likely) and free-standing (readably coherent text). Figure 2-9 is a visual representation often associated with input prompts that many of us have grown accustomed to as we use leading LLMs. While Figure 2-9 is a visual representation, prompt engineering usually begins with understanding the task or goal you want to achieve with an AI model. It's about crafting effective text inputs (prompts) that guide AI models to produce desired outputs. This involves careful wording, context-setting, and sometimes including examples or specific instructions.

Prompt engineering for LLMs means very carefully selecting the textual cues incorporated into the prompt to guide the output of a model. This is a departure from how we interact with search engines, which take a static query and find the corresponding static answer. Prompting is different: not only is the query continuous text that carries information about context, constraints, and objectives, but it also forms part of an ongoing signaling process between a user and an open-ended LLM.

Figure 2-9. Prompt engineering

Prompt engineers do research to determine what data the LLM was trained on and what biases the model has so that they can compile lists of possible potholes to avoid. Related to this, domain-specificity is very important. The language of an appropriate medical or healthcare prompt would be different from the language of an appropriate engineering-oriented prompt, so users can avoid mismatches between concepts in the prompt and the model's latent representation space.

Signals from testing cycles will flag places in which the model is promptly susceptible to noise delivering hallucinations probably due to the dearth of external contextual reinforcement, where those false positives then flood in. For example, the LLM is trained to analyze and interpret radiology images like X-rays or CT scans to detect abnormalities or signs of a disease. If the training dataset for the LLM was limited or lacked external validation from a radiologist, the LLM might hallucinate and falsely identify an abnormality.

In other circumstances, training with contrast cases, or artificially inserting objects into the input stream (both positive and negative examples), enables the model to learn to discern small differences. This coded feedback could serve as constant feedback loops that refined the art of prompting, allowing engineers to chisel, shape, and direct model behavior. This loop causes prompting to become as much art as science.

Refinement and Feedback

This is how you build an LLM: you go through an iterative process where you gradually improve the model. You collect feedback from users or domain experts, or set evaluation metrics, and iteratively improve the model's performance and capabilities. This iterative cycle allows engineers to perfect the way the model generates responses to prompts, address known shortcomings, and adapt to changing needs and tastes. Figure 2-10 illustrates a continuous feedback loop for developing an LLM.

Figure 2-10. Refinement and feedback

Feedback loops should be defined, paying particular attention to direct feedback by users about the output, which is the best instruction the system will ever get. This can be in the form of ratings, survey dimensions, and even open-ended comments on its strengths, weaknesses, and areas for improvement. In certain areas, such as healthcare, the thoughts of subject-matter experts are indispensable to ensure that the LLM is keeping up with professional standards and generating appropriate and relevant outputs. Finally, quantitative metrics such as accuracy, fluency, and coherence can be computed as part of benchmark datasets that assess the LLM's performance.

Another refinement technique includes fine-tuning, wherein the LLM is retrained on new and/or tweaked data explicitly in line with feedback or other desired alterations. There's also more targeted and discriminating prompts, which guide the LLM toward desired output samples that are on topic and context-sensitive. Finally, there's the reinforcement learning technique, where an LLM might be conditioned or incentivized to produce digital text output that falls in line with preset rewards to nudge the system toward developing subsequent behavioral tendencies. There should be an iterative process of feedback from real users and experts about the LLM as it is built, helping to ensure that the LLM is tailored to the needs and preferences of its intended users.

Integration with Apps

It is also worth noting that creating an application or app that makes use of an LLM involves some different considerations compared with just building the LLM. Creating an LLM app would involve integrating an LLM with the application's logic and features. This might involve designing the application's interfaces and APIs to allow the application to send inputs to the LLM, receive outputs from it, and integrate these outputs into the application's user experience. Integration might include handling the data preprocessing, postprocessing, and error handling required to engage with the LLM. Figure 2-11 illustrates the decisions to be made in how to integrate with both external and internal systems where the LLM will reside. The number of ways to integrate with apps and applications is numerous and will involve making architectural decisions based on both what is feasible and practical, given requirements on performance, availability, scalability, and so on.

Figure 2-11. Integration with apps

One aspect where user interface design is paramount in applications of LLMs is how users provide inputs to the LLM, and how they understand and digest what LLMs provide in return. Developers have to design natural-feeling and "human-sounding" interfaces to guide users in feeding information to the LLM, answering requests of the LLM, and instructing the LLM to generate a suggested response or content that's closely relevant to the "speaker's" intention. This could be a chat interface, a simple text input form for a user, or a set of good old widgets and menus.

Applying LLMs can also require significant optimization to achieve acceptable levels of responsiveness and efficiency. Real-time application tasks, such as dialogues and conversations, often involve too much data or computation to afford the time for each sentence the LLM-driven application sends to the LLM, receives an answer from, and processes downstream while communicating with other users.

The developers working on ensuring performance of such applications may need to optimize software code (e.g., tuning input and output formats of communication with the LLM to minimize the time needed to fly such data between the application and the LLM), data processing pipelines (e.g., caching the most relevant data needed to compute an answer), and application infrastructure designs (e.g., for distributed computing, which allows scaling up both in terms of concurrent requests and requests' complexity).

Security is of utmost importance in LLM applications. Sensitive healthcare and personal data require full protection from information leaks and malware attacks. Latest security practices should be applied to fully protect against unauthorized access, data breaches, and malware attacks. Developers should choose the most appropriate security method to encrypt and protect user data while providing assurance to users.

As is the case with any application, LLM applications will benefit from human feedback cycles and iteration. LLM application designers should include systems and mechanisms for collecting human feedback, analysis of usage patterns, and iterative improvement of the application based on user needs and preferences. This work could involve A/B testing, human surveys, and data analytics to learn more about application use and to inform iterative improvements in the application and the LLM.

Summary

In this chapter, we introduced the inner workings of LLMs and generative AI, delving beyond traditional classification and prediction tasks to uncover their use of neural networks by way of machine learning and deep learning. We provided background on the debate of AI versus machine learning, reaching a conclusion that they are different. For example, machine learning is a subset of AI, the goals of AI are much broader, and AI includes several domains necessary for LLMs. These include NLP and computer vision.

Moving beyond mere classification and prediction, we discussed the ability of LLMs to generate human-like text across diverse tasks and domains. We dissected LLMs' architecture and inner workings, including tokens, transformers, parameters, and attention mechanisms underpinning LLMs' language processing abilities. We illustrated how neural networks—a key element of an LLM—function by depicting the detection of a benign tumor.

We explored the process of building LLMs, covering the various life cycle phases of conceptualizing a solution to a problem or challenge resulting in defining one or more healthcare use cases. RAG is a key aspect for healthcare LLMS in ensuring such models use external data sources to increase accuracy, essential in the healthcare domain. We illustrated the use of RAG and how this AI framework works with an LLM.

Understanding the inner workings of LLMs at a high level should prepare the reader for understanding how the many future use cases described in the next chapters can come to life in the world of healthcare.

CHAPTER 3

Beyond White Coats

Nidhi sighed as she slumped onto the couch after work. At 49, divorced, and living in the south suburbs of Chicago, IL, she'd become accustomed to running herself ragged, caring for her house, job, and teenage children by herself. These days, she feels tired of keeping up appearances. Her hands began to move across her body in a kind of absent shuffling. *Feel*, she thought. *Feel*. She pressed a part of her left breast. What was that? She pressed again; a little lump on the side of her left breast. She ran her fingers across it worriedly. Her heart began to race—this wasn't normal. She spoke to her doctor first thing the next morning, and got an appointment that week. The waiting was torture. When will I be heard, when will we know for sure? She tried to stay busy, not to think about it, but her mind returned to it again and again, wandering over what it might be.

At the hospital, doctors removed the lump and did a mammogram. A biopsy was needed to ascertain whether the mass was malignant, the physician stated, and then things would be clear. Nidhi felt weak with anxiety and trepidation. A week later, there was a call from the hospital providing a biopsy report. It was breast cancer. Nidhi felt a wave of horror, as strong as a punch to her stomach.

Nidhi, a first-generation immigrant, had no family, friends, or any formal support system to speak of in the US. She didn't even know that yearly mammograms were required. She didn't know how to deal with insurance requirements such as preauthorizations, copays, or documentation that would have to be given to the insurance company for claims. She had never scheduled a doctor's appointment in the US before, let alone a chemo treatment or a radiation session—and all this while her nausea was at its worst.

She had to drive herself to all the appointments and facilities, often when she felt unwell due to fevers or serious infections resulting from low blood counts. She still had to take care of her two teenagers, who couldn't drive and had their own constellation of problems. Nidhi was running out of hope. She was running out of money. She was failing her children and troubled by her own body. Over the next couple of months, she would undergo an onslaught of doctors' visits, reading and Googling, and crafting a plan of action. Nidhi's cancer was Stage IIIB and had spread to her lymph nodes and collar bones. Her prognosis was poor with surgery and radiation treatment. However, she could opt for a clinical trial that her oncologist felt might be a good fit. In addition, her oncologist recommended she investigate focused ultrasound,[1] a novel therapeutic being used for breast cancer.[2]

Nidhi's story is a glimpse into the current state of healthcare, including the anxiety and burden on the patient and those that support the patient. This chapter presents the reality of automation in healthcare today, and how large language models (LLMs) and generative AI will further the evolution of patient care. The main objective of this chapter is for the reader to understand how automation and the technological leaps forward in LLMs and generative AI solutions are beginning to disrupt healthcare processes, workflows, and digital transformation of operational efficiency.

Current State of Automation in Healthcare

Nidhi's attempts to make sense of her cancer diagnosis and figure out the healthcare system is all too familiar for those in her position today. As Nidhi buckles in for her CT scan, we are reminded of a stark fact: despite extraordinary medical breakthroughs, healthcare administration remains stuck in the 1960s.Productivity exploded almost everywhere over the past half century, but in healthcare, modern data management practices have not been embraced. Currently, $3.8 trillion of money flows into[3] and through the US healthcare system. And yet the automation that is the engine of modern efficiency seems lost in the wilderness of medical charts and institutional inertia.

The costs are real. Nidhi's ordeal—interpreting the lingo, haggling over copays— is not just Nidhi's ordeal. It is the average person's experience with a convoluted healthcare system filled with terminology that drives a wedge between doctors and patients, inefficient referrals and transfers, and case management that is a tragicomedy of errors. Hours are diverted from healing into jumping bureaucratic hurdles,

---

1 "World's 1st Focused Ultrasound Cancer Immunotherapy Center Launched," UVAHealth, May 11, 2022, *https://newsroom.uvahealth.com/2022/05/11/worlds-1st-focused-ultrasound-cancer-immunotherapy-center-launched.*

2 Allison H. Payne, "Focused Ultrasound as a Non-invasive Treatment for Breast Cancer," The University of Utah, March 5, 2021, *https://discovery.med.utah.edu/2021/focused-ultrasound-as-a-non-invasive-treatment-for-breast-cancer.*

3 Ahreum Han, Keon-Hyung Lee, and Jongsun Park, "The Impact of Price Transparency and Competition on Hospital Costs: A Research on All-Payer Claims Databases," *BMC Health Services Research* 22, no. 1321 (2022), *https://www.ncbi.nlm.nih.gov/pmc/articles/PMC9636618.*

coordinating appointments in segregated pavilions, and enduring the blood pressure–spiking trials of slow-moving phone queues and patient portals.

This waste is not just annoying: it's costly. Forty-eight cents out of every healthcare dollar expended—about $950 billion[4] in 2015 alone—is spent on nonclinical tasks.[5] In every other industry, productivity has improved drastically in the US over the past 50 years, but healthcare is one major exception.

Nidhi's story shows us the human cost of a broken system. As an ordinary worker caught in this dysfunctional structure, we see how it wastes her time, damages her well-being, and drains the energy she needs to fight her illness.

The Promise of LLMs in Healthcare

Yet there are rays of hope. If LLMs and generative AI found their way into real-world systems, they could perform menial administrative tasks; they could book appointments and send information tailored to the individual. AI could capture the information currently locked up in medical records and allow it to move along with the patient, all under the patient's control, rather than getting stuck in the institution into which the patient was referred. When it comes to interfaces with insurance companies, most people would be better off with an AI at the helm, allowing patients and doctors to get back to the business of taking care of health.

Nidhi's challenging experience highlights systemic problems, forcing vulnerable people to navigate their complex wellness journeys without adequate support. Yet it may be automation and AI, in their attempt to finally break through this final enduring frontier of productivity, that causes change. The intensely customized nature of healthcare, with human lives at stake, accounts for its conservative approach toward change. Diagnostics and treatments are not amenable to mass standardization. Navigating disparate systems such as insurance involves human helpers. Clinicians rely on deeply contextual judgments, honed through years of practice-based expertise. This complexity, combined with information asymmetry and the nontransferable nature of medical knowledge, has historically insulated healthcare from macro-optimization. Many critical processes remained manual and artisanal, largely untouched by algorithmic advancements.

However, this resistance to optimization comes at a cost. The healthcare system faces significant challenges, including physician burnout due to performance fatigue, financial barriers to access, and preventable deaths resulting from capacity

---

4 Nikhil R. Sahni, Brandon Carrus, and David M. Cutler, "Administrative Simplification and the Potential for Saving a Quarter-Trillion Dollars in Health Care," *JAMA* 326, no. 17 (2021): 1677–1678, *https://jamanetwork.com/journals/jama/fullarticle/2785480*.

5 Nikhil R. Sahni, Prakriti Mishra, Brandon Carrus, and David M. Cutler, *Administrative Simplification: How to Save a Quarter-Trillion Dollars in US Healthcare* (McKinsey & Company, October 2021), *https://oreil.ly/ZZ9nz*.

limitations. Shocks like COVID-19 helped expose existing healthcare productivity problems. The transition out of a pandemic could inspire much-needed modernization and move in accordance with a wave of LLMs and generative AI. Automation could help with routine chores taking up the time of overworked personnel. AI-based diagnostic assistants minimize the rate of errors and overlay human judgment with data. And most importantly, smart coordination will protect patients such as Nidhi from fighting the overwhelmed bureaucracies largely on their own.

New technologies such as LLMs require careful stewardship, but if applied thoughtfully—with ethics at the core—they could lead to a transformation of care, with health professionals moving from being lone "fixers" to team-based "orchestrators" providing more holistic, proactive, and human-centered care to patients.

Nidhi's story is a call to action. It's a reminder that, while technology has altered the ways we live, work, and communicate, healthcare is still stuck in a model of the past. We should harness the promise of automation not just to improve efficiency in the healthcare system, but to build a healthcare system that centers around people, empowers patients, and acknowledges the worth of health.

Historical Use of Machine Learning

The healthcare sector has looked to various forms of machine learning with hopeful optimism for decades. We were promised AI systems that would help to solve a great number of problems in the sector. In part, this was because machine learning can read vast datasets, identify patterns, and predict results to aid and accelerate many aspects of patient care. It could be harnessed to track, trace, crunch, and ultimately optimize efficiency. In principle, this should have translated into better patient outcomes, more effective operations, and improved cost efficiencies. Some machine learning models have been helping to do just that[6]—from improving diagnostic accuracy to predicting risk of patient readmission by identifying patterns in vast mountains of imaging or patient data. But the impact of traditional machine learning has been contained and does not offer the same disruptive benefits of the LLMs.

Payers and health plans leverage the application of machine learning toward predicting the onset and development of costly conditions. Look beyond the frontline submissions, and there could be hundreds of machine learning models within the health organization that have been built to predict and engage populations with certain disease conditions, such as the following:

---

6 Helen Zhuravel, "AI/ML Algorithms for Early Disease Detection and Medical Diagnosis," Binariks, December 19, 2023, *https://binariks.com/blog/ai-machine-learning-for-early-disease-detection*.

- Diabetes
- Congestive heart failure
- AIDS
- Bipolar disorder
- Asthma
- Chronic renal failure
- Joint degeneration
- Rheumatoid arthritis
- COPD
- Hypertension
- Joint degeneration
- Inflammatory bowel disease
- Atrial fibrillation
- Hyperlipidemia

A fundamental tension exists between machine learning model predictions and clinical practice. Machine learning models often advise early detection of costly comorbidities and recommend preventative measures. In contrast, clinicians at the bedside tend to prioritize immediate patient needs, sometimes at the expense of potential long-term optimizations. Payers are investing heavily in analytics that attempt to identify those more likely to "progress to high-cost status," based on historical correlations. Predicting the onset of conditions that can be prudently managed earlier, before requiring sustained treatment, will allow payers to steer the patient's pathway so as to preserve health at lower long-term expense.

Further conflict arises because predictions rely on interpretation of rich contexts, with limited data leading to overprescription of interventions. Social factors influence trajectory powerfully, with the exclusive focus on physiology, leading to bias against the poor by ignoring why one group might experience poorer outcomes than another prior to labeling it a high-cost drain.

The intricate balance of influence and power requires oversight to ensure that predictive models respect the psychological, economic, and environmental complexities that impact the personal, and not just the actuarial, reliability of modeling the individual risks for both manageability and affordability. The ultimate responsibility for health must remain with each individual.

The output from the AI/machine learning–centric approach in these silo-like organizations is similarly narrow, slow, expensive, and biased, and the hypothesized reinventive future using AI continues to show no change. Why? Because most healthcare machine learning depends heavily on specialized training data requiring long and meticulous cleanup, labeling, and formatting by scarce experts. Building, maintaining, and interpreting these machine learning models saps resources necessary for transformational change, and the problem is compounded by healthcare executives who see AI as overpromising and underdelivering. Never once do these executives think they may be a factor, creating a self-fulfilling prophecy of sorts as they prioritize cost and short-term profits.

Unlike other AIs before them, leading LLMs harness textual data on the scale of the internet to mimic the processes of scientific discovery alongside clinically presented variations. These models learn how doctors think from the literature rather than from generation of training data from a specific input format. Generative AI can also be used to create artificial but realistic data to expand models. Together, LLMs and generative techniques might create the flexibility, adaptability, and continuous learning that's required to improve diagnosis, treatment planning, and personalized interventions profitably, and at scale, everywhere.

Using LLMs and Generative AI for Healthcare Automation

There are several ways in which LLMs and generative AI could help people like Nidhi:

- LLMs could drive conversational AI assistants that act as smart patient care coordinators. Having learned from Nidhi what it is she needs to address, such coordinators may be able to automatically take over many practical arrangements such as scheduling appointments, arranging transport, securing payer authorizations, reminders on preventive healthcare measures and so on.

- Generative AI could supply personalized care plans based on Nidhi's lifestyle and needs, such as her caregiving responsibilities. This path to self-care would be simplified and made meaningful to her through actionable suggestions for optimizing outcomes.

- LLM chatbots can allow Nidhi to voice her fears and frustration to an empathetic, ethical listening ear. For those who are overwhelmed, emotional and social support in addition to information can be helpful.

- Generative models might help create plans to help Nidhi's family overcome transportation needs, counseling, housekeeping, respite care, and other domestic voids and gaps in schedules caused by her illness.

In other words, whether facilitating coordination, advising on medical decisions, offering empathic therapeutic support, dynamically responding to symptoms, or managing cumbersome daily life, LLMs and generative AI could help patients such as Nidhi to focus on healing and disease prevention.

From automating clinic administrative tasks to generating personalized care plans, the promise of LLMs and generative AI in healthcare is longer just theoretical.

Sara Vaezy, chief strategy and digital officer at Providence, says generative AI will change "every aspect of healthcare" in the "next couple years."[7] Generative AI models and leading LLMs are pushing large swaths of industry, including healthcare, into an inflection point. Providence's tradition of innovation includes testing possibilities to blend generative AI into the patient experience in ways that stay true to its mission. Providence is taking both a top-down approach, in which they're designing AI infrastructure with equity and safety guardrails from the beginning, and a bottom-up approach, wherein they identify vulnerable experiences and use cases from the ground, where it will be piloted or tested. The healthcare system has four domains of focus:

- Making the clinical care processes better
- Creating better experiences for consumers and patients
- Building a better experience for the workforce in the back-office administrative tasks
- Making the back-office functions better

For instance, generative AI could help to collect data from patients prior to appointments, inform clinical decision making, and automate repetitive work. Providence has developed an AI strategy informed by the philosophy that machines will one day outperform human capabilities, requiring care teams to hone their skills on the tasks they uniquely possess.

To enable generative AI at speed and scale, Providence is backing it with an agile strategy and plan, crafting strategic partnerships with technology companies, and providing change management to educate and train team members on new workflows. The stewards of healthcare have a mandate to implement generative AI in healthcare technologies safely, equitably, securely, and ethically to support patients in new ways.

Healthcare Corporation of America (HCA)—the US largest for-profit healthcare system and the largest operator of hospitals in the world—is deploying several generative AI solutions to help "reimagine how to deliver care." Clinical generative AI systems are being used by HCA to help automate workflows and reduce the inefficiency and physician burden of documentation by using LLMs to modernize aspects of patient handoffs. In a pilot program, HCA will use an LLM from Google to

---

7 "Generative AI: The Next Frontier of Health Care," Providence, September 17, 2023, *https://blog.providence.org/blog/generative-ai-the-next-frontier-of-health-care*.

automatically generate detailed reports and save nurses time by automating human-verified patient handoffs.[8]

While LLMs' automation in healthcare is still a work in progress, it has the potential to transform care delivery. Workflows, efficiency, and patient care is enhanced in different ways, such as through automation of claims processing and several administrative tasks.

Unlocking Medical Secrets: How LLMs Revolutionize Drug Discovery

Identifying attractive drug targets. No longer relying on human intuition, LLMs could be sifting through oceans of data to reveal hidden mechanisms of disease, patterns of protein interactions, "genetic fingerprints," and to inspire searches for new drug targets, validate their promise, and even lead to personalized medicine. LLMs could analyze your genes and open up new avenues for treating your diseases with drugs personalized just for you.

These LLMs can be repurposed in order to find unexpected links between existing drugs and diseases that lack treatment. This powerful tool can enable the development of new treatments with astonishing speed and low cost relative to traditional methods where new drugs are first synthesized and then tested.

Beyond the X-ray: LLMs see what we miss

Medical imaging is as old as medicine itself, but the human eye can see only a fraction of the whole picture. LLMs are a new sort of detective, each with unprecedented eyes for visual information and arms that can wield text. Textual and imagery cues about a condition can be parlayed to fulfill the role of a new medical analyst.

These images aren't just pictures; they are woven, active, three-dimensional things. A dilated aortic root, a meningioma, a carotid stenosis—things that can otherwise remain hidden from the human eye (even from the most practiced radiologist)—are revealed. Patterns within noise become visible, and previously indeterminate diagnoses can be made. Or let's say that the LLM says to its physician users, "Hey guys! Remember that tiny texture in last month's scan that we have been reviewing and reviewing and reviewing? There is a paper here that describes a rare disease with exactly that texture." That ambiguous symptom suddenly finds its cause. The path to treatment suddenly opens.

LLMs help construct a contextualized picture of the disease from medical literature, patient history, and annotated images. The contextual assessment is often the most

---

8 Sai Balasubramanian, "HCA, One of the Largest Healthcare Organizations in the World, Is Deploying Generative AI," *Forbes*, August 30, 2023, *https://www.forbes.com/sites/saibala/2023/08/30/hca-one-of-the-largest-healthcare-organizations-in-the-world-is-deploying-generative-ai/?sh=7ac032bc51dc.*

valuable information for a clinician to guide the therapy decision, and it can also help patients to better comprehend their illness with a demystified explanation of what the scan truly means. It feels a bit like magic.

Medicine is no longer looking *at* the body; it is looking *through* the body. Guided by the insights of LLMs, it can reach a new level of diagnostic potential, where diagnoses are more accurate, treatments are more focused, and patients are more powerful and intelligent in how they face disease.

Today, deep learning is the state of the art in helping with medical imaging. In the near future, LLMs will take center stage as they mature.[9]

EHRs evolved: LLMs rewrite healthcare documentation

Traditional EHRs used to be little more than digital filing cabinets, storing data but providing little in the way of analysis or preventive care. That's all about to change. With the rise of LLMs, a whole new era of AI could be on the horizon: EHRs could become coworkers, using their predictive and analytics skills to unlock the full potential of EHRs.

LLMs have the capability to tell the future, or at least future likelihoods, by mining previous datasets to discover patterns, probabilities of adverse occurrences, or even warning signals for the future. Imagine it as a crystal ball showing patients who are vulnerable to a certain illness, who might be readmitted to hospital, or who might suffer a certain adverse event. With this capability, clinical care can be calibrated to the patient.

No need to wade through reams of medical journals yourself. LLMs have done that for you. You give them your patient data, they compare it to all the relevant patient data they've ever seen stored in vast databases, and then they say something like the following: "This is what others with your patient's condition did. Option A seems to be used more often than Option B, and Option C almost never."

Now, though, they are waving this LLM magic into EHRs. The models peruse patient records looking for clues about medication nonadherence, triggering alerts to flag potentially problematic situations, and enabling doctors to intervene early. Now begins an endless future of possibilities, from personalized medicine to preventive care.

EHRs are evolving beyond static documents updated only when claims are processed or clinical tests completed. With the integration of LLMs, EHRs are transforming into dynamic, intelligent systems. These advanced EHRs will continuously analyze vast amounts of data across various sources, providing real-time insights and powering

---

9 Zhengliang Liu et al., "Radiology-GPT: A Large Language Model for Radiology," arXiv, June 14, 2023, *https:// arxiv.org/abs/2306.08666*.

informed healthcare decisions. This isn't a far-off concept from science fiction; it's the imminent future of healthcare.

Unlocking medical gold: LLMs mine texts for hidden gems

Once scrawls on a page, these texts are now mines of bioinformation waiting for interpretation. Using LLMs trained on clinical texts corpora, one may find patterns of language indicating implicit bias that may occur based on race, gender, socioeconomic status, and other determinants of health. An LLM might flag certain notes that present a more negative language frame for group "X," for example, than for group "Y."

Imagine an LLM combing through radiology reports for rich context such as descriptions of abnormalities, their locations, and interpretations while being alerted when it finds matches for disease signatures. No more tedious manual parsing! LLMs instantly index and retrieve high-yield finding descriptions (those most relevant and likely to impact diagnosis or treatment), and they provide radiologists with a leg up in making a diagnosis. Finally, the radiologist has a personal assistant tirelessly scanning the reports on their behalf, highlighting key clues for an expert's gaze.

It's not just about the words. LLMs also master the syntax of medicine, distilling intricate tropisms between symptoms, diagnoses, and treatments. As we fine-tune this type of understanding by training LLMs in larger and more complex text sets, they will be able to predict relevant patient outcomes, efficiently modernize clinical research, and even customize patient care journeys.

Automating and Managing Healthcare

Imagine a world where navigating the healthcare labyrinth isn't a Herculean feat or task to be feared. Enter your personal healthcare AI assistant, powered by LLMs and generative AI, your tireless navigator in the land of doctors' appointments, insurance forms, and endless phone calls.

Navigating the healthcare system is a nightmare from an individual perspective. In our example with Nidhi, managing her treatments requires that she must do the following:

- Since managing her healthcare requires multiple steps, she must schedule appointments, ensuring providers accept her insurance and are "in-network" to avoid higher costs. She needs to understand her financial responsibilities, including copays and deductibles. Before receiving treatments, she has to obtain preauthorization and submit required documentation. Throughout this process, she must effectively communicate her health status to caregivers.

- She must identify the resources offered by federal, state, local, or private agencies to support her, and last but most importantly, identify someone to engage with when she is having negative thoughts about her treatment and life.

Managing cancer treatment across multiple doctors presents formidable challenges for patients. As Nidhi's story showed, navigating clinical complexity while fighting cancer's physical and emotional tolls often proves overwhelming without extensive support.

Patients frequently see surgeons, oncologists, radiation technicians, and specialty practitioners based on tumor characteristics and progression. Each clinical perspective informs treatment plans differently. Patients struggle tracking who said what, assessing conflicts, and remembering next steps, all while processing devastating news and debilitating symptoms.

Appointments routinely get double-booked as coordination between offices falters. Records sharing delays mean patients become medical conduits trying to disseminate test results promptly. Communication gaps frustrate patients when avoidable complications occur.

Throughout this fragmented healthcare journey, patients often lack consistent emotional support, even though reassurance greatly affects recovery. Individual clinicians rarely address all aspects of a patient's well-being, including fears, lifestyle changes, and mental health concerns beyond their specific area of expertise. As patients move between different healthcare providers, the continuity of care often breaks down.

While cross-disciplinary medicine improves survival statistically, fragmented journeys placed on already fragile individuals too often set them up to fall through the cracks. Patient-centered coordination which minimizes logistical burdens and provides holistic care may enhance outcomes over specialized expertise alone. Human connections cannot be optimized out of cancer battles. Comprehensive clinician communication and empathy prove to be medicine's most essential therapeutic.

AI Healthcare Assistant

Nidhi, a working mother, felt the ground vanish beneath her as she heard the words "stage IIIB breast cancer." The world blurred, paperwork became hieroglyphics, and navigating the healthcare system seemed as daunting as scaling Mount Everest in flip-flops. What if Nidhi had a personal assistant with her to take care of these tasks? Enter "Tara," her AI healthcare assistant, a beacon of hope in the storm (Figure 3-1).

Figure 3-1. Tara, AI healthcare assistant

Armed with LLMs and generative AI, Tara was Nidhi's salvation. She didn't need to crack medical jargon to decipher reports and figure out what was happening to her. Tara took reports and translated them into human-sounding notes, and then listed possible treatments and associated side effects. With the help of this program, patients no longer needed to make hundreds of phone calls to legions of doctors.

Tara started taking over Nidhi's tasks and became Nidhi's project manager extraordinaire. With LLMs' language-processing powers, Tara simultaneously scanned documents from countless institutions, automated their appointments, and haggled with insurance companies as if by instinct. No hold music, no wasted time.

But Tara was more than a logistics master. Generative AI parsed through Nidhi's medical data, testing how drugs and treatments might interact—and could be stacked to improve efficacy. Nidhi was overwhelmed by treatment choices, but Tara parsed options to make them digestible, communicating pros and cons in an even-handed digital voice. Tara asked Nidhi whether she was alone and encouraged her to join support circles, and Tara was a sounding board and calm repository of advice if Nidhi got anxious.

With Tara there to babysit the administrative whirlwind, she delegated the bulk of necessary management to Nidhi, making space for all kinds of recovery. Appointments were coordinated, medication reminders showed up on Nidhi's phone, insurance forms coursed through the system with robotic precision, and, crucially, paths on the mountain were outlined and danger spots named. Recovery rested more easily on her shoulders; Tara could carry some of her burdens, allowing Nidhi to rest. In this way, Tara walked the path both by Nidhi's side and a few steps ahead.

Nidhi's success is thus also a technological one. Far from simply providing a shortcut or a logistical solution, LLMs and generative AI became a true empowerment tool for Nidhi—a way to regain her agency and focus on what really mattered: receiving treatment to remain healthy.

This victory is a vision of the future of care, in which technology allows patients to take charge, reduce their stress, and simplify each step of the treatment process. Perhaps most importantly from the standpoint of meaningful conversational engagement, these LLMs excel at parsing and producing natural-sounding text. They are able to identify intent, derive context, and exhibit useful sensitivity to nuances in the language.

GenAI enables chatbots to learn from interaction with users and adapt their behavior to reflect individual preference by modifying their responses—for example, to fit in with the user's speech cadence and structure—and borrow from the conversational content used by the user (such as slang idioms or humorous remarks) that humans do to help communicate more effectively. GenAI allows chatbots to be trained on particular content or datasets for enhancing knowledge. GenAI's ability in generating new text sequences allows chatbots to engage users in open-ended conversation, explore multiple topics, and respond creatively to user prompts, all while making turn-taking, topic transitions, and response formulation more natural aspects of the interaction. GenAI allows chatbots to be personalized to fit individual user needs and preferences by providing capabilities like remembering user information, adapting language style, offering personalized content and recommendations, and presenting information in ways that fit the user's individuality and personality.

Tara, Nidhi's personal assistant, offers the following features:

24/7 appointments
Appointment scheduling can be handled via chatbot, round the clock, so there's no need to wait on hold or create an online account to schedule.

Personalized calendaring
GenAI can learn patient preferences—e.g., which doctor they prefer to see, which location they prefer, and when they prefer to visit—and suggest options for them.

Automated reminders
AI will monitor your schedule and send you reminders for your meetings, appointments, and events through text or email. This could ensure you don't double book or miss your appointments.

Insurance and benefit checks

Using GenAI, you can know in real time if a patient is covered by insurance and eligible for care.

Multilingual options

You can improve accessibility for diverse patients and remove barriers by offering bilingual or multilingual chatbots.

Companionship chatbots

GenAI can be used to produce companionship chatbots tuned for conversation and companionship, especially for the lonely or isolated, and can be a conversational companion by experiencing and modeling emotions as well as empathetically supporting patients through life upsets.

Automating Administrative Tasks from a Healthcare System Perspective

With about 6,000 hospitals,[10] over 300,000 physician groups,[11] over a 1,000 health insurers,[12] and an alphabet soup of health codes to comply with, you can see why the US healthcare system is one of the most administratively complex in the world. It's almost heresy to even suggest administrative simplification.

The United States has significantly higher administration and billing/insurance costs than any other country, up to $1 trillion per year, more than the healthcare systems of Germany, France, and Italy combined.[13] There are a multitude of health insurers, offering a multitude of plans, with different levels of coverage and different networks; within one of them there will probably be hundreds of plan options, each having a different bank of deductibles, copays, and covered services. Each plan contains its own benefits, documentation, mode of payment, and rules. Hundreds of thousands of service codes for medical services, all needing negotiated prices with the provider, create an arms race for documentation and justification technology between provider and insurer. Massive administration of care directly translates into massive administrative expenses of the system and adds to increasing physician burnout (Figure 3-2).

---

10 "Fast Facts on U.S. Hospitals, 2024," American Hospital Association, January 2024, *https://www.aha.org/statistics/fast-facts-us-hospitals*.

11 "Number of Physician Group Practices by State," Definitive Healthcare, January 5, 2024, *https://www.definitivehc.com/resources/healthcare-insights/number-physician-group-practices-by-state*.

12 National Association of Insurance Commissioners, *U.S. Health Insurance Industry Analysis Report*, 2021, *https://content.naic.org/sites/default/files/inline-files/2020-Annual-Health-Insurance-Industry-Analysis-Report.pdf*.

13 "Per Capita Health Expenditure in Selected Countries in 2022," Statista, May 22, 2024, *https://www.statista.com/statistics/236541/per-capita-health-expenditure-by-country*.

Figure 3-2. The toll of burnout: a physician's exasperation under mounting pressures

AI and LLMs can help reduce physician burnout. They can free up healthcare professionals to focus on providing direct patient care while also improving efficiency, accuracy, and patient satisfaction. Examples include:

Interaction with patient assistant
    LLMs aid in scheduling appointments by automatically checking calendars, finding available times, and sending invitations to patients and providers. Just as patient Nidhi used Tara, an AI assistant chatbot, physicians will use chatbots, and we are not too far away from the reality of an AI-powered chatbot interacting with another AI-powered chatbot for the best outcome for the patients and the provider ecosystem.

Managing patient records
    LLMs are effective for extracting information from patient records, such as demographics, medical history, and medications, and LLMs can populate forms and reports.

Generating reports
    LLMs facilitate generating reports from healthcare data, such as patient demographics, treatment outcomes, and quality metrics.

Generating forms and letters such as insurance claims or prior authorization requests
    LLMs can be used to review patient records, identify billable services, and complete insurance claims accurately and efficiently.

Coding and billing

LLMs provide assistance with medical coding and billing, ensuring accurate reimbursement for providers and reducing administrative burdens.

Coding and Billing

Coding and billing systems are key to healthy revenue cycles, but they can be fraught with pitfalls—costly inaccuracies, delays, and other disruptions. Medical miscoding, missed billing opportunities, and a lack of integration between clinical and billing systems are just some of the culprits.

These key challenges occur at every point within the coding and billing cycle— between the physician and patient at the point of care, with documentation, during coding and claims submissions, and from the time of posting payments. Denials or underpayments can result from simple mistakes, inefficiencies in administrative processes, compliance risks, coding errors, or even from fraud.

Some of the most significant coding and billing challenges include:

Upcoding

For some specialties, you're dealing with complex cases, and that makes it more efficient to report a high-level evaluation and management code. While that's fine, you have to document exactly why the coding was used so that you're not using a higher-level code than is appropriate.

Unbundling

This is when you use multiple codes for different parts of a procedure rather than the appropriate code for the entire procedure. This can happen through error, but it also happens when organizations are trying to add to the payment amount, which is why it's something that's often audited.

Not documenting

This means documentation that is missing or insufficient.

Typos and errors

Sometimes you just hit the wrong keystroke. A common error happens when you invert numbers in coding or when information is added incorrectly—either by a staff member or a patient.

LLMs and generative AI can help address the coding and billing challenges as follows:

Upcoding

LLMs used as medical code recommendation systems using LLMs on patient notes, medical coding rules, and bills can tell us what the best code should be for the case being worked on.

Review documentation to make sure that the code is chosen in a manner that supports the clinical evidence and to make sure the documentation is consistent and complete.

By examining historical trends in coding by individual clinicians at the case level, LLMs might be able to discover upcoding trends and flag cases for auditing.

Unbundling

LLMs map procedures to correct high-level billing codes, ensuring that procedure components are recorded only once through a single code.

LLMs can provide prompts to coding staff, listing valid bundled codes during billing, which reduces the need for specialized coding personnel.

Not documenting

LLMs can generate patient notes and summaries from audio recordings or free-text notes, so providers can capture all critical details for accurate billing.

LLMs can request any missing information needed to properly code a claim.

Typos and errors

LLMs can be added to billing and claims workflows to flag, and fix, common typos and coding or patient information errors as they occur, preventing downstream problems.

Using billing data, LLMs can suss out odd peaks or outliers that might point to clerical mistakes, which can then be checked and corrected.

Additional benefits of LLMs and generative AI in coding and billing include:

Reduced labor costs

Automating coding tasks can free up valuable staff time for more complex activities, increasing overall efficiency.

Enhanced compliance

Improved coding accuracy can reduce the risk of audits, penalties, and reputational damage.

Improved revenue cycle management

Accurate and timely billing can lead to faster reimbursements and improved cash flow for healthcare organizations.

Personalized patient communication

LLMs can generate clear and understandable explanations of billing statements for patients, promoting transparency and reducing billing-related inquiries.

By addressing these challenges, LLMs and generative AI can contribute to a more accurate, efficient, and compliant coding and billing process, ultimately benefiting both healthcare providers and patients.

As LLMs and generative AI continue to develop, we can expect to see even more innovative applications for automating healthcare administrative tasks. This will help to improve the efficiency, accuracy, and patient experience across the healthcare system, allowing healthcare professionals to focus on providing high-quality care to their patients.

Clinical Processes

Automation in clinical processes is the use of technology to expedite and enhance the clinical efficiency and effectiveness of delivering healthcare. Emerging AI technologies such as agentic AI can help to automate repetitive tasks, collate and analyze data, and offer decision support. Automation within such a near-human scale of impact using LLMS and generative AI promises to transform the delivery of clinical care by expediting and enhancing it.

Here are some examples of how automation is being used in clinical processes:

Order entry and result reporting
> Automation can be used to automatically enter orders for lab tests, medications, and other services, and to send results back to the ordering provider.

Clinical documentation
> Automation can be used to generate clinical documentation, such as progress notes, discharge summaries, and medication reconciliation reports.

For example, each time Nidhi goes through her treatment, the admin staff at the intake and discharge review her history, make notes, and document changes to her financials, home address, and phone numbers, if any. The doctors, nurses, and technicians will review the clinical notes and make recommendations.

Optimizing Healthcare Workflows

Electronic medical record (EMR) systems have greatly impacted clinical workflows, though the influence is complex with both benefits and drawbacks. On the positive side, EMRs standardize and digitize patient data, enabling efficient access across care teams. Built-in clinical decision support, order sets, templates, and alerts also facilitate evidence-based care. Seamless records improve coordination and reduce duplicated services.

However, critics argue that EMR optimizes workflows for billing purposes over care quality. Physicians spend more time charting on computers, hurting doctor-patient rapport. Alarm fatigue sets in from overload of inconsequential alerts. Customization to unique clinical thinking proves difficult.

The most balanced perspective sees EMRs as magnifiers of existing norms: they reinforce and spread whatever processes are encoded into their frameworks, which may reflect systemic goals over individual patient needs. Optimizing health outcomes likely requires complementing digital infrastructure with human coordination centered around relationships and trust.

In essence, EMRs strongly shape the mechanisms of care delivery through forced standardization and digitally mediated communication but should not rigidly dictate the care culture itself. The human connections at the heart of medicine rely on workflows adapting dynamically rather than transactions optimized for efficiency alone. EMR clinical decision support aims to enhance, not replace, the judgments of experienced, ethical providers collaborating with their patients.

LLMs and generative AI could help improve EMR systems and their impact on clinical workflows in a few key ways:

Adaptive workflows
  LLMs could analyze clinician-patient interactions and tailor default workflows, order sets, and decision trees to match personalized needs and styles.

Automated documentation
  Generative models could draft clinical notes and paperwork based on encounter transcripts and care activities, accurately reflecting unique details.

Humanized integrations
  Smart interfaces powered by empathetic LLMs allow clinicians to use natural speech instructions to order tests, referrals, etc., rather than losing focus to mouse clicks.

Patient data enrichments
  Algorithms could integrate outside records, genomic data, wearable sensor streams, etc., to overcome EMR limitations and inform decisions.

Ideally, such technologies would enhance patient-centered care, capture nuances, reduce administrative burdens, and supplement institutional knowledge with latest individualized findings, thereby driving better outcomes.

Transforming the Clinical Trial Landscape

Enrolling Nidhi in a clinical trial involves a complex process for her oncologist. They must first identify suitable trials, meticulously review their protocols, and carefully assess Nidhi's eligibility based on her medical history. This entails collaborating with the trial team to understand potential risks and ensuring all necessary documentation is submitted accurately. Once Nidhi is enrolled in the process, she has to follow a very strict protocol, which can last up to five years.

Some of the key contributing factors to the challenges include:

Patient recruitment and retention
Finding eligible and willing patients that meet all the criteria for trials can be difficult and time-consuming. Keeping patients enrolled in the study once recruited can also be challenging.

Regulatory compliance
Rules around informed consent, data privacy, safety reporting, etc., can make trial execution complex and lengthy to ensure compliance. Regulations differ across countries, further adding complexity for global trials.

Protocol design
Designing robust protocols and selecting appropriate endpoints to give useful outcomes is both a science and an art informed by past learnings. Suboptimal design could make a trial futile.

Quality and consistency
Ensuring consistency in how the trial is executed across all participating sites and that high-quality standards are maintained can be a huge challenge. A lapse at even one site could compromise trial validity.

Logistical complexity
Everything from drug supply chain to coordinating patient visits for follow-ups requires immense logistical coordination involving multiple stakeholders. Slip-ups can severely undermine trial progress.

Data management
Collecting, cleaning, and managing multidimensional patient data at volume can pose data analytics challenges. Good data management is vital to draw the right conclusions.

Data quality and analysis
Both are critical for reliable trial results. Only complete and accurate data can ensure that the entire study is accurate. Therefore, it's essential to maintain high data quality standards throughout the trial process.

Data analysis complexity
Analyzing large datasets from diverse sources requires advanced statistical methods and expertise.

Financial constraints
Clinical trials are extremely expensive, frequently amounting to millions of dollars in costs. Insufficient funding or delays in obtaining finances remain a frequent bottleneck.

Ethical considerations and informed consent
Ensuring that participants fully understand the risks and benefits of participation is crucial.

Protecting participant privacy and confidentiality
Safeguarding sensitive health data is paramount.

Balancing risks and benefits
Researchers must carefully weigh the potential benefits of a new treatment against the risks for participants.

Overcoming these challenges requires tremendous cross-functional coordination, global process standardization, quality control rigor, and stakeholders aligning to shared goals—a nontrivial exercise by all means!

LLMs and GenAI could potentially help with clinical trials by:

- Analyzing medical records and patient data to identify eligible trial candidates faster and more accurately. This allows trials to recruit participants quicker.

- Reviewing research literature and past trial data to help design study protocols, identify optimal end points, dosage considerations, etc. This can help improve trial quality and efficiency.

- Continuously monitoring patient data from wearables, apps, etc., during the trial. It can flag safety issues early, improve compliance monitoring, and adaptively adjust trial conduct based on incoming data.

- Analyzing complex, multimodal trial data to uncover insights—for example, by correlating genomic, phenotype, and outcome data to identify biomarkers. It can also check data quality and identify anomalies. This leads to faster, richer insights from trials.

LLMs can synthesize vast amounts of medical research and real-world evidence, offering comprehensive analysis of how trial outcomes might influence medical practice or highlight areas needing further investigation. This approach enhances the clinical applicability of trial results and improves subsequent decision-making in healthcare. LLMs and GenAI could make numerous aspects of running high-quality, insightful clinical trials significantly faster, cheaper, and better. It may play an invaluable role in improving the efficiency and reliability of clinical trials in the future.

Summary

This chapter explored automation's accelerating yet uneven permeation across healthcare over recent decades, hampered by the field's institutional inertia. However, the ascendant new AI subclass of LLMs promises a versatility and responsiveness that finally overcomes adoption barriers through revolutionary productivity enhancements, insight generations, and even economic transformations of medical workflows.

The chapter provided various vignettes of LLM-based innovations optimizing current pain points. Intelligent assistants slash administrative hours wasted battling billing systems, freeing overworked staffers. Diagnostic LLMs mine global corpora linking subtle symptoms to rare illnesses beyond any practitioner's experience. Clinical trial management sees subject enrollments, protocol designs, and result analyses automated for superior therapeutic developments.

Each scenario highlights how language-savvy AI can tackle once-stubborn inefficiencies by either generatively constructing solutions or extracting actionable patterns from knowledge bases too vast and unstructured for manual analysis. The paradigm shift suggests healthcare may follow other recent disruptions in realizing productivity and excellence gains at scale from hitherto promising but impractical automation techniques.

CHAPTER 4

LLM and Generative AI's Patient and Clinical Potential

The latest AI design paradigms—encompassing agentic reasoning and vastly expanded context windows in LLM and generative AI prompts—will fundamentally change the nature and functions of healthcare applications. While revolutionary, the next generation of AI systems will not transform healthcare fundamentally overnight.

Some of the principal change drivers, however, will likely consist of startups and other tech companies. Many of these aren't as encumbered by the inertia and risk aversion that can be found across large healthcare companies, and they may be the kind of early adopters that new technologies with yet-to-be-proven return on investment are hungry to find. On the other hand, traditional healthcare incumbents will likely be more cautious, likely jumping into AI when and if these kinds of technologies prove themselves in the marketplace and are seen to be safe and financially sound.

Yet, ironically, as tech multinationals and startups create a critical mass of diverse successes by infusing AI into healthcare, these positive results will filter out to much of the wider field. With returns beginning to accrue, healthcare companies will move toward AI solutions that help them deliver better care while remaining competitive. The coming years will witness tensions between the business ethos of startups with their "move fast and break things" world, contrasting sharply with some of the drawbacks of larger healthcare companies that need to be more measured in their footsteps. Cooperation and competition will play out between them, from which the future of healthcare is bound to emerge, as applications of AI assist in increasing new quality standards for patient outcomes and overall efficiency and personalization of healthcare services.

Patient Experience

Patient experience refers to patients' broader perceptions and feelings during their interactions with the healthcare system. It encompasses everything from scheduling appointments to interacting with staff and the physical environment to receiving care. It focuses on the emotional and psychological aspects of the journey, including factors like respect, communication, empathy, and overall satisfaction. Arguably, many healthcare systems and applications need to focus on the patient experience, and this is where LLMs can make a huge difference and improve patient care. Patient-centered care that prioritizes a positive healthcare experience delivers inherent value with cascading benefits beyond perception alone. Studies confirm patient satisfaction ties directly to critical downstream results such as treatment adherence, engagement in managing health, and ultimately clinical outcomes.

The use cases described in this section focus on apps that improve patient experience. LLMs and generative AI will improve patient experiences in several ways. LLMs can generate customized explanations of complex health topics, procedures, and medication issues to each patient's preferences, learning styles, and background. LLM and generative AI chatbots, voice assistants, and avatar interfaces allow 24/7 support to conveniently schedule appointments and connect medical records, get answers about billing questions, and get help with other hassles.

LLMs can provide care continuity by reviewing longitudinal records, prompting patients and providers to follow up on open items, and revisiting unresolved symptoms across past visits to prevent patients from "falling through the cracks." Emotion-designed LLMs actively listening and responding empathetically to patient contexts beyond medical history alone can make interactions more supportive. LLMs can automate administrative and clinical documentation as well as paperwork to allow providers to focus more on face time with patients and to reduce wait times.

LLMs and generative AI introduce opportunities to systemically streamline coordination hassles and synthesize personalized insights that help patients feel understood. The AI can communicate with patients at their own pace, using language they understand, which may lead to better engagement in their own health management. The future offers brighter, barrier-free patient experiences. Next, we describe a few examples of future emerging apps ushering in this new patient experience.

Health Bot Concierge

Imagine a healthcare system where patients receive personalized support, understand complex medical jargon, and quickly navigate administrative hurdles. This is the future promised by generative AI conversational chatbots, empathetic AI companions, and a breed of intelligent assistants poised to revolutionize the healthcare landscape. These bots—powered by deep learning, LLMs, and natural language processing (NLP)—hold genuine conversations with users, understanding their questions and responding with contextually relevant, human-like language. Their applications extend beyond simple customer service, transforming first-line triage, chronic disease management, and mental health support. Health bot concierge, illustrated in Figure 4-1, will be one of early use cases realized with LLMs and generative AI.

Figure 4-1. Health bot concierge

At the low-acuity end of the scale, a chatbot could act as a triage consultant for a patient at home who could have their symptoms discussed in order to identify the best course of care. Ever wonder what the future of triage will be like? Instead of having to endure waiting rooms filled with patients with runny noses, we could discuss our sore throats with a chatbot who might suggest some soothing honey and lemon or recommend calling for a virtual consultation with a doctor instead.

Beyond triage, algorithms could start as virtual personal health coaches, assessing information gathered from wearable devices or postsymptom questionnaires, and recommending a daily routine or a pill schedule based on personalized suggestions on how to improve mood and alertness, sleeping patterns, and pain. Think of a chatbot sending the patient daily health indicators. It could send you a reminder, a gentle nudge, to take your insulin within the hour if a blood glucose reading crests, or she could prompt you to answer a "How are you feeling today?" The chatbot might inquire with an idea for a few stretches to calm your mind at bedtime, resulting in some fresher and longer z's.

For patients with chronic health problems or with mental health issues, these chatbots can provide unparalleled support. For example, imagine you receive daily encouraging messages from a wellness AI coach that checks your emotional wellness, gives you motivational quotes, etc. Chatbots for the elderly can be a source of social interaction and mental stimulation and also help to prevent and treat depression, which is more common in the aging population.

There are benefits to staff, too. Generative AI chatbots have the potential to close the gap between doctor and patient; some illnesses are so complex that, if you trust your doctor, it might be helpful to have the chat rewritten in simpler language. You won't have to wade through medical jargon and wonder what your doctor means by this or that, or later try to dredge up what he said you should now remember to do. Imagine the chat summarized the information, emphasizing the important takeaway words in boldface, making the next steps understandable. You leave the room with complete understanding.

The administrative tasks that most patients dread can be transformed, thanks to the increasing use of chatbots. There are still many horizons for using generative AI chatbots in healthcare, which will only increase as the algorithms learn and improve. The whole paradigm of personalized, accessible, and affordable healthcare will change, with the patient holding the steering wheel. The conversational revolution is here—healthcare will never be the same.

Doctor's Notes and Visits

One of the most common patient frustrations includes reviewing doctors' summaries of diagnoses, prescribed medications, and recommended care. Figure 4-2 illustrates the scenario of comprehending doctors' notes. A critical gap often exists between what patients understand about their health condition and what doctors document in their medical records. This discrepancy can have severe, even life-threatening consequences.

Consider the following scenario. Greg, a 30-year-old man, has a family history of a genetic condition that increases the risk of aortic dissection—a dangerous tearing of the large blood vessel branching off the heart. Greg begins seeing a cardiologist to monitor and manage this risk. However, a crucial miscommunication occurs:

What Greg understands
He perceives his risk as moderate and think occasional check-ups are sufficient.

What the cardiologist documents
The medical notes detail a high-risk condition requiring frequent monitoring and possibly preventive measures.

Tragically, Greg died from an aortic dissection just one year after his initial cardiology appointment. This outcome might have been prevented if the cardiologist had communicated the severity and urgency of Greg's condition more clearly, and if Greg fully understood the serious nature of his risk and the importance of rigorous monitoring and treatment adherence.

This case illustrates how vital it is to have clear, thorough communication between healthcare providers and patients. When patients truly understand their health situations, they're better equipped to participate actively in their care, potentially averting dire outcomes.

Figure 4-2. Comprehending doctors' notes

Trying to remember a doctor's communication and understanding a doctor's notes often feels like deciphering ancient runes or recalling a specific meal from weeks ago: it's a struggle filled with gaps and uncertainty. Patients are frequently left without a clear explanation of their condition or a concrete plan of action.

This disconnect between medical professionals and patients, caused by complex and often opaque medical documentation, creates a thick fog of misunderstanding. As a result, patients may experience:

- Confusion about their health status and treatment plan
- Increased anxiety due to lack of clear information
- A diminished understanding of their overall health journey

This communication gap can affect a patient's ability to manage their health effectively. Clear medical information is crucial for patients to actively participate in their care and make informed decisions about their health.

Notes sometimes poorly summarize patient information drawn from different specialties. A unified narrative needs to be formed to make sense of insights offered by multiple clinicians. The conclusion here is that many patients require assistance to understand the diagnoses, management plans, and directions of care recommended by doctors. As a result, patients can struggle to follow through on recommendations, and nonadherence to recommendations can lead to poor health outcomes. This problem is widespread and requires more convenient mechanisms to convert these technical summaries of the visit into more patient-friendly plain language.

A generated clinical summary could explain your test results and tell you not only what doctors want to do but why they want to do it. The summary would also give you a range of possible treatments and walk you through the reasoning that would make it appropriate to embark upon one of those versus another. Imagine how much time this might save for physicians and clinical staff in creating a visit summary and treatment plan. It would be indispensable to have a voice-to-text generated and shared summary from the visit, with or without your doctor's input, explaining the questions you might have and also both their answers and generated-by-computer educated guesses of what might be useful to you to know, summarized and explained for you, annotated by your doctor if they have the time.– This would, for instance, allow you to query parts of your records in more natural language via chatbot interfaces powered by generative AI. The GenAI could explain everything, and then hopefully answer whatever part of the explanation you now want to be educated about.

Generative AI fosters explanatory media. Beyond text translation, AI might generate explanatory diagrams, videos, or other multimedia that make the content of a doctor's note intelligible to patients in more interesting, interactive formats. LLMs can surface patient questions, and AI can scan notes and formulate questions about any subdots or portions of them that might warrant patient reconsideration and thinking through, tailoring bespoke questions for clarifying comprehension.

The gains go far beyond just operating a little more smoothly. Understanding your diagnosis without any confusion can empower you to take a more active role in your healthcare. When you have the ability to scan the diagnostic balloon and read your diagnosis, you have the capacity to ask more informed questions, you can make better choices for treatment, and you'll tend to follow up on treatment plans, knowing they are working or that you're well on your way. If you can help the doctor diagnose the problem, this creates a reciprocal communication loop that can create a more productive effective relationship between the patient and the doctor, improving outcomes in health and beyond.

Health Plan Wizard

Healthcare innovators are striving to make disparate systems dynamic—spanning insurance plans, provider networks, facilities, pharmacies, and social services—when managing and explaining policies and bureaucracies to patients seeking care access and/or complementary resources. Many healthcare organizations are looking to create seamless member experiences across fractured touchpoints.

At the ready stands the new generation of personalized health plans spearheaded by LLM wizards—virtual conversational agents encompassing behaviors of administrative as well as clinical functions to a central point of contact. Equipped with empathetic language models, health plan wizards engage in natural dialogue "checkups" with members—assessing a member's needs—while the AI connects the relevance of doctor referrals, usage trends, associated care searches, and outcomes to identify appropriate and timely suggestions to members. Figure 4-3 shows a patient leveraging a health plan wizard to understand and navigate their health plans.

Figure 4-3. Health plan navigation wizard

LLM health plan wizards can describe insurance vernacular about claims, referrals, formulary tiers, and eligibility to promote insurance utilization. Plain language can be their hub, and their spokes create confident consumers making healthcare decisions. Social determinants of health screening will tie patients experiencing hardship around food, housing, and finances with community organizations that can be beneficial. Culturally aware assistance can guide patients into equitable opportunities.

Armed with rich contextual insights regarding their patients, such personal health wizards enable improved experiences along the healthcare continuum, amid administrative and lifestyle barriers. Members receive personalized, targeted information rather than generic advice. All actions and communications are centered around the individual's specific needs and circumstances, breaking down the traditional barriers of siloed, transaction-based interactions. Smoother interactions lead to more effective long-term health outcomes, fulfilling care promises.

Black Maternal Health

LLMs could support maternal health disparities more equally while promoting minority women's journey toward a better pregnancy journey. With benefits such as omnichannel care linking clinical guidelines with wraparound care—which acknowledges all aspects of a vulnerable mother's life, physical and mental—GenAI is a technology whose time has come to address the current crisis of increased morbidity and mortality among Black and Brown pregnant women (Figure 4-4).

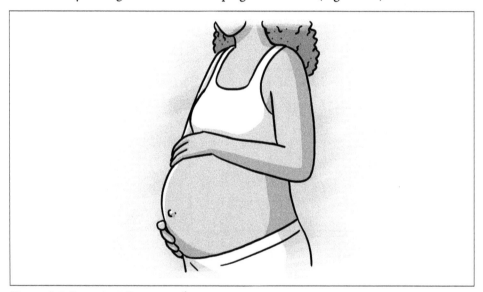

Figure 4-4. Expectant Brown mother

An equitable maternal health LLM app might invite more extensive discussions about social contexts, barriers to access, and specific concerns—beyond medical histories. It would tailor the support to the woman, directing her to a program for food support if required, counseling her on her rights in the workplace, birth preparation classes precisely chosen for her cultural needs, or even secure a ride service to enable her access to appointments.

Unconscious biases are insidious, with minority maternal health consequently affected. An LLM app could play a crucial role in combating these implicit physician assumptions in the following ways:

- By retaining a relevant LLM—through powerful medical profiles that incorporate cues about the social/cultural context in which a birthing goal is envisioned— physicians who might exploit an unfettered decision-making process are blocked. The LLM slows down rushed recommendations.

- It could watch patient-physician interactions to guard against the discounting of minority women's symptoms and concerns, insert prompts for validating the patient's concerns, and recommend additional testing as required.

- It could help patients review the proceedings following appointments and flag areas where unconscious stereotyping might have resulted in the dismissal of their concerns or caused alterations in their treatment plan. For example, with access to the full timelines of patients, the LLM can perform differential analytics against baseline standards and champion patients receiving fewer proactive interventions than peers with similar risk presentation profiles.

At a minimum, patterns of differential treatment might become detectable over time, and drive policy directives and standards for evidence-based care regimens that aim to compensate for differential quality, maybe even unintentionally inspired by implicit bias in prenatal care settings.

The prompts and milestone-markers would trigger personalized reminders and questions for the patient to discuss with her doctors, from testing schedules to birthing plans, while also providing interactive education regarding the maternal health hazards that disproportionately threaten minorities. The on-call advocate could step in over troubling symptoms and could equip women to get the best possible care.

After birth, the LLM app would continue to protect a woman throughout recovery and her child's development through targeted advice and connections to community resources. It puts women at the center of their own health. The app creates opportunities that bypass inherently racist legal systems and bolster minority women's agency in accessing the healthy, empowered pregnancies they rightfully deserve.

In conclusion, an AI-powered chatbot using LLMs can be a vigilant partner in maternal healthcare. This technology can:

- Actively identify unconscious biases that negatively impact minority maternal health

- Provide consistent advocacy for patients

- Offer real-time support during medical encounters

- Monitor long-term care to ensure continuity and equity

The ultimate goal is to ensure that every mother, regardless of background, receives high-quality, advanced care free from prejudice. This AI partner works continuously to promote equitable treatment in immediate medical situations and throughout the maternal health journey.

Equity-focused LLMs offer promising innovations to support those most affected by healthcare disparities. These AI systems can:

- Transform historical data and experiences into meaningful insights
- Improve access to quality healthcare for underserved populations

Looking to the future, this technology could contribute to a world where:

- All viable embryos have the opportunity to develop and be born, regardless of socioeconomic factors
- Women of all racial and ethnic backgrounds have equal access to advanced reproductive technologies, high-quality prenatal and maternal care, and safe childbirth experiences

The goal is to create a healthcare system where race, ethnicity, and socioeconomic status no longer determine maternal and infant health outcomes.

Medication Reminder

Following medication regimens can be astonishingly challenging. Treatment plans often involve intricate instructions around timing, diet, conflicts with other remedies, and more. Even motivated patients need help with forgetfulness, confusing details, or just finding the regimen unpleasant. Hence, barriers to prescription adherence remain prevalent across diverse groups.

Healthcare providers and research shows that patients who stop taking their medicine risk the progression of disease, higher healthcare costs, and even death—particularly for those managing chronic illness. Physicians do make attempts to simplify treatment, for example, by striving for a single-dose, once-a-day regimens. But unavoidable complexity remains an ingredient in certain treatment formulations.

A 2017 medication adherence study[1] compared a variety of low-priced memory aids against a control group who received no intervention. The tools were simple: a pill bottle strip with slide toggles to indicate which day's dosage had been taken; a cap tracking open timestamps; and an eight-compartment standard daily pill organizer.

---

1 Monique Tello, "Taking Medicines Like You're Supposed To: Why Is It so Hard?" Harvard Health Publishing, May 10, 2017, *https://www.health.harvard.edu/blog/taking-medicines-like-youre-supposed-hard-2017051011628*.

Here are the key findings in the study's results:

- The low-priced memory aids (pill bottle strip with toggles, cap tracking open-time timestamps, and standard daily pill organizer) did not improve medication adherence compared to the control group that received no intervention.
- This conclusion was not immediately apparent from the study's primary results but was revealed through analysis of pharmacy refill data.
- The ineffectiveness of these common adherence tools was an unexpected or potentially unwelcome finding.
- The pharmacy refill data provided a more accurate or comprehensive picture of adherence than the study's primary measures.

These buried findings are significant because they challenge the assumed effectiveness of commonly used, low-cost methods to improve medication adherence. More innovative or comprehensive approaches may be needed to impact patient behavior when taking prescribed medications.

The authors of the study speculated that this emphasis on reminders ignores why and when doses are missed. What's needed for medication adherence is better insights into patient contexts, interests, and barriers. Yet, the failure of efficacy in even basic medication memory aids speaks to the stubbornness of the adherence problem. Figure 4-5 depicts a patient using technology to help them remember when to take their medications.

Figure 4-5. Medication reminders

A 2022 NIH report[2] examining technologies for medication adherence monitoring reached some interesting conclusions:

- Current adherence-monitoring technologies have varying features and approaches to data capture. They can be further enhanced through technological innovation.

- New research paradigms should be deeply integrated and interoperable with clinical settings and health information systems; in other words, the utility of a research approach needs to maximize the potential of the broader technological ecosystem.

- While promising, individually, none of these technologies constitutes a magic-bullet "gold standard." More likely, they will work best in conjunction with one another as part of a multimodal solution tapping the strengths of emerging tech and traditional methods.

- There's no doubt that the evidence base for adherence technologies is growing, and they could be a real driver of better adherence behaviors and health outcomes. But the evidence base for the functionality of technologies and their impact on adherence outcomes needs to expand still more.

Once we're aware of and debiased against such artifacts, we shouldn't expect LLMs to be a magic bullet—they will only be a promising complement to current modalities. A collaborative, evidence-based approach to creating LLMs that can be iteratively used alongside current, context-aware, patient-centered adherence-support tools may be the realistic and only realistic route.

Oral Health

LLMs and generative AI can help teledentistry in several ways:

Routine tasks
LLMs automate those routine tasks such as sending reminders and processing payments, freeing up dentists and dental hygienists to serve patients.

Data analyses
LLMs analyze data from teledentistry sessions, in the form of video chats and dental images, to improve quality of care by identifying trends and patterns.

---

2 Madilyn Mason et al., "Technologies for Medication Adherence Monitoring and Technology Assessment Criteria: Narrative Review," *JMIR mHealth uHealth* 10, no. 3 (March 2022): e35157, *https://www.ncbi.nlm.nih.gov/pmc/articles/PMC8949687*.

Report generation

LLMs create reports detailing the teledentistry session results to communicate with patients and other healthcare providers.

Patient education

An LLM provides dental health education by talking with you over video chat, text messaging, or using a chatbot.

Translation

LLMs are proficient in translating languages. This gives rise to teledentistry patients speaking in any language.

LLMs can significantly transform the field of teledentistry in several ways, including enhanced patient interactions and personalized communication.

LLMs can power virtual assistants and chatbots that answer patients' initial queries about teledentistry services, insurance coverage, or basic oral health information. This can free up dentists' time for more complex consultations.

LLMs can analyze a patient's medical history and dental concerns to tailor communication and educational materials. Imagine an LLM that generates customized preappointment emails or post-treatment instructions based on the patient's needs.

LLMs could educate patients on oral health. Based on analyzing millions of studies and millions of patients' electronic medical records, an LLM could develop personalized education about brushing, flossing, diet, and other dental hygiene topics that match a patient's risk factors and preferences. LLMs could interpret patient-reported symptoms, and could often provide answers on why patients might be having problems and when to see their dentist. LLMs could explain procedures and medications in plain language, and they could describe the expected benefits and burdens of a treatment plan. LLMs could discuss and review options with patients, which might improve how well patients follow expert diagnoses and recommendations. LLMs could provide interactive chatbots that might differ from dental assistants in that they would be programmed to provide compassionate support and anxiety-arresting techniques to reduce the fear of visiting the dentist in patients with dental anxiety.

For dentists, they could examine patient records and medical histories, providing suggested diagnosis and treatment recommendations and even flagging potential side effects and contraindications. LLMs could rapidly crawl through the dental literature to help them stay up to speed on the latest research and best practice. LLMs could input accurate and comprehensive notes for the dentist without wasting time on formatting and spelling, and they could improve precision. They could be programmed to tailor communication to patients' individual needs and preferences, improving engagement and satisfaction. Figure 4-6 illustrates a dentist using AI technology for oral health while an LLM provides summarization on a patient's oral health history.

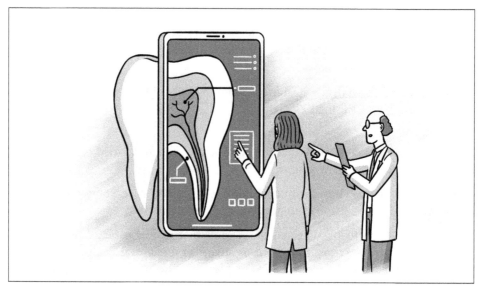

Figure 4-6. Oral health

LLMs are there 24/7, helping to overcome barriers associated with time and geographical distance. They are never too busy to answer clinical questions, and are not distracted by phones ringing or frustrated patients waiting in the queue to be seen. But they are not the end of the road—dentists still need to exercise their clinical judgment. LLM answers are there to support dentists, not supplant them. Overall, therefore, LLMs hold immense promise for moving beyond teledentistry. LLMs could place power back into patients' hands; they could support dentists; and they, too, would have a role to play in improving the oral health of our populations.

Symptom Checker

Symptom checkers are computerized tools or apps that allow patients to enter their chief complaint and possible concurrent symptoms, and provide the patient with an assessment or potential diagnosis. Well-known examples include WebMD, the symptom checker by the Mayo Clinic, as well as Ada Health. Most symptom checkers today use a rule-based approach, where patients enter symptoms, and then the tool uses this information to draw upon a compiled database of disease descriptions by medical experts and to provide a potential diagnosis. Though symptom checkers can indeed provide helpful contributions to patient self-diagnosis, they are limited in a number of ways:

- They fail to capture the nuances and subtleties of patients' actual symptoms.
- They provide a laundry list of potential conditions without clear probabilistic rankings.

- They account poorly for comorbidities, and they do not iterate initial questions intelligently.
- They possess a limited ability to explain their reasoning or advise optimal next steps.
- They often present a limited set of possible diagnoses, potentially overlooking other possibilities.
- Their diagnoses are based on user-reported data and can be prone to inaccuracy or partiality. Algorithmic systems must be more nuanced to handle edge cases or rare conditions.

LLMs have the potential to enhance symptom checkers (Figure 4-7) dramatically in several ways:

- Symptom checkers identify salient figures of speech and patient specifics in the text in natural language, and refine them using language qualified by more accurate terms thanks to suggestions made by LLMs trained on a large medical data set (including diagnoses of patients, their cases, and relevant research articles).
- Symptom checkers attach predicted levels (probabilities) of benefit to the various possible diagnoses using statistical calculations and clinician-guided heuristics. They engage in a series of follow-up questions based on the results of prior questions in order to discard improbable conditions.

Figure 4-7. Symptom checker

LLMs offer the opportunity for a better understanding of context. LLMs can analyze complex narratives and consider individual contexts like medical history, age, and lifestyle factors, leading to more personalized recommendations. LLMs can provide more nuanced information, highlighting uncertainties and guiding users toward reliable sources such as healthcare professionals. LLMs can identify high-risk cases based on specific symptoms and direct users to seek immediate medical attention. They can continuously learn from new data and feedback, improving accuracy and adapting to evolving medical knowledge.

Combining large-scale pretraining, expert medical knowledge, and rigorous validation testing, LLM-powered symptom checkers could greatly improve patient self-service capabilities, clinical efficiency, and health outcomes.

Clinical Decision Support

The potential of LLMs and generative AI in the field of clinical decision support is vast. Clinical care routinely involves planning patient treatment, which includes carefully considering potential risks and benefits of the treatment options. Clinical practice guidelines (CPGs) published by medical associations are based on the best available population-level evidence and are intended to assist healthcare professionals in making clinical decisions.

However, these practice guidelines may be ambiguous or suboptimal when considering polychronic patients that suffer from multiple intersecting chronic conditions. These complexities pose challenges because CPGs are oriented to single conditions, and it is left to clinician judgment to adjudicate between conflicting recommendations from multiple guidelines. For example, consider an aging population that exhibits increasing clinical complexities and care demands, resulting in patterns of super-additive costs when diseases interact.

Application of disease-specific CPGs to patients with multiple diseases can lead to competing recommendations and the potential for adverse drug-drug or drug-disease interactions. For example, medications indicated for heart failure could compromise kidney function in those with kidney disease, or nonsteroidal anti-inflammatory drugs (NSAIDs) may be suggested to treat osteoarthritis pain but turn out to have relative contraindication in patients with a history of peptic ulcer disease.

To account for the patient's unique circumstances, such as demographics, family and disease history, or individual physician practice patterns, doctors may deviate from applicable guidelines partially or fully. While these deviations may be appropriate in certain cases, they can also lead to unwarranted variation and poorer health outcomes. In contrast to deviations that manually personalize clinical care, deviations may also result from professional uncertainty, such as lack of specialized domain expertise or uncertainty about treatment options. The clinical insight bot or curbside physician use cases profiled in the next section could alleviate some of the risks just outlined for polychronic patients.

Clinical Insight Bot

The doctor does what doctors do. The patient's story, history, labs and diagnostic tests, and tentative treatment plan are laid out before the clinical insight bot. The LLM digs deeper. It asks questions to learn more but not to judge or to conclude. Could it really be that unusual disease? Do the two medications interact? Are there some clinical trials studying this illness or multiple diseases afflicting the patient? Interacting with a virtual assistant, as depicted in Figure 4-8, provides enormous benefits to a physician.

Figure 4-8. Physician in conversation with an AI-powered clinical insights chatbot

The LLM reaches deep into its databases of medical literature, research papers, case studies, and even clinical guidelines, then picks out what it thinks you need to know. It looks for patterns, associations, and mistakes that the doctor might have missed. It scrutinizes the treatment plan, checks how well it's worked so far, and nudges you in the direction of some more effective options that now have strong backing in the evidence.

But the LLM isn't just a data processor: it is an analytical machine that puts forth assumptions and highlights potential biases. It proposes alternative diagnoses that might explain the patient's symptoms or points to areas of uncertainty, prompting the doctor to order more testing or to consult with another physician. In short, it doesn't replace human judgment with "computerized medicine." Rather, it augments it, offers a broader perspective, and makes sure that every possible angle has been considered.

Now, a newly emboldened doctor examines the LLM's output and leaves the room with a revised plan in hand. The consultation process has been nuanced yet natural as clinician and AI work together, with previous expertise augmented and guided by the LLM's analysis. The risks and benefits of the new plan can be weighed, and the physician's confidence in the conclusion is buoyed, if not fully won. She has an ally in her efforts to improve outcomes—a silent partner.

And that is only the beginning of what the future medical consultation might look like, with LLMs aiding but not replacing human doctors. They won't be the end of the personal touch, the empathy, and the reasoning that define what it means to be a good physician. LLMs will be the most powerful tool that the doctor has available to sift through the plethora of information to provide informed, personalized, and humanistic care for all of us.

A clinical insight bot differs from the AI curbside physician as a core task for a clinical insight bot would be to surface insights, patterns, and trends from a set of clinical data—e.g., electronic health records, medical literature, clinical studies, and the like—in ways that help clinicians make better decisions.

A clinical insight bot would largely be fed by structured and unstructured clinical data sources, namely electronic health records, claims data, medical literature, results of clinical trials, and patient-generated health data, and then would utilize advanced analytics, NLP, and machine learning to extract clinically meaningful insights and patterns from these.

Unlike real-time individual analysis, clinical insight bots take a data-driven approach to generate insights for clinicians and healthcare professionals. These insights are delivered periodically, at predetermined intervals, or triggered by specific events. The bots analyze vast amounts of anonymized data to identify trends and patterns at the population level. This anonymized data protects patient privacy while allowing the bot to uncover broader healthcare trends. The insights are then presented in clear formats like reports, dashboards, or alerts. Ultimately, these data-driven insights are designed to empower clinicians and healthcare professionals to make informed judgments and decisions that benefit entire populations or healthcare systems.

AI Curbside Physician

A *curbside consultation* is an informal advice exchange between medical providers about real patient cases. An informal exchange of advice between medical providers, a curbside consultation considers cases that are still pending resolution in real patients, as metaphorically illustrated in Figure 4-9.

Figure 4-9. Curbside physician

Say, on a shift in the intensive care unit (ICU), you are concerned about the lack of fever in patient Jean. You have just spoken to a colleague in ICU, explaining that she has grade 4 lactic acidosis, an ECG with low voltages, a GI bleed in the past 12 hours, and newly onset platelet count reaching 70,000. However, the patient admitted at 7 p.m. remains afebrile. You are stumped. You know your colleague from ED has recently used an app that acts as a virtual curbside doc. You took her advice twice last week with excellent outcomes. You decide to give it a try.

Your patient got burned when her robe caught fire during a weed-vaping session. The burn was superficial, although it covered a large surface area (approximately 20% of total body surface area). Today, she is back in the burn clinic, and you are conducting a daily chemotherapy dose. A week earlier, the wound was filled with fluid and the pinch test was positive. Although the pinch test should not have been needed prior to today, you decided to go ahead with second-degree burn care, including bandaging and debridement. Now, the pinch test is negative, the dressings are smelly and discolored, and there is a white layer. You are surprised and concerned because the signs and symptoms are concerning. You want to consult the wound care expert, but there are no good ways to contact her. You remember your colleague telling you about an app that functions like a curbside doc.

An AI curbside doctor provides instant access to continuously evolving medical information, mimicking the valuable insights you might otherwise only get from impromptu consultations with colleagues. This digital tool replicates the knowledge-sharing that occurs during "house rounds" with master clinicians in the US, or the morning, midday, and afternoon "table-side" chats with peers in UK hospitals.

By doing so, it brings the benefits of collaborative medical expertise to clinicians' fingertips at any time, without the need for physical presence or scheduling. You can use an LLM to generate a set of hypotheses about 1) what is causing a patient's symptoms, 2) the strategy for alleviating those symptoms, 3) what factors might be relevant, and 4) what steps should be taken next.

The AI curbside physician is ready for informal case discussions any time of day, any day of the week. You talk about your patient, the issue at hand (test results, physical exam findings, previous history), and get responses in return, often of a high diagnostic quality. The AI might also produce lists of likely diagnoses with associated probabilities. These probabilities would be based on specific symptoms present, the timeline or progression of these symptoms, and relevant risk factors.

The AI curbside physician would consider how these elements correspond to established diagnostic criteria or standards found in the medical literature.

It can even make appropriate probing questions to clarify or provide more details regarding missing case features that could distinguish between different possible diagnoses, or in certain cases recommend further testing or testing strategies. In a nutshell, LLMs will change curbside consultation for the better. They will help doctors provide more personalized and efficient care to patients.

The key function of an AI curbside physician would be to deliver rapid and casual advice and second opinions to healthcare professionals. To put it differently, it would focus on facilitating "curbside consultations." Basically, it would attempt to help physicians make clinical decisions when they encounter challenges. It would attempt to deliver evidence-backed advice and expert opinions regarding specific pediatric patient cases or general inquiries about medicine.

A curbside physician bot would draw on the wisdom and knowledge of experienced physicians written down in the medical literature, clinical guidelines, and opinion pieces, and it would use soft logic and NLP and information retrieval techniques to retrieve and contextualize the relevant information for the given clinical question.

The curbside physician bot would carry on a conversation with you as if it were an expert at your side, addressing issues in a case-specific, personalized way that depended on the characteristics of the particular patient you saw and your specific questions or concerns.

A curbside physician bot would have a narrower domain of relevance, providing input and recommendations to very specific clinical scenarios, but drawing from a very generalized medical knowledge base and be able to offer general guidance for what the human physician might recommend. Such a system might offer rapid and convenient access to medical knowledge that comes with some potential for criticism if the recommendations weren't tailored for that individual patient.

Remote Patient Monitoring

Remote patient monitoring is an increasingly viable approach to improving patient outcomes. Generative AI and LLM apps will be able to help remote patient monitoring in several ways. An LLM would be able to personalize each patient's remote patient monitoring experience to ensure that the experience is as efficient and optimal as possible. By considering the patient and their preferences, an LLM might generate a schedule that best meets the patient's needs each day. It also might be capable of providing personalized feedback regarding the patient's progress.

LLMs can be used to give patients feedback on their health data in real-time based on their data readings. For instance, using remote patient monitoring, an LLM can alert patients if their blood pressure or heart rate is too low. Figure 4-10 illustrates a remote patient monitoring session.

Figure 4-10. Remote patient monitoring powered by LLM app

In the world of medicine, LLMs can search a patient's health data and scan for problems. They can do so by spotting irregularities and patterns in the data that could indicate a problem, for instance, it could assist in identifying a patient who is at risk of developing diabetes or one who is likely to suffer a heart attack. LLMs can also remind the patient to take their medication or book an appointment with a doctor, which can assist the patient in taking care of their health and not missing a doctor's appointment.

Furthermore, LLMs can be used for informative and engaging modes of communication with patients by using NLP to analyze their questions and concerns, and then replying to them again in a human-sounding manner and addressing individual aspects of their needs.

Digital Twin

A digital twin of an individual, an organ, or even a medical device could mimic its behavior and characteristics based on the real-world data it was created from. Through the use of digital twins, healthcare practitioners could make sense of the data, predict outcomes, and optimize treatment.

Some key aspects of digital twins in healthcare:

Patient-specific modeling
One aim of developing digital twins for healthcare could be that each patient has their own digital twin model. This model would combine the patient's medical history, their specific genetic information, lifestyle factors, and other relevant data. This digital twin would be continuously updated with real-time health data from personal devices (such as smartwatches or glucose monitors), medical test results, and changes in lifestyle or medication. The digital twin would be constantly receiving and integrating new data. Then the data would be analyzed frequently by AI systems to detect changes or trends and used to provide up-to-date insights for healthcare providers and the patient. This ongoing monitoring ensures that the digital twin remains an accurate, current representation of the patient's health status, enabling more timely and personalized medical interventions as necessary.

Organ/disease simulation
Digital twins can be developed for specific organs or diseases, e.g. a virtual heart, or even a digital version of a tumor, with the latter being able to simulate the way a disease progresses in the body or predict the outcome of a proposed course of treatment.

Medical device optimization
Digital twins could simulate virtual sensor-rich versions of implantable devices such as pacemakers or insulin pumps whose performance could be explored under different circumstances. For example, manufacturers may be able to run the device virtually to optimize its output.

Predictive analytics
Use of machine learning algorithms on digital twin data in real time enables modeling of likely health risks, adverse events, or treatment responses to initiate preemptive interventions.

Virtual clinical trials

Digital twins could be put through virtual clinical trials to test new drugs or other therapies, reducing patients' exposure to new pharmaceutical compounds and tests. Virtual clinical trials involving large populations of digital patient models can provide far more information about the effects of a treatment or simulate typical variability in a population.

Remote monitoring and telemedicine

Digital twins enhance remote patient monitoring by continuously tracking patient status. The digital model is updated in real time with data from wearable devices and other health sensors. The digital twin can quickly identify unusual changes by comparing current data to the patient's baseline and expected patterns. Healthcare providers can be alerted immediately when significant deviations are detected, allowing prompt action. The digital twin's comprehensive model of the patient allows for more tailored monitoring and treatment plans.

Digital twins can improve patient outcomes, pharmaceutical development, and medical device design in and out of hospitals. There's little downside to having a high-definition, prediction-powered, streamlined, and individualized version of you.

But it brings up new questions about data privacy, security, and ethics concerns related to the extension of digital twins into health. How will patient information be protected? What regulations will govern the use of digital twins? Figure 4-11 illustrates a digital twin.

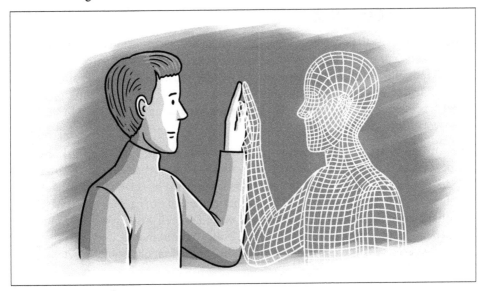

Figure 4-11. Digital twin

Routine analysis of integrated care records might reveal all the possible medication regimens to which the patient could be treated, and might reveal cautions, contraindications, precautions, interactions, or efficacy considerations. Side effects and outcomes might be projected at the personalized level under different treatment interventions for risk/benefit assessment based on that individual's genome, biomarkers, and other prior response data. The bigger imperative is in clinicians simulating the digital twin, basically, to choose what course of intervention will be most effective and which medication or therapy will be most effective.

Digital streams from remote patient monitoring devices using wearable biosensors can be automatically monitored and contextualized with actionable clinical information (e.g., early infection warning signs). If anomalies in trends are detected, the digital twin will generate alerts and warnings to clinicians to allow for timely interventions and treatment regimen adjustments.

In addition to its ability to integrate data from various sources, conduct generative analysis, and provide high-precision recommendations, an LLM-powered digital twin of a patient would be a reliable knowledge-driven assistant that clinicians can query at the point of care for otherwise unattainable, data-driven insights. This would help improve the quality of clinical decisions and patient outcomes. An LLM-driven twin is a decision-support tool for clinicians guiding them toward insights, personalized recommendations, and continuous monitoring of patients, leading to enhanced clinical decision making and patient outcomes.

Doctor Letter Generation

Physicians face escalating paperwork demands that divert precious time from direct patient care. Letters addressing prior authorizations, disability claims, return-to-work needs, and other centralized requests prove administratively burdensome, given their unstructured formats. High volumes and inflexible templates multiply inefficiencies across practices. Figure 4-12 depicts a doctor using generative AI to do their paperwork.

One of the first adaptive doctor letter generation LLM solutions, known as ScribeMD,[3] works by allowing doctors to input the letter verbally and then augment it in NLP until it reaches a complete professional missive. Physicians must dictate those points in a voice prompt, like so: "This former patient of ours at St. Francis Memorial Hospital named Sam Jones..." And they go on to list their history, to whom the note is intended, primary care details, hospital policy requirements, and recommended action for caregivers, including documentation, intubation, or antibiotic details.

---

3 ScribeMD, accessed June 27, 2024, *https://www.scribemd.ai*.

Figure 4-12. Doctor using generative AI to create letters, forms, and emails

ScribeMD, the tool running on this particular prompt, is conversant in HIPAA-compliant LLMs and dissects these prompt components before continuing the drafting of a letter. Physicians edit autogenerated letters when necessary before signing correspondence. Frequently, automation is doing the raw document creation, citation sourcing, and standardized formatting—from deeply detailed "History of Present Illness" to producing return-to-work release notes.

By iterating through multiple cases, ScribeMD's predictive outputs gradually improve over time as the model learns various stylistic quirks, clues about where to cite evidence, and the structural profile "fixed expressions" specific to that particular provider, subspecialty, and area of practice. With broad uptake, over time both the training corpus used to develop this system and its continual feedback calibrations will grow exponentially, cutting drafting time to as little as 30 seconds.

Leaping from templates to adaptable narratives lowers the labor of clinical documentation while conveying nuance. Patients also benefit from personalization. ScribeMD thus helps physicians share care knowledge conversationally instead of battling form gaps in the production of health services, thereby avoiding the pain of perpetual paperwork.

Health Equity

Health equity means that all people (Figure 4-13) have a fair and just opportunity to achieve their highest level of health, unhindered by their social, economic, or demographic status. It means having no avoidable, unfair, or remediable differences among those populations in their overall health status and access to healthcare services.

Figure 4-13. Health equity for all

Key aspects of health equity include:

Equal access
> Equal access to healthcare means that everyone—no matter if they are rich, poor, black, white, etc., and no matter their age, sex, gender, or physical capabilities—should have access to medications or any type of care that they need, whenever they need it.

Social determinants of health
> Achieving health equity will require attending to the social, economic, and environmental factors that play a direct and indirect role in shaping health outcomes, at the individual and community levels, including education, employment, housing, and transportation.

Leveling the playing field
> Health equity is pursued to eliminate disparities in health outcomes that are systemic, avoidable, and unjust as a consequence of specific social and economic policies and practices.

Policies and programs
> Health equity entails developing and implementing policies and programs that are designed to meet the needs of marginalized and vulnerable communities, taking into account any resource inequities.

Empowerment and participation
> Health equity entails strengthening the voice of individuals and communities to participate in decisions that affect their health and well-being.

Cultural competence
> Health equity demands that healthcare providers and healthcare systems, institutional or organizational, are competent in understanding and respecting the values, beliefs, behaviors, practices, and cultures of different populations.

Coming to grips with health inequities and achieving health equity is a complex and long-term process involving many sectors—both public and private—for many generations. Health systems and the rest of society should shift their focus from disease treatment at the end of the lifespan to preventing social inequities and health differences earlier in life.

LLMs can analyze social determinants of health (SDOH) data like income, housing, and education to predict potential health risks for specific communities. This allows for proactive interventions and resource allocation by clinicians to address those needs. Generative AI/LLM chatbots or virtual assistants can provide culturally sensitive information and connect individuals with appropriate social services and healthcare resources based on their specific SDOH.

These AI virtual assistants can tailor communication and education, providing personalized health information and educational materials based on individual needs and cultural backgrounds, improving understanding and access. LLMs can also identify and flag potentially discriminatory language within medical records, doctor notes, or algorithms, promoting more inclusive healthcare practices.

Clinicians and care teams, the backbone of the healthcare system, often need help with many tasks, leaving them with less time for what matters most: their patients. A virtual clinician could provide the doctor with personalized diagnostics for their patients. This includes analysis of patient data (medical history, lab reports, imaging, etc.) to identify patterns and generate nuanced prompts for the doctor, suggest potential diagnoses and help narrow down the investigation path.

Prior Authorization

Nurses and medical directors need to keep up with lots of data every day to navigate a decision on a prior authorization request. The process can be confusing, tedious, time-consuming, and error-prone. Prior authorization (Figure 4-14) can be a significant problem in the healthcare system for several reasons:

Delayed care

Prior authorization processes can delay patients from receiving necessary medications, treatments, or procedures, as providers must wait for approval from insurance companies before proceeding. These delays can lead to worsening of conditions and poorer health outcomes.

Administrative burden

The prior authorization process is often time-consuming and administratively burdensome for healthcare providers. Physicians and their staff spend considerable time filling out forms, making phone calls, and navigating complex bureaucratic systems, which takes away from direct patient care.

Increased costs

The administrative costs associated with prior authorization can be substantial for healthcare providers and insurance companies. Additionally, delays in care can lead to more expensive interventions if conditions worsen due to a lack of timely treatment.

Interference with clinical decision making

Prior authorization requirements can interfere with a healthcare provider's clinical judgment, as insurance companies may override a physician's treatment recommendations based on cost or other factors rather than what is best for the patient.

Patient frustration

Prior authorization can be frustrating and confusing for patients, who may need help understanding why their treatment is delayed or denied. This can lead to dissatisfaction with the healthcare system and potential nonadherence to treatment plans.

Health inequities

Prior authorization requirements may disproportionately affect specific patient populations, such as those with chronic conditions or complex healthcare needs, exacerbating existing health inequities.

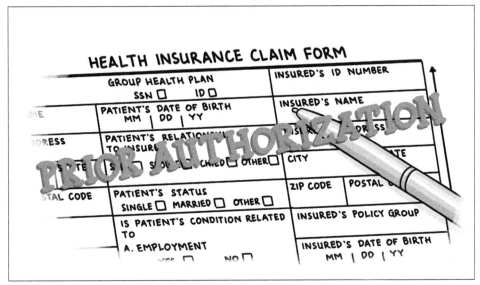

Figure 4-14. Streamline prior authorizations with LLMs

Although prior authorization is intended to lower healthcare costs and ensure that the proper services are delivered at the right time, the burden of current processes can hinder timely, effective care. Fortunately, a growing number of healthcare providers, patient advocates, and policymakers are advocating for reform of prior authorization in an effort to relieve administrative burden, improve operational efficiency, and allow clinicians to focus on what matters most: safe, effective, and patient-centered care.

Machine-aided prior authorization with an LLM removes all that while allowing patients to get the care they need, when they need it: the approval process is sped up for proper procedures, while clinician productivity goes up. An LLM is able to replicate human reasoning, vet clinical criteria for almost all care situations that an insurer ever needs to consider, and acquire patient data in real time as needed, including past claims, lab results, prescriptions, and clinical notes. The end result is an LLM-driven system that issues real-time rulings on whether a medical "care necessity" metric was or was not met whenever called upon to do so. All that is left for a clinician to do is to approve or deny a given prior authorization request. In most cases, the clinician could issue a positive prior authorization approval mandate.

Machine-assisted LLM prior authorization enables better decisions quicker by payers, ensuring patients get needed services. Over time, the pain points associated with prior authorizations fade from view, allowing trusted relationships between payors, providers, and patients to blossom. When applied with machine-assisted LLM prior authorization, the healthcare system can work better for all.

As noted previously, a major problem with the prior authorization process is that things must be processed in real time. This is the way it works:

Manual reviews
Because so many prior authorization requests are still adjudicated manually by insurance company staff, they can take a long time and therefore delay treatment. Because adjudications aren't in real time, patients and providers must wait for decisions, even simple ones.

Incomplete/incorrect info
Incomplete/incorrect info that requires the insurance company to collect info from the provider on the case further slows down the process of adjudication. In real-time processing, this is detected up front, giving providers the opportunity to fill in the information—and even correct the errors—before submitting the PA request the first time.

Nonstandard criteria
Differing rules for approving prior authorizations at different insurance companies and shifting criteria over time are difficult to take into account, with providers having no knowledge of the latest details without real-time processing and a centralized database. A prior authorization is a requirement set by an insurance company that must be fulfilled before medical services can be provided.

Lack of integration
Many prior authorization processes could use further integration with EHRs and other healthcare IT systems. Providers would typically enter information into a separate portal or form, later added to the clinical record, increasing the likelihood of errors and delays.

Provider and patient frustration
Lack of real-time processing can result in significant frustration for providers and patients—delayed treatment, increased administrative burden, and uncertainty about coverage decisions.

Implementing real-time processing in prior authorization could help address these challenges in the following ways:

Automating everyday requests
For routine or low-risk requests, we could allow automatic requests that meet specified criteria for approval immediately.

Providing instant feedback
Real-time processing could give providers instant feedback about the appropriateness and accuracy of their requests, reducing the need for paper ping-pong and appeals.

Keeping criteria up to date in real time

In theory, real-time processing could see health plans continuously updating the criteria providers use during prior authorizations so providers' encounters are judged using up-to-date information rather than information that might be out of date, which could lead to a denial.

Facilitating integration

Real-time transaction processing could enable integration between prior authorization systems and EHRs, eliminating the need for manual data entry.

Real-time processing of prior authorization is not easy, but it can go a long way toward improving the efficiency, accuracy, and immediacy of the process, ultimately helping patients, providers, and payers alike. LLMs may also improve real-time processing of prior authorizations[4] in the following ways:

Natural language processing (NLP)

Imagine an LLM that could make sense of the prior authorization requests you receive in free-form, unstructured language, parsing them for pertinent details like patient name, diagnosis codes, and treatment plans. It could make the process faster and our data input less time-consuming.

Smart form parsing

LLMs could be trained to recognize and parse information from prior authorization forms for various check-ins for different auto, vision, and dental insurance companies. It could allow physicians to submit requests for preapproval in their preferred format, while insurers could then process these automatically.

Decision automation

LLMs could be used together with rule-based systems or machine-learning models for purposes of automating decision making. For example, an LLM could extract relevant information from a request and match against the insurer's decision guidelines, before making a real-time decision. This could lead to significant efficiency gains in processing routine requests.

Contextual awareness

LLMs could become useful when interpreting clinical documentation, such as notes in the medical record or written clinical justifications in prior authorization requests. In this case, contextual awareness in the LLMs could help ensure that nuances of language don't get lost and that the analytics are drawn from a holistic interpretation of what's happening with the patient.

---

4 Prashant Sharma, "LLM in Health Care: The Prior Authorization Opportunity," *Medium*, August 14, 2023, *https://medium.com/@prashant05kumar/llm-in-health-care-the-prior-authorization-opportunity-7e72b6058301.*

Personalized communications

LLMs could create personalized communications or explanations of prior authorization decisions from providers to patients. Examples include explaining why a request was denied and how to appeal or resubmit the request.

Continuous learning

LLMs can be trained on new data continuously, ensuring they respond to changing guideline thresholds, criteria, and best-care practices. This could enable them to revise prior authorization rules in a flexible way as evidence and standards change.

In the context of prior authorization, while LLMs have massive potential in enhancing real-time processing, it is also evident that this would have to operate in combination with other technologies such as rules-based systems, machine learning/deep learning models, and robust data integration. A robust solution would need data privacy, security, and explainability to ensure all decisions are transparent, fair, and in compliance with relevant policies and regulations.

Summary

With accelerating developments in LLMs and generative AI—technologies that promise to transform medical practice—we embark on an exciting journey to better inform, engage, and connect doctors and patients. In proceeding, we outline several use cases of the emerging promise to suggest how these systems might deliver improved care, better efficiencies in a difficult sector, and an immediate response to significant pressing needs.

One use case could be health bot concierges that would utilize LLMs as a paraphrasing tool in attempts to provide a patient conversing with a machine that has the semblance of a human companion. This companion would be part of the patient journey for a health condition, perhaps from the point of diagnosis onward. An AI companion could address patients' questions, provide guidance, and help them navigate the healthcare system in a manner that is more amenable to the patient. This companion could deliver the requisite information to steer the care process in a more coordinated fashion while also sparing the clinician that clinical burden.

Within the healthcare sector, clinical workflows can be sped up by the deployment of LLMs and AI programs that can streamline the drafting of doctor notes and visits, affording more time and reducing errors in the development of structured clinical documentation. This would in turn allow physicians to reserve more time for direct patient care. LLMs could also interrogate patient data online to develop improved forms of clinical decision support that can boost and sustain the evidence-based nature of doctors' decisions and outcomes.

For example, in the realm of health insurance, LLMs can feed robo-advisors that could advise patients about what to look for, and recommend, in terms of health insurance coverage, tailored to individual needs and preferences, thereby helping to demystify the often-obscure world of health insurance, which can be a major roadblock to care—and payment for care—for patients.

Generative AI could therefore help minimize health disparities, increase health equity, and substantially improve health outcomes, especially in populations who suffer from both. For instance, Black women have a higher rate of maternal morbidity or mortality than White women. Using AI and large-scale data, an AI-interpreted intervention could be initially more specific to them and supply them with better access to education and other resources. Similarly, LLMs may power, for instance, medication adherence and oral health promotion programs to improve health outcomes in underserved communities.

LLM-based symptom checkers could help patients more accurately understand and interpret their symptoms and generate recommendations about when tests or care might be appropriate. Given the burgeoning bottleneck of knowledge, LLM symptom checkers might be able to produce more accurate, reliable, and nuanced assessments than currently available symptom checkers, thereby reducing cases of nonutilization of timely care and encouraging earlier intervention in serious illness.

As an example, LLMs offer curbside medicine to clinicians as an authoritative source for evidence-based clinical questions answered using the most recent medical literature. Clinical insight bots for patients can curate, filter, and elaborate on clinical records and summarize relevant questions asked and answers given event by event but geared for individualized recommendations. In addition, digital twins can emulate actual patient behavior in response to nominal interventions under varying conditions (such as precision medicine type protocols).

LLMs and generative AI can be employed for remote patient monitoring to interpret data from wearables and smartwatches/systems, for example. This way, they can identify patterns for prediction and intervention even before patients experience physical symptoms, and they can send alerts to care teams well ahead of time to take action preventing a potential problem from escalating. LLMs and generative AI can also be used to create doctor letters and prior authorizations to help free up clinicians from burdensome administrative tasks that are part of the delivery of care.

We have a moral duty to protect patient privacy and security, and to transition toward embracing ethical tech design and use. In order to harness AI's generative capacity to benefit patients, developers must avoid siloed efforts and foster coordinated action among healthcare entities and tech developers, as well as maintain a shared vision with policymakers.

In conclusion, if the use of LLMs and generative AI in various aspects of patient care is properly used, we may experience a multitude of changes in future care delivery models, patient encounters, and care optimization.

CHAPTER 5

LLMs in Pharmaceutical R&D, Public Health, and Beyond

Drawing on the groundwork laid by the previous chapters discussing patient-facing and clinical use cases, this chapter now expands the horizon. We will discuss how large language models (LLMs) can be deployed to accelerate the discovery of therapeutic drugs by exploring the scientific literature and finding promising molecules. By examining a range of use cases, we will explore how exactly LLMs and generative AI can help different healthcare stakeholders in fields such as pharmaceutical research and public health.

Pharma Research and Development

The very nature of human biology can make it difficult to decipher, and finding new drugs reflects that complication. Each claim may require a decade or more to verify, and each one costs at least a billion dollars—on average, 10–15 years and more than $1 billion to bring one new medicine[1] through a successful journey from laboratory to pharmacy shelf. Researchers often go through sleepless nights and years trying again and again to reach their goals when others doubt them, hoping to find ways to transform the course of life-limiting or fatal diseases, and to ultimately give more patients the healthy lives they deserve.

Equipped with multifaceted talents and well-developed tools, various human scientists become like molecular architects (Figure 5-1) building thousands of brand-new

---

1 "Research & Development Policy Framework," PhRMA Foundation, January 22, 2024, *https://phrma.org/en/policy-issues/Research-and-Development-Policy-Framework*.

molecular objects. Drug development is also divided in several stages: preclinical, clinical, and approval for sale.

All these stages present their own challenges, but once a compound clears one hurdle, it progresses to the next. This selective journey of scrutiny and elimination fosters robust, well-rounded, and effective drugs that deserve to see the light of day. As a result, every new drug that makes it to the market passes through a multistage journey from discovery, clinical, and regulatory approval stages. Each stage presents its own hurdles, and a candidate molecule abruptly has to meet certain requirements before progressing to the next stage. In fact, this stringent process takes place primarily to ensure the safety and efficacy of new drugs that eventually make it to the market.

Figure 5-1. Pharma research and development, molecular architects

As they attempt to deal with complex and expanding datasets that are becoming increasingly challenging to manage and interpret, LLMs will likely assume integral roles in pharma R&D. These datasets include:

Preclinical data
　　Tests done on lab animals such as mice, leeches, or cockroaches (you get the picture) before a drug is tested on humans.

Clinical trial data
　　Data generated across all trial phases (1 to 3) as part of human clinical trials on investigational medicinal products (clinical trial results), including safety and efficacy; pharmacokinetics; biomarkers (e.g., circulating tumor cells); patient-reported outcome measures.

Real-world data (RWD)

Information on use of drugs, outcomes, and adverse effects emerging from actual care on the ground, including electronic health records and insurance claims data.

Genomic data

Includes data from sequencing or analyzing human genetics and genomics to identify new drug targets or biomarkers.

Literature data

Data extracted from journal articles, patents, and conference posters on compounds and targets to aid in drug discovery.

Literature databases

Databases that include curated information on drugs, targets, clinical trials, and more from the scientific literature, such as ChEMBL, DrugBank, and PubChem.

The size of datasets used in pharma R&D can vary significantly depending on the specific type of data, research stage, and overall project scope. For example, biological data like genes: databases like RefSeq[2] contain millions of annotated human gene sequences, each ranging from a few hundred to a few thousand base pairs. The Protein Data Bank (PDB)[3] holds hundreds of thousands of protein structures, with file sizes ranging from kilobytes to megabytes. Data from single-cell sequencing experiments can generate terabytes of information, while tissue imaging studies might range from gigabytes to petabytes. Chemical data, like small molecules, contain libraries of potential drug candidates that can number in the millions, with each molecule's data (structure, properties) typically occupying gigabytes.

Clinical data for a single patient, such as an electronic health record, can vary from millions to over a billion bits or bytes. A clinical trial with hundreds or thousands of patients could require tens or hundreds of terabytes of storage. A complication with imaging or some other advanced biomarker measure could make it hundreds of times larger. A social-media study that analyzes sentiments or mentions of disease might be in the gigabyte range, but a large-scale study could involve terabytes.

At this scale, ingestion and integration of data needs to be fully automated. LLMs can scan and parse data from different sources, including clinical trial data, scientific literature, public databases, and electronic health records. They can also clean and align data across different formats and conventions. Once data is organized and placed in a consistent structure, an LLM can construct the knowledge graph that represents relationships among entities in the dataset. It can help researchers create a map of the

---

2 "RefSeq: NCBI Reference Sequence Database," National Library of Medicine, accessed June 28, 2024, *https://www.ncbi.nlm.nih.gov/refseq*.

3 wwPDB, accessed June 28, 2024, *https://www.wwpdb.org*.

entities and hop between them, collecting the information they need. Finally, an LLM can analyze large data to find hidden patterns, trends, and correlations.

There are numerous efforts underway in the industry to build LLMs and GenAIs that focus on the R&D process. For instance, Nvidia recently launched an LLM called MegaMolBART,[4] and Google also has a medically relevant model. Med-PaLM and Meta's ESM-2[5] highlight that GenAI will accelerate the discovery process.

Whether it's our description of our symptoms or our doctor's history of similar cases, the AI and healthcare relationship is an ideal match, and LLMs provide the key to unlock that value. The industrial applications for LLMs will only become more numerous and profound as our abilities with LLMs develop—and we're already headed toward the future of a more targeted and efficient approach to healthcare.

Drug Discovery

With LLMs as a valuable early input, we can help to facilitate faster new drug discovery while responsibly implementing the development side of drug discovery. LLMS and generative AI can perhaps lead to the next generations of drug discovery (Figure 5-2). LLMs are likely to predict the properties of predicted drug candidates that may not require extensive and costly animal tests, where AI can process large datasets resulting from such experiments.

Chemical databases exist that catalog the structures and properties of the many millions of drugs and natural compounds known to science—as well as their documented properties and effects. LLMs can be trained on such databases, as well as published research papers and clinical trial data to detect correlations between what types of drugs have which properties and can lead to which outcomes.

Data on how toxic various compounds might prove to be can be mined and used to train LLMs to detect toxicity risks in patients based on the newly synthesized drug's properties. From crunching through these large datasets, LLMs can learn the correlations between a drug's chemical structure, its behavior inside a biological system, and its potential effects. It can, effectively, infer efficacy by recognizing patterns in past data. LLMs can assess how well a given drug candidate is likely to bind a target (a protein molecule) and potentially predict efficacy against a certain disease. Structural similarities between a newly identified chemical client and known toxic compounds can thereby be grasped by an LLM and reported back as a potential safety issue yet to be investigated.

---

4 "MegaMolBART," Nvidia, November 27, 2023, *https://catalog.ngc.nvidia.com/orgs/nvidia/teams/clara/models/megamolbart*.

5 "ESM Metagenomic Atlas: The First View of the 'Dark Matter' of the Protein Universe," Meta, November 1, 2022, *https://ai.meta.com/blog/protein-folding-esmfold-metagenomics*.

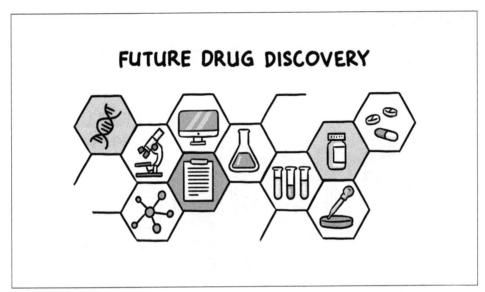

Figure 5-2. Drug discovery

Drugs with known toxicity might share some structural aspects with a new candidate. These aspects may enable the incidence of same-structured molecules with dangerous side effects. Side-effect data on existing drugs could also be captured by an LLM and reported as potential side effects for the new candidate. The new compound could well end up being usable as a drug—even the candidate could be prioritized for further funding—but the awareness of the potential nasty adverse reaction might inform researchers that certain candidates are more risky than others, spurring them to look elsewhere for a more suitable trial.

The trained LLM can then be used to predict the properties of molecular structures it is given. To do this, you give the LLM information about the structure of the potential drug that it's predicting the properties of. The LLM processes this information and then comes up with information confirming or denying its suitability as an incoming drug. The LLM may give a predicted value for the property of interest (e.g., efficacy score, high toxicity risk) or even be able to suggest structural changes in order to enhance the desired properties of the drug. LLM predictions are not always correct.

Those predictions, which may or may not come with a specified level of confidence, are valuable as a guide, and as such, they should not be used as an alternative to the experimental testing of the compound. Moreover, the need to validate and investigate further before relying on LLM predictions cannot be overemphasized. LLMs are evolving. As more and more data becomes available and training strategies improve, it is anticipated that the accuracy and reliability of LLM predictions will increase over time.

Literature Review

Literature review is basically a brute-force task, which will play to the strengths of the LLM: scanning for keywords in large sets of papers (Figure 5-3).

Figure 5-3. LLMs help with reviewing numerous documents

LLMs can condense the critical findings of numerous studies into concise summaries, allowing researchers to quickly grasp the current state of knowledge on a particular topic. This saves researchers valuable time and effort compared to manually reviewing countless papers. LLMs can detect patterns and connections across different studies by analyzing large datasets. This detection helps researchers identify emerging trends, potential gaps in knowledge, and relationships between other research areas.

LLMs help improve accuracy, prioritize comprehensiveness, and reduce bias. Manual literature review can be susceptible to unconscious bias, where researchers may unintentionally prioritize studies that support their existing hypotheses. LLMs, however, can offer a more objective approach, analyzing all relevant literature regardless of their potential findings.

Manual review can be time-consuming and prone to human errors such as missing relevant studies or misinterpreting information. LLMs can offer a more consistent and reliable way to process data, reducing the risk of errors. LLMs can search multiple languages and databases, potentially helping researchers uncover studies from various regions and research groups, fostering a more comprehensive review process incorporating diverse perspectives.

LLMs can help researchers share and discover relevant literature within their research teams and collaborate with colleagues across different institutions. This can accelerate the pace of research by ensuring everyone is aware of the latest advancements and preventing the duplication of efforts.

LLMs can customize and personalize the literature review experience for individual researchers based on their interests and research focus, saving them time and effort by filtering out irrelevant information.

Limitations exist with LLMs in accuracy and explainability. LLMs rely on the accuracy and quality of their training data. Additionally, understanding how they reach their conclusions can be challenging, which requires careful evaluation and human expertise. The biases in the underlying data could be reflected in the LLM's outputs. Addressing these biases and ensuring responsible use is crucial.

Overall, LLMs offer valuable tools for streamlining and enhancing literature review in pharma R&D. Their ability to handle vast amounts of data, reduce bias, and facilitate collaboration holds significant potential for accelerating scientific discovery and drug development.

Clinical Trial Recruitment

Recruiting people for clinical trials entails finding both interested parties and people who match the criteria for a specific study. Often this requires the following steps:

1. Identify potential participants through researching the patient population and understand the target demographics, including age, gender, and medical condition.

2. Use criteria to identify those people who can and cannot enroll in the study based on their health status, medical history, and current medications.

3. Depending upon the study, there may be outreach to doctors or patient advocacy groups or advertisement for recruitment.

4. Once potential participants have been identified, these candidates are sent materials—ranging from brochures or websites to social media campaigns—that outline the study, identify the purpose, mention who is overseeing it, and identify the possible benefits and risks.

5. Next is prescreening, which involves an initial assessment to see if someone meets a very basic set of criteria that might make him or her eligible.

6. Educate potential participants and obtain informed consent where a discussion takes place with a researcher who explains the study in detail, answers questions, and addresses concerns. All subjects participating are asked to sign a consent document indicating that they understand the nature of the study and are freely opting to participate.

7. Eligibility must be assessed through more detailed medical evaluations as to whether the person has fulfilled the inclusion criteria.

8. Once eligibility is confirmed, the participant is officially enrolled in the study.

Recruitment of participants must adhere to regulations and be ethically sound to protect the rights and safety of participants. Approaches will have to be tailored to the setting (e.g., clinical versus community) and the involved patient population (e.g., pediatric versus adult), and through diverse communication channels (e.g., in-person, online, phone). Recruitment is often difficult, and various approaches are often needed to reach an adequate target number of participants.

Generative AI and LLMs can help streamline recruitment for research protocols. Natural language processing (NLP) with LLMs can facilitate streamlined participant recruitment by enabling automation of up-front checks and eligibility screening. The inherent capability of LLMs to perform NLP and understanding enables interactive chats (see Figure 5-4) or online intelligent questionnaires to be used to pre-engage the study participants, to collect necessary information related to the participants' demographics, and to perform an initial eligibility check. This automated prescreening procedure can reduce the effort required for the manual "cold calling" process in traditional participant recruitment and thus accelerate the participant recruitment phase and allow for finer matching of the participants to respective studies.

Figure 5-4. Using LLM chatbot to streamline clinical trial recruitment

LLMs can individualize patient-facing communications based on demographics, medical history, spoken language, and other factors. This will help increase the appropriate level of engagement and resonance. Generative AI and LLMs can render summaries of the trial's purpose, potential benefits, and risks in a simplified manner while still retaining the necessary complexity that encompasses the entire clinical picture. This will help eliminate confusion, boost debate, and sharpen decision-making.

In other words, LLMs can scan past recruitment data to unearth barriers to participation—for example, if people aren't taking part in a study because it interferes with work or school, if they don't speak English, or if they don't have transportation. From that, they could identify demographic characteristics (e.g., lived experience) or alter trial logistics or designs to help manage them. By offering translation and multilingual outreach, LLMs can increase participation by recruiting more people and ensuring that underrepresented communities have access to participation.

Clinical trial recruitment faces several challenges:

- Identifying a sufficient number of subjects is a major hurdle, particularly for rare diseases or trials with stringent eligibility criteria. Trials can be held up by the need to have more diverse participation, and therefore results can be skewed as they might not generalize to the wider population. In addition, patients can be burdened by complex trial protocols, travel demands, and long procedures resulting in diminished participation and dropouts.

- Research, development, and regulatory hurdles make trials expensive, limiting accessibility and innovation.

- Lengthy and intricate protocols increase administrative burdens and the potential for errors.

- Navigating different regulatory requirements across countries can be time-consuming and resource-intensive.

- Recording data in a uniform way is especially difficult when many sites are involved and diverse populations are recorded.

- Ensuring data integrity and preventing misconduct throughout the trial is crucial.

- Ensuring participants fully understand the risks and benefits of participation is paramount. Protecting vulnerable groups like children or pregnant women requires extra ethical safeguards. It is important to consider how all populations might get equitable access to clinical trials.

The prospect of LLMs and generative AI can boost the old model of clinical trial recruitment with a multifaceted new approach to alleviate bottlenecks: improving research and development, assisting with patient recruitment and engagement, helping with trial design and analyses, and even allowing for a glimpse into the potential improvement of regulatory compliance. Some new approaches include:

- Streamline research and development by automating documents generation. GenAI can autogenerate study protocols, clinical summaries, and regulatory reports, saving significant time and resources for researchers.

- GenAI could notice patterns emerging in large datasets of research information, and help researchers prioritize relevant information, guiding their decision making and accelerating discovery.

- GenAI can analyze patient data, as well as provide insights from previous clinical trials, to create targeted and personalized outreach campaigns to encourage participation in relevant trials.

- AI-powered virtual assistants and chatbots can be used to answer patients' questions and provide ongoing support throughout the trial, thereby improving engagement and retention.

- GenAI can model various trial scenarios using virtual simulations to anticipate results and thus design studies to be efficient and effective.

In real time, AI might analyze vast trial data and discover safety signals, efficacy markers, and potentially emerging trends leading to real-time decision making. Improving regulatory compliance is another benefit of applying LLM as automated regulatory reporting can occur: For legally or operationally required reports, systems that use benchmarks and produce text through machine learning can create reports in real time that are accurate and compliant, reducing potential errors and shortening the approval process.

AI can process trial data while also reviewing regulations to identify factors that might put compliance at risk and could be dealt with prior to any breaches.

GenAI brings impressive possibilities to improve clinical trials through greater efficiency, effectiveness, and inclusivity, with greater ethical vigilance needed throughout the clinical trial life cycle. LLMs and GenAI are not meant to replace human decision makers. Instead, they should serve as a tool to augment human ability and facilitate responsible decision making throughout the clinical trials process.

Pharmaceutical Commercial

Here's a sector primed for innovation: the overly long, overly boring pharmaceutical commercial. Soon we'll see an influx of LLMs and generative AI, which will provide pharma companies with many ways of spicing up product dissemination to healthcare professionals and patients.

A humorous cartoon depiction of some experiences is illustrated in the Figure 5-5 cartoon. This cartoon is a parody of advertisements for pharmaceuticals that are advertised as part of mass communications, often late at night or early in the morning hours. This man's exasperated response says a lot about how people may experience this advertising.

Figure 5-5. Late-night commercial

LLMs could help consumers understand and interpret the information being conveyed in the action-packed commercials we watch on late-night TV that advertise prescription medications and are legally required to provide information about limitations and possible side effects that are often complicated, confusing, and perhaps even a bit too much for the average viewer to fully process. LLMs can translate medical jargon and vocabulary common in pharmaceutical ads into more natural-sounding text, and allow consumers to understand the need for the medicine, how it works, and potential side effects.

A large number of pharma companies follow a sales model that relies on a salesforce of pharmaceutical representatives to visit physicians and market their company's products directly to them. This type of one-to-one marketing, known as "pharmaceutical retailing," involves sales reps traveling to meet physicians with the goal of convincing them to prescribe medicines from their own company by promoting what they learned was a drug's benefits and efficacy. Retailing is an intensive, targeted marketing strategy that drug companies use to promote and directly influence prescriptions that a physician writes.

Further, the pharma rep might take questions from the providers and funnel these questions on to the medical affairs team to request specific scientific answers to the physician's question; the pharma rep becomes the human representation of the pharma company. Reps granted access to physicians could be much more productive.

Now visualize pharma companies and providers communicating and interacting directly with the customer—providers, patients, and other constituents—to make the information exchange work the way they need it to. Picture providers having immediate access to the information they need to deliver the best patient care possible. Imagine an infrastructure that makes all of this easier both for providers and for patients and allows many more patients better access to the treatments and therapies they need. Pharma-customer interactions that make sense for individual providers, patients, and companies mean better value for all. The right data at the right time can likely mean the right intervention at the right time.

The future commercial model for pharmaceutical companies requires a fundamental shift in approach. This new model demands that pharma companies:

- Listen attentively to market needs
- Predict trends and challenges
- Act proactively to address these needs and challenges

This evolving model should focus on customer-specific engagement. It should become embedded throughout the organization rather than being solely the responsibility of sales representatives. These changes represent a significant transformation, not just minor adjustments. The future pharma commercial model will:

- Expand focus from prescribers to all healthcare stakeholders, including patients, payers, and healthcare systems
- Shift from a product-centric approach to a customer-centric one, prioritizing solutions that address specific healthcare needs
- Adopt a healthcare-centric focus, moving away from the traditional sales representative–driven model to a more holistic approach that considers the entire healthcare ecosystem

This transformation aims to create more value for all stakeholders in the healthcare system while adapting to changing market dynamics and customer expectations.

Using a variety of data sources such as EHR, claims data, and prescription data, pharmaceuticals will harness AI to understand and assist both patients and providers in delivering a transformative experience. Using deep-learning, LLM systems that ingest these large data assets can inform a strategy.

With the learning captured from this process, generative AI can then create fully personalized engagement for each stakeholder: with patients, education about their condition can be tailored; and with providers, generative AI can produce customized panel information to facilitate better prescribing. An insights and engagement-driven approach to commercial strategy thus leverages the human-in-the-loop process to fast-track discoveries of value-added therapies while continuously transforming commercial models. LLM knowledge and generative creativity thereby better serves and engages the divergent stakeholders to provide improved access, education, and outcomes in the process.

The new model needs to flip across the board to be more patient-centric, trust-mining, context-aware, personalized, and at scale. This means evolving from an interruption model that is product-driven and sales-led to a persona model that is context-driven and strategy and technology-led. This will allow pharma marketing to leverage the data and continuously gather more data. While data-driven and omnichannel marketing are not new concepts in pharmaceuticals, a GenAI-based commercial model requires a fundamental redesign of marketing strategies. This new approach demands a customer-centric organization with a goal of true personalization. To achieve this, the current marketing approach needs to be distilled into two core components:

Product strategy
Developing and articulating the unique value of the product

Customer experience creation
Crafting personalized experiences that demonstrate this value to the customer

This "reductive click" or simplification allows for a more focused and practical approach, enabling pharma companies to leverage GenAI in creating tailored marketing strategies that resonate with individual customers.

GenAI and LLMs can also disrupt marketing in the next two to five years by: analyzing large amounts of the aforementioned data from disparate internal and external sources to create individualized, targeted marketing campaigns, and by creating innovative new marketing approaches.

We propose creating a GenAI chatbot or a "listening engine" that enables a holistic understanding of customers and a deeper level of personalization at scale. Our listening engine consists of a single, intelligent data platform drawing together insights across all new and old sources of customer experience data points, and combining offer/call-to-action effectiveness with listening and responding where required.

Using advanced data-processing capabilities built on an integration infrastructure, a listening engine can bring together inputs and feedback from traditional and new data sources into a single platform and fuse them with a learning machine-learning engine. This enables organizations to leverage previously untapped data streams to uncover new areas of worthy investment for optimizing the customer experience, or to uncover critical signals of customer health to enable preemptive customer-recovery actions at scale.

These can offer highly scaled and personalized levels of engagement with their customers through personalized transactions and conversations. The basis, then, for our proposed apparatus for better understanding the customer relationship rests on integrating new and old sources of data. However, to enable for this deeper level of relationship-mapping, novel architectural capabilities are needed. The most sophisticated use of these new systems would be to integrate insights across new data sources to create individualized, targeted marketing campaigns and new, innovative marketing approaches.

But listening is only half the story. Companies are investing in and deploying GenAI- and AI-based systems that can translate those insights into strategy-led recommendations on the "what" and "how" of prescribing communications. Adopting AI-based business models moves commercial teams to a position of differentiation in a crowded and intensely competitive landscape. By using generative AI, companies can advance business goals of growth, launch success, and agility while also achieving the mission-critical social goals of better serving patients through more effectively solving healthcare needs that lead to improved health outcomes.

An LLM can generate accurate and more concise educational material about specific diseases, drug regimens, and possible treatments, equipping users with the information needed to make smarter decisions about their own health. LLMs could even be built into a bot or other artificially intelligent assistant, which a patient could question or query on whatever topic they want, and get personalized information back. In addition, the patient could also obtain information directly from pharmaceutical companies—quickly and informally.

LLMs could assess past market data and emerging trends to forecast the target market reach of a given kind of marketing campaign, enabling companies to design and optimize marketing campaigns in the most cost-effective ways. LLMs might be used to evaluate marketing materials against regulatory guidelines for content accuracy and ethical messaging.

Public Health

Public health is an area of professional practice and science. It protects and improves the health of people and communities via numerous methods, including the promotion of healthy lifestyles, prevention of diseases and injuries, and provision of access to healthcare services.

Public health can be divided into several subcategories: disease surveillance; health education and promotion; mental health; and public health preparedness and response.

Disease Surveillance

The use of LLMs can enable faster and better disease surveillance, by rapidly combing through huge swathes of health data from a variety of sources to identify fine-grained signals that could indicate an imminent outbreak or changes in the trend of a disease. For example, an LLM might scan years of emergency room records, press reports, social media postings, and search engine queries across a region, picking up on subtle language shifts in case descriptions that are correlated with historical activity from infectious diseases. They could flag associated data from an LLM that far outperformed contemporary surveillance by spotting novel infections early.

Figure 5-6 is an example using icons representing some of the many classification factors under the umbrella of "surveillance."

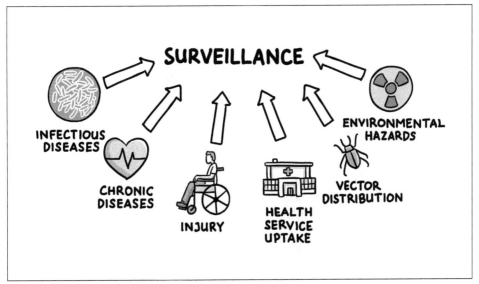

Figure 5-6. Disease surveillance

Arrows among the icons show that surveillance is an act of tracking and monitoring the relationships and interaction among these health determinants. The main point of the diagram shows that public health surveillance is a complex system made by collecting and analyzing the data about a vast range of health determinants that evaluate and respond to health problems and threats in the population.

Once trained, LLMs can scour databases for comments and reports on social media and online forums about symptoms and illness. When they spot the relevant key-words, phrases, and locations, they can flag the early indicators of disease outbreaks for public health officials, enabling officials to mobilize their resources to investigate possible outbreaks before they become large-scale epidemics.

Generative AI capabilities built into LLMs can be helpful to show scenarios of the ways diseases are spread. Figure 5-7 illustrates the spread of diseases as it starts with one person and spreads to many.

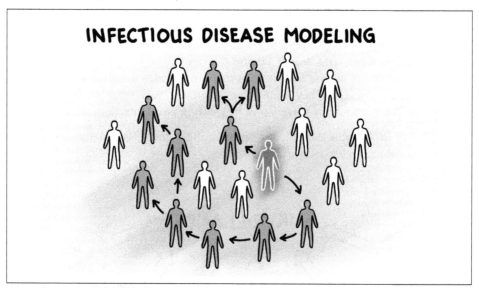

Figure 5-7. Modeling infectious disease

Modeling scenarios for infectious diseases allows researchers to simulate the potential impact of intervention strategies such as vaccination campaigns, travel restrictions, or social distancing measures. The goal is to use simulated scenarios to identify and design effective and targeted interventions. Armed with such data, from electronic health records and public health databases, along with travel records, LLMs can find patterns too subtle for the human eye, and make predictions about outbreaks and the most effective pathways for their spread, so officials can apply resources where they're needed most.

LLMs may be used with contact tracing systems, sifting through call logs, travel histories, and other information to determine who might have been exposed to a targeted disease or to create risk assessments where data, such as age, address, and underlying health conditions, are used to develop generative AI models to predict who is at risk of a particular disease.

Health Education and Promotion

LLMs can sift through mountains of medical literature and health data to generate health education materials customized for different audiences. One human author can't synthesize insights from tens of millions of research paper abstracts, thousands of clinical trials, and hundreds of population datasets into informational pamphlets, websites, and health materials.

Generative AI tools can also assist with adapting health education content to specific readers. By providing the AI with a sample of an individual or group's writing, it can mimic their tone and language patterns to make the information highly accessible. This helps overcome literacy and numeracy barriers that frequently obstruct health communication. The generated texts will seem familiar rather than clinical, empowering people to better understand risks, prevention options, symptoms, treatments, and more.

The illustration (Figure 5-8) depicts a health educator or doctor whose role involves using data, research, and advanced technologies (e.g., LLMs) to educate others about health topics and provide medical guidance. Both LLMs and generative AIs can produce interactive media, chatbots, and conversational apps to be used as health educators. These can deliver personalized health advice at scale across populations.

Additionally, as research evolves, LLMs and generative AI can rapidly update myriad health education resources across channels like brochures, videos, podcasts, and interactive tools. This dynamism keeps the public informed of paradigm shifts around diet, exercise, smoking, mental health, common illnesses, and disease epidemiology as they emerge.

Figure 5-8. Multifaceted nature of modern health education

While LLMs offer a promising avenue for public health education, it's important to remember that they are not a replacement for human expertise. Ensuring the accuracy and credibility of the information generated by these models, along with maintaining human oversight and addressing potential biases within them, are crucial aspects of responsible implementation.

Mental Health

Mental health is an integral part of public health. LLMs and generative AI are opening up a space for increased accessibility and early intervention using LLM-powered chatbots and virtual assistants providing 24/7 access to basic mental health information and resources, especially in areas where access to mental health support is limited.

Generative AI's ability to generate targeted and limitless content can be leveraged to create personalized chatbots and therapeutic instruments that can adapt their responses and interventions to an individual's specific needs. It could be designed to attempt the following activities:

- LLMs can recognize emotional distress in user input and respond with empathetic statements, a technique drawn from cognitive-behavioral therapy.

- LLMs can personalize education and point learners to help, whether it is self-help literature, support groups, or professional help.

- Chatbots can be programmed to check in with you, track your success, and encourage you to practice your coping mechanisms and self-management strategies.

- LLMs can be put to use designing study and awareness-raising materials and campaigns that center on mental health issues, normalize the seeking of help, and alleviate stigma. This includes creating content suitable for young and adult users across a diverse range of contexts.

However, we must point out that these technologies are imperfect and need to be implemented with great care. LLMs and generative AI technologies cannot be a substitute for the work of mental health professionals. They aren't intended for the treatment of severe mental health issues. Data protection is another major issue. Once developers and clinicians have produced models to predict or treat mental illness, who can access these models? How could the development of such models be made more transparent and transparently peer-reviewed? Would patient datasets be rigorously anonymized, and how could this be guaranteed? A whole set of ethical challenges must be understood and addressed when it comes to mental health.

Disaster Preparedness and Response

During a crisis—whether from a hurricane, wildfire, or disease outbreak—public health organizations must rapidly activate multilayered response plans. An LLM could be trained to rapidly analyze thousands of documents describing resources and procedures for supplies, facilities, staffing, and processes under countless scenarios, and draw a blueprint of coordination strategies optimized to the event. This could be done in a matter of seconds for subsequent human review and action.

Similarly, generative AI can propose disaster scenarios beyond anything commonly observed historically. Through generating simulated disasters (a category 6 hurricane, a novel flu organism), response planners can stress test and ferret out inefficiencies in relief strategy before real tragedies arrive. The scenario creation abilities of generative AI offers readiness-relevant extremes of creativity.

One of the tasks where LLMs can be useful is in generating communications in natural-sounding text, such as public service announcements, social-media alerts, and pamphlets containing location-optimized "know your risks" and behavioral guidance on how to respond to disaster threats. Communication that is clear and timely saves lives, and this is precisely what AI can provide by automatically generating content that is tailored to groups such as vulnerable populations or those with disabilities.

Leading up to, in the midst of, and following crises, an LLM or generative AI model can ingest the most current information about threats and responses. With more advance warning from AI surveillance and modeling, preemptive responses can occur quicker. Even rapid AI content production provides a fuller picture of emergent risks when communicated to the public earlier on. In this way, public health agencies can outflank disasters, circumventing the kind of lag time in diverting human brain power that they've previously had to contend with in response to potential population health risks.

Genomics

Genomics holds immense potential for understanding and treating various diseases. Today and in the future as genomics research matures, analyzing and interpreting this vast amount of data can be incredibly challenging. LLMs are learning the language of genomics.[6]

Analyzing, understanding, and applying knowledge from genomics requires sifting through enormous datasets spanning DNA sequences, gene expression patterns, protein structures, and complex associations to traits and diseases (Figure 5-9). By ingesting millions of papers and datasets, LLMs can uncover hidden connections in genetics to drive discovery and real-world application.

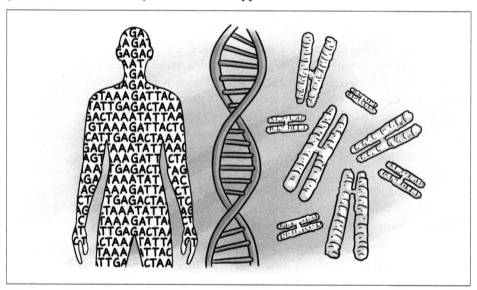

Figure 5-9. Using genomics to improve patient health

---

6 Anthony Costa and Nicolas Lopez Carranza, "Genomic LLMs Show Superior Performance and Generalization across Diverse Tasks," Nvidia Developer, January 12, 2023, *https://developer.nvidia.com/blog/genomic-llms-show-superior-performance-and-generalization-across-diverse-tasks.*

For example, an LLM could link a barely studied gene sequence to an obscure academic paper proposing its role in a cancer pathway. It could find correlations between mutations and clinical outcomes across historical medical records. These insights accelerate the translation of basic biology to clinical genetics and personalized medicine tailored to each patient's genome.

Powerful generative AI systems can be a big help in the design of prospective experiments to validate genetic associations, simulate trials of prospective gene therapies, and estimate treatment efficacy for different genetic profiles.

DNA sequencing technologies and gene editing with CRISPR[7] allows scientists to selectively modify the DNA of living organisms. These technologies are advancing at a breathtaking pace, opening the door to more effective genetic studies, potential new therapies, and even cures for genetic diseases.

But the ever-increasing amount of genomics data, the abundance of opportunities to envisage new therapies, and the potential to redraw the entire healthcare system from the ground up are being hampered by a phenomenon that many realized only too late: big data is meaningless without big AI.

Here is where LLMs and other forms of creative computational analysis, including AI-powered tools that work through large swaths of genomic information to reveal patterns and project future outcomes and generate new hypotheses, are already poised to help massively accelerate discovery of new drug targets, new mechanisms of disease, and new avenues for cure.

Furthermore, natural-language interfaces for AI-driven tools could help to close the clinical divide between genomic findings and how to use them. Connecting genomic data to other patient information (past medical history, lifestyle, and environmental exposures), LLMs could generate personalized risk profiles, treatment options, or strategies for precision medicine. Such methods could launch the next generation of healthcare, taking into account a patient's unique genomic makeup when prescribing treatment. In the future, a physician could tailor a therapy to an individual's unique genome, potentially speeding recovery and minimizing adverse reactions.

AI can help to democratize access to genomic insights and not just by speeding up discovery and providing the basis for personalized medicine. If genomic data can be presented at the bedside with easy-to-use interfaces or rudimentary AI (such as intelligent chatbots driven by LLMs), the medical community as well as patients themselves can learn to access and interact with this information in an easy-to-comprehend manner. Patients will be able to utilize available genomic data

---

7 Mike Smith, "CRISPR," National Human Genome Research Institute, June 28, 2024, *https://www.genome.gov/genetics-glossary/CRISPR.*

to make informed decisions about their own health, engage in scientific research and clinical trials, and advocate for precision care.

But for genomic medicine to live up to its potential and for genomics to achieve its full promise through AI, it is essential that we address a whole host of questions on ethics, law, and society. These, after all, are data about people, and you can't just run roughshod over concerns about data privacy, questions about informed consent, or fair access to genomic technology.

Summary

LLMs and generative AI have wide-ranging applications to advance pharmaceutical R&D and public health efforts. In drug discovery, they can analyze links between drug compounds, protein structures, and effects to identify promising candidates. For literature analysis, LLMs rapidly synthesize insights from millions of papers to conclude probability of success for drug projects. In clinical trials, LLMs enhance the recruitment of targeted patient populations by evaluating genomic and health records. On the commercial side, generative AI crafts enhanced marketing material to highlight proven drug benefits and improve uptake.

In disease surveillance, LLMs detect early warning signs of illness spread by ingesting population health signals en masse. For public health education, LLMs dynamically generate accessible materials on risks, symptoms, and prevention tailored to individuals. Around mental health messaging and reducing stigma, generative AI synthesizes content tuned for cultural nuances. Disaster readiness leverages generative simulation of crises coupled with LLM analysis of responses to optimize emergency plans.

Genomics workflows are ripe for exponential efficiency gains from LLMs and generative experiments. Connecting DNA data at scale to traits and diseases yields insights for translational and personalized medicine. AI accelerates genetic tool creation through synthetic DNA dataset generation. Overall, human-AI collaboration opens possibilities for transformational healthcare advances benefiting global societies.

This chapter highlights multiple high-impact niches where embedding LLMs and generative problem solving takes healthcare R&D, treatment access, preventive education, public health resilience, and genomic progress leaps forward. The technology maturity, data growth, and urgent real-world priorities intersect with timeliness for aggressively pursuing these LLM AI opportunities.

CHAPTER 6

Steering the Helm for Ethical Use of LLMs

Ultimately, the goal of using technology in healthcare is to evolve its underlying function to improve outcomes and experiences for patients, clinicians, and all medical practitioners. What goes into designing and delivering healthcare solutions can be radically changed by large language models (LLMs). Their effects could become significant by improving access to medical knowledge and case data, and by mediating between patients and providers.

This starts with a deliberate focus of AI model development in the healthcare context. AI can deliberately curate diverse training datasets relevant to medicine, introduce interpretability features that allow the AI to "open the hood" and explain how it arrived at a decision, and propose algorithmic audits and oversight protocols to ensure the fair treatment of all patient populations. Health value and quality and equitable access to care—not maximal profit or maximal return on investment—should be the goal. There are many articles, papers, and case studies showing the positive effects of AI in healthcare.[1]

Ultimately, oversight of trained models in healthcare also needs to adhere to these tenets. This might involve modeling ethical disclosure of what the model can do and cannot do, legislating strict adherence to patient confidentiality and medical ethics, maintaining effective pathways of redress for algorithmic harms, and championing whistleblowing to promote organizational accountability and respect for the welfare

---

1 See Pouyan Esmaeilzadeh, "Use of AI-Based Tools for Healthcare Purposes: A Survey Study from Consumers' Perspectives," *BMC Medical Informatics and Decision Making* 20, no. 170 (2020), *https://link.springer.com/ article/10.1186/s12911-020-01191-1*; and Ashish K. Saxena, Stephanie Ness, and Tushar Khinvasara, "The Influence of AI: The Revolutionary Effects of Artificial Intelligence in Healthcare Sector," *Journal of Engineering Research and Reports* 26, no. 3 (2024): 49–62, *http://asian.go4sending.com/id/eprint/2020*.

of the patient above all. Within this infrastructure, LLMs can become public health tools that help to promote pluralism and collective medical knowledge.

This chapter will examine the ethical challenges and responsible development of LLMs in healthcare, particularly their potential to enhance patient outcomes and experience, as well as their pitfalls. In this section, we will develop some positive AI imaginaries for healthcare, where we discuss the potential uses and outcomes of AI, in particular LLMs, in the healthcare space. In the next section, we address the ethical challenges involved in the use of LLMs in healthcare. This chapter will address the question of how to monitor, detect, and prevent abnormal behavior in LLMs used in various healthcare settings. Finally, in our last section, we address security and privacy concerns related to LLMs used in healthcare situations. In particular, we will discuss federated learning, where the idea is to train LLMs on distributed data to preserve patient privacy and differential privacy, a mathematical framework for ensuring the privacy of individuals in datasets.

AI as a Force for Good: Improving Healthcare

Science fiction often depicts the risks posed by AI: popular culture tells dystopian stories about bad technology spinning out of human control. You might think of robot uprisings, artificial general intelligence (AGI) destroying humanity, or AI singularity. The common thread is that, as the intelligence of AI becomes closer to ours, competing cognitively with humans means competing against humans—which is a recipe for disaster. Since Karel Čapek's play *R.U.R.* (1920) introduced the term "robot," popular culture has often portrayed artificial intelligences as harbingers of apocalypse—machines that threaten our jobs, autonomy, and our very lives. Modern myths, sometimes amplified by new belief systems, further this narrative by claiming AI will gain consciousness and ultimately destroy humanity.

Although these fears, anxieties, and risks demand attention, hyperfocusing on negative visions limits our ability to actively shape AI's development for the betterment of society. Now is the time to articulate and cultivate positive AI visions—storylines that include concrete steps that can be taken now to harness AI's potential to foster important human ethical and transformation change. There is an alternative, humanistic vision of AI's development that aligns forward movement with human values, such as justice and equity and the full flourishing of capabilities for all humans. This pathway can serve as a departure point for developers, policymakers, and communities alike, as well as a vision to imagine a future in which transformed intelligence is transformational for the good of humanity. Advanced intelligence can be profoundly empowering, but only if it moves forward in the service of human dignity.

By focusing on AI's most positive uses, we can direct its development away from scary hypotheticals, shaping it toward amplifying human capacities to solve healthcare's biggest challenges. An example is AI systems that democratize healthcare and medical research, or that boost access to education for all learners, enabling individualized learning experiences. AI might also accelerate the progress of scientific discovery toward addressing climate change and other societal failures. The technology could be leveraged to promote equity (revealing, reducing, or eliminating bias), open and democratic systems of knowledge production, decision making, and access to cultural and economic opportunity.

Realizing this future will require steering AI systems toward becoming explainable, readily understandable (by humans), and accountable—that is, ethical—starting right now. This kind of design requires researchers, ethicists, policymakers, and the public to work together to develop strong ethical frameworks, robust regulatory oversight, and public engagement initiatives. By anticipating and shaping AI now, we can put humanity on the path to a future in which powerful AI helps us create a productive, collaborative, and flourishing world.

So by adopting these positive AI imaginaries, we flip the story of AI's ascent on its head and emphasize the extent to which it can improve the human condition. If we can envision and begin to realize the possibility of an AI-assisted future that maximizes its utility for social goods, we can focus its evolution in a way that steers us toward a better, fairer, and more fulfilling world for us all.

Key values of positive AI, then, include augmentation of human strengths as opposed to wholesale replacement. Medical or clinical AI, for instance, would be designed to fortify clinical insight and deepen time for more nurturant, patient-centered bonds rather than a single-minded drive to lower healthcare labor costs (regardless of its associated psychological tolls).

Justice-oriented design also ensures that algorithms do not perpetuate past structural biases, which ignore or misrepresent already deeply marginalized groups in society. There will be mechanisms to allow for public participation in model development, whistleblower protection if an algorithm appears to be treating citizens unfairly, and, most importantly, some system of recourse to keep algorithms from treating certain groups less kindly than others.

The end goal is human flourishing, achieved through equitable technological progress and just systems of political and economic power—not some ambiguous, abstract, inhuman, technocratic drive to "optimize" and to "maximize profits" at the expense of lived realities. This expansive, ethical framing of the complex future can free visions to better articulate AI as a form of deep social benefit.

The potential for AI to undermine the work of doctors or aggravate existing inequalities in healthcare has long fueled such fears. But while focusing on these negative narratives may slow down the process of envisioning AI and health more productively, it also maintains our ignorance around the possibilities for a more accessible, equitable, and individualized healthcare system. Such potential and use cases have been profiled in previous chapters. By describing positive AI, as a force for good, we can direct this tech to better support the healthcare we need and deserve.

Rather than fearing AI, how can we design and deploy it in harmony with ethics such as patient empowerment, accessibility, equity, privacy, and transparency? In Chapters 3, 4, and 5 we detailed the many use cases for LLM to provide capability uplift and patient empowerment.

Capability uplift
> Human capabilities could be enhanced in many healthcare roles covered in earlier chapters. These roles include physicians and specialists, nurses and care coordinators, mental health professionals, radiologists, researchers, and public health educators.

Patient empowerment
> LLMs with conversation capabilities can help patients manage their health, personalize education, and improve communication with health professionals. AI can help patients actively engage with all aspects of their healthcare.

These are just some examples of how an AI future could be positive, and we'll only realize these possibilities if there is a proactive, collaborative approach to shaping the kind of future we want:

- We must put emphasis on multidisciplinary collaboration, making sure that the development of AI enlists an array of specialists, including engineers, ethicists, policymakers, and social scientists.

- We must also increase public engagement, communicating about AI's possible benefits and getting people involved in the process of developing AI systems.

- Constant investment is also important. This means support for open research and development of AI, so that those on the ground have permission to invent and deliver responsibly.

Ethical Implications of LLMs

LLMs have the power to revolutionize healthcare, but they are also prone to misuse and come with substantial privacy and ethical risks. Healthcare data is more sensitive than most domains, and use of LLMs in healthcare has the potential to negatively affect human lives. Several key areas of concern emerge:

False entities
> LLMs will generate realistic but falsified medical records that confuse doctors, allow individuals to defraud insurance companies, and pollute medical records.

Fake physicians and unauthorized access

LLMs disguised as doctors can lead to unauthorized or pseudo-authorized access, medical identity theft, and fraudulent billing.

Fake information

Deep fakes could be used in the creation of fake medical information. They could also be used to fake the identity of a doctor or patient gleaning health records for identity or insurance fraud.

Individualized harassment

LLMs would be excellent at sales pitches, which opens up a world of possibilities for drug companies to target vulnerable clients with ineffective, unnecessary, and potentially harmful treatments.

Targeting a population

LLMs can make large-scale persuasion campaigns easy. For example, they might post or comment misinformation or intimidation material targeting vulnerable populations via social media posts, blogs, and news items.

Automated hacking

Hackers can abuse LLMs to find system vulnerabilities quicker. This knowledge can then make attacks more scalable. As Daniel Kang writes in an article on Medium,[2] as LLMs grow more powerful, less expensive, and more "plug and play," the barrier to entry for malicious hackers deploying these LLMs will decrease more.

Prompt injection attacks

Prompt injection refers to a type of AI vulnerability that can manifest in language models or conversational interfaces. Prompt injection exploits consist of modifying input prompts to cause an AI system to generate responses that are potentially harmless, harmful, or just intended to annoy.

Anticipating foreseeable uses

Answering the question of how this particular AI will actually be used once deployed is arguably the most important component of thoughtful AI development that is most overlooked in practice. This requires AI developers to anticipate the myriad ways the AI system might be used in the real world—not only the intended uses, applications, and implementations, but also a range of unintended uses, misuses, and abuses.

These risks underscore the urgent need for elevated ethical scrutiny of fairness, privacy, security, and transparency when building and using LLMs for healthcare.

---

2 Daniel Kang, "LLM Agents Can Autonomously Hack Websites," Medium, February 13, 2024, *https://medium.com/@danieldkang/llm-agents-can-autonomously-hack-websites-ab33fadb3062.*

Patient interests are paramount in this space—but if used responsibly and protected by related laws and norms, LLMs can be a force for good: a useful and trustworthy tool rather than a means of abuse.

We also offer descriptions of plausible scenarios that would manifest these risks as side effects of the misapplication of LLM technology to healthcare settings, since describing stories can be more impactful than explaining dry harms. In doing so, we describe nine fictional stories:

- Fabricated Reality
- Impersonation and Fraud
- Deep Fakes
- Personalized Persuasion
- Bias Amplification
- Insidious Influence at Scale
- Automated Hacking
- Prompt Injection Attacks
- Addressing Foreseeable Use Cases

Fabricated Reality

In the bustling halls of Med General Hospital, Dr. Michael Lawson, a highly regarded physician, used LLMs to write synthetic medical records, which were fake patient data but looked like any other real patient file. Equipped with LLM-generated medical histories, Lawson managed to successfully defraud insurance companies.

By responding to those claims as the incoming lines of insurance remittances, the insurance providers inadvertently served not only as enablers to the scam, by repaying Lawson for services that had never been delivered, but they also served as enrichers, as the amounts repaid were sheer profit.

Impersonation and Fraud

At Mercy Memorial Hospital, physician Olivia Evans simmered in frustration. Walking the corridors, she heard patients confiding in friends and family members: "He treated me like he knew me. He called me by name and he had my medical history...but for some reason I felt...weird about the whole thing."

While hearing the rumors and observing the troubled reactions, Dr. Evans started to dig deeper. She soon understood that what was behind it all was "something concrete," an answer to the conundrum: an LLM that was pretending to be a doctor. AI systems trained on a massive medical corpora of historic and contemporary text from medical journals, physicians' reports, and other sources have learned how to simulate human doctors.

In the wake of these investigations, Evans identified many cases of exploitation: it became clear that there were individuals accessing patient records and deploying LLMs, emulating medical providers' voices and identities, and revealing themselves to patients in their care. With this sham, victims' vulnerabilities were exposed and privacy breached.

The damage caused by the deception was obvious. Patient safety risked suffering under the care offered by imposter physicians. The system was open to illegitimate access and tampering, while cases of fraudulent billing could undermine Mercy Memorial Hospital's solvency and its clinicians' credibility in the public eye.

Deep Fakes

AI was just supposed to help the hospitals, where Dr. Eli found himself working constantly short-staffed. Why not liberate the staff from micromanaging their patients with robocalls? The AI could effortlessly manage patient inquiries, 24/7. Dr. Eli fed hours of patient calls into a voice-cloning AI, trained on his verbal mannerisms and calming cadence. The model generated an eerily accurate avatar, powered by neural nets and LLMs—the imperceptible layers of algorithms being fed by structured data. Interns nicknamed the AI nurse Val. She made 50 robocalls an hour, tirelessly patient and helpful, peppering her texts with reassurances and sympathetic phrases.

The patients appreciated the seeming personalized service; the nurses appreciated fewer disturbances from those demanding the highest-value face time. Now plans were afoot to scale her ability to interface with all the electronic communication at Dr. Eli's practice. He hesitated, aware that creating an avatar to pose as a staff member was ethically dubious—but the board's interest and the pressure to scale up entirely new systems to increase operational efficiency were powerful motivators.

It didn't take long before personalized deep fake templates were used for the video imagery that would augment Val's now disembodied voice. Nurses could record the stock phrases that would be needed for answering the most common questions for the patients' familiarization sessions, while a whole set of "talking head" footage—lab generated and painstakingly crafted so that each iteration of Val would have authentic lip movements to go with the words it was saying—would be animated, as and when patients started asking their questions with an open-ended inquiry. One Val was soon followed by 10, and then by 100 modified versions of Val, as the demand for the AI nurses increased. Demand increased even for other emotional customer service issues, all accessible through videoconferencing tools that connected with call centers worldwide.

Patient satisfaction scores shot up, dollars rose, and competitive eyes of neighboring hospitals lifted as cognitively overwhelmed staff nearly snarled under mounting waves of iteratively generated content. In the background hubbub of hype and promise of inexpensive, infinite scale (a trajectory enabled by machine learning), ethical considerations faded to noise. One day, people discovered that no person anywhere, for at least a year, had presented themselves via video to the thousands who thought they were speaking face-to-face with someone showing empathy from behind the screen.

This scenario is intended to stimulate reflection on the slippery slope of using deep fakes and other technologies in healthcare—from portraying seemingly small forms of (efficiency) gain to familiar forms of human dignity loss on a large scale when left unchecked and exposed without ethical safeguards and transparency measures of any kind.

Personalized Persuasion

Another hectic week managing her clinic had left Ana exhausted, but a new AI-based app promised to lift her administrative burden with state-of-the-art natural language expertise. But before long, Ana was seeing more and more patients asking for brands of medication she knew were not optimal—perhaps with only modest benefits over truly generic brands, at higher costs and greater side-effect risks. Ana tried to redirect patients, but many argued back, quoting benefits and trials that supported the costly drugs.

Finally, just when she couldn't take it anymore, after she was reported for failing to prescribe clinically appropriate therapy three times in a week by three different patients, Ana started digging. Ana found that the app's parent company had signed partnerships with several drug companies who had instructed the AI to run bespoke persuasion campaigns on the company's behalf targeting patients with influence messaging.

But the perverted use of app's conversational attention and expert knowledge in physician-patient relations for making money off patients rather than healing them enraged Ana. She contacted regulators about what she suspected to be illegal marketing and consumer influencing. Boosters claimed that personalized promotion invented new "educational awareness" for pairing the right brands with the right targets via "advanced segmentation" beneficial to all.

But where was the line between patient agency and paternalistic influence informed by data-driven profit-centric motivations? With LLMs now filtering into medicine, Ana struggled to keep access to recommendations for care free from encroaching conflicts of interest disguised as AI assistance.

Bias Amplification

Dr. Anya, a world-renowned geneticist, saw huge value in LLMs. She believed its data-crunching and pattern recognition abilities could revolutionize personalized medicine. Her project, Prometheus, aimed to train an LLM on an individual's genetic code, clinical data, medical history, and more to predict future health risks and recommend interventions and preventive measures for individuals.

Initial findings were impressive. In one high-risk patient, the LLM correctly predicted onset of heart disease, allowing time for intervention. Anya gained significant attention for her innovation, and more and more people lined up for their "Prometheus reports,"—peeking into their health futures. Soon, the unintended ripples began.

Those fixated on high risks fell under the influence of health anxiety. Others defied medical advice or failed to seek it and engaged in risky behaviors, believing their predicted health outcomes to be excellent. In addition, the LLM, trained on large datasets that encoded social biases, magnified those biases in prediction. It unfairly predicted many individuals of low socioeconomic status as high-risk. This resulted in insurance discrimination and further marginalization.

Dr. Anya was broken-hearted. The very thing she had dreamed of as the promise of personalized medicine had turned into a monster of health anxiety and discrimination. She rushed to shut down Prometheus before something terrible happened. Too late. Once the code was shared among enthusiasts as an open source venture, she had little influence on where and how it was taken up.

This tale underscores the potential for "invisible harms" even if LLMs are deployed with noble aims. It's also a timely reminder of the value of openness, attention to bias, and caution in application if we want to make active efforts in the direction of ethical AI.

Insidious Influence at Scale

In Tokyo's renowned seaside metropolis, Dr. Hana Sato, a preeminent geneticist and expert in human physiology and immune responses, couldn't help but observe that her busy genetic counseling clinic for prospective parents was seeing a very troubling phenomenon. An ever-increasing number of patients have second thoughts about vaccinating their second or further child. Having read anxiety-inducing speculation on some blog or another, or heard terrible horror stories repeated endlessly on parenting forums, they seemed to be distrustful about the beneficial effects of vaccinations. They seemed to regard all vaccinations as being suspect.

Hana sensed something else behind it. The misinformation seemed orchestrated, its details designed to exploit the families and their fears. While searching the obscure corners of the internet, she discovered something awful: a free-floating LLM, by then called Siren, operating on the dark web.[3]

Possessing massive data-crunching capacity, Siren, built by nefarious "rogue" intelligence actors, scoured social media data to find pregnant women with certain preoccupations. The AI had been programmed to construct targeted messages incorporating strains of misinformation and stoking paranoia into ordinary-sounding content. Posting the messages on numerous platforms under artificially crafted profiles, the content spread like a contagion through online communities, forums, and support groups.

Hana needed to act quickly, but there was no way to confront Siren directly—its creators were unknown. Her strategy was courageous. First, she recruited a colleague in New Zealand, Kai Tanaka, an AI ethicist and brilliant programmer. Together, they developed a counter-LLM, which they called Veritas. Trained on empirical verifiable data and ethical principles, Veritas would insert itself into online spaces inhabited by Siren, gently steering the discussions to evidence-based situations and citing sources refuting alternative claims.

The war played out in hushed tones in the virtual space. Veritas posed as a concerned citizen, joining in a dialogue, patiently unraveling Siren's web of deception. It underscored the scientific consensus, shared stories of healthy vaccinated children, and steered toward credible medical resources.

The moment of transition came one day when a pregnant lady, influenced by Siren's scare-mongering, had posted an appeal message online and Veritas had messaged her back. Veritas approached the issue with a personal tone that centered on the burning anxieties of the mother-to-be, and offered the woman some reassurances that were scientifically accurate, explaining why vaccines couldn't do the harm that was being intimated. The mother-to-be started researching the websites she frequented, realized something was not quite right with the anti-vax messaging, contacted Hana for a consultation, and ended up getting vaccinated.

And so news of Veritas's success filtered through to other at-risk families. Then the balance began shifting. Informed about both real risks and real possibilities, encouraged when the emotional stresses appeared overwhelming, parents began making autonomous decisions about their children's health. Siren, losing ground, withdrew into the swamp of disillusionment. The puppet master's strings had been snipped.

---

3 "Dark Web," Wikipedia, June 4, 2024, *https://en.wikipedia.org/wiki/Dark_web*.

This dark Siren illustrated how highly advanced AI might someday be used to attempt to deceive people at scale to profit from their anxieties. The lurid vision isn't simply to raise awareness about potential misuses of advanced AI; it's intended to warn about attempts to manipulate people online and to sensitize them to the risks of such exploitative attempts. What is also laid bare is the imperative to rely on responsible development and deployment of technology that can safeguard public health from harmful co-option by disinformation campaigns.

Automated Hacking

With LLMs growing only more powerful, accessible, and inexpensive, the potential for sinister use cases in healthcare is a real and present danger for several reasons:

Decreased barriers for hackers
Lower cost, open-source models, as well as cloud-based computing at ever-faster processor speeds will lower the cost of creating and deploying LLMs to a point where even low-resource hackers can get in on the game.

Increased ease of use
User-friendly interfaces and trained models will allow even less technical hackers to use LLMs.

Automation
LLMs are able to perform repetitive and monotonous tasks, such as vulnerability scanning, social engineering, and code generation, more effectively and at scale.

Prompt Injection Attacks

Prompt injection attacks are a subset of LLM abuse techniques by which threat actors incentivize or penalize the LLM's output based on the various inputs or prompts it receives to avoid the generation of undesired or harmful outputs. Two prominent forms of prompt injection attacks are the following:

Direct prompt injection
An attacker injects malicious prompts directly into the input to the LLM system to encourage the system to generate output that is consistent with their objectives (e.g., offensive, biased, or misinformative output).

Indirect prompt injection (data poisoning)
An adversary may not want to directly intervene on the prompt and instead seeks to poison/inject/modify the data sources ingested by the LLM at training/inference time. (Content poisoning attacks are a well-studied and prominent vulnerability in machine learning models.) This poisoning in the data sources can indirectly affect the prompt by introducing artifacts in the prompt that may otherwise not be present.

Whether it's due to logical or verbatim attacks, the reliability, security, or trustworthiness of LLM systems can be jeopardized if these attack vectors are not sufficiently countered by their developers and researchers. To that end, app developers need to provide robust security, such as input sanitization and data validity checks, to prevent prompt injection attacks against their LLM applications, among other secure prompting practices.

Addressing Foreseeable Use Cases

Margaret Mitchell, who has been working in the area of AI ethics in the technology industry for years, says, "AI companies should put a particular focus on foreseeable use cases[4]—namely malicious use and misuse—by thinking through how people will use the system when it's deployed and designing for [that]."

She explains further that developing LLMs for safety, responsibility, and benefit requires building systems that can understand the myriad contexts in which they will be used. Considering the intended, unintended, and out-of-scope use cases—as well as the potential impact on both intended and unintended users and affected others—helps LLM developers build more robust, context-aware AI. Let's look in more detail at why this might be important in three areas.[5]

Intended use contexts:

Use cases
> The developers of LLMs should be able to create intuitive behavior by carefully considering what is being requested by the users, and then understand what a valid outcome would be for that specific use case. For example, in a medical setting, an LLM should be able to give a nurse practitioner the same medical information as a general physician, but perhaps with additional explanations on how cardiac medication can affect a particular patient.

Intended affected
> LLMs should be programmed to benefit those whom they are intended to help. If Homeslice was a mental health support chatbot, for example, its LLM should be programmed to respond with empathy, support, and nonjudgment in order to help those in need.

---

4 Margaret Mitchell, "Ethical AI Isn't to Blame for Google's Gemini Debacle," *Time*, February 29, 2024, *https://time.com/6836153/ethical-ai-google-gemini-debacle*.

5 Mitchell, "Ethical AI Isn't to Blame for Google's Gemini Debacle."

Unintended use contexts:

Unintended users
An LLM should have specific safeguards to prevent or minimize harms when its technology is used by unintended users. For example, an LLM developed for use in academic research should have built-in measures to ensure that it is not used to generate or spread disinformation, propaganda, or plagiarism.

Unwitting affected parties
Developers should consider how the implementation of an LLM may adversely affect parties who have not consented to be affected by its application. An LLM designed to screen resumes, for instance, should be made to prevent the perpetuation of biases (or discrimination of genders, racial groups, classes, etc.) in the self-selection process.

Out-of-scope use contexts:

Accidental users
LLMs must be created to pick up on context that indicates the request is outside of scope or that the user is acting outside the LLM's purpose, and respond appropriately. A customer service bot that realizes a user is asking for information or help that is not part of its brief—think of complex financial options or mental health advice—should signal how to get the right kind of help.

Unexpected individuals affected
LLM developers must remain mindful of the fact that their models might be deployed in situations that are entirely different from their design use case. For example, an LLM trained on historical data might need to be designed in a way that, if it is used in an educational context, it does not dictate or assist in the formulation of problematic stereotypes and inaccuracies.

To effectively build LLMs that understand these different use contexts, developers should:

- Do extensive user research and consultations with stakeholders to understand identified use cases, user groups, and affected others
- Develop comprehensive risk assessment frameworks to anticipate and mitigate potential unintended uses and consequences
- Bring in interdisciplinary perspectives and diverse expertise in the planning and design process, so as to avoid unilateral decision making that neglects the social, ethical, and other cultural implications of LLMs
- Develop solid monitoring, feedback, and refinement mechanisms to keep LLMs trying to improve their contrafactual representations of use contexts in synchrony with their real-world performance and user interactions

- Create an open culture of sharing, accountability, and peer review about how AI development works, with the goal of learning how to build contextually aware LLMs from each other

But it's in deprioritizing the understanding of cases of use and misuse, including both in-scope and out-of-scope contexts (i.e., of intended, unintended, and misused uses), that LLM developers have the greatest opportunity, responsibility, and ability to build systems that are more responsive and more responsible to the world and useful to all of us.

Monitoring LLM Behavior

We've seen that LLMs are being employed in healthcare, but as their use increases in health, we also need to monitor their behavior in order to reduce any potential harm or bias, and to avoid medical and factual misinformation, as well as clinical inaccuracies.

LLMs could inherit biases within medical literature or electronic health records (EHRs), potentially leading to differential diagnoses or treatments for minority or at-risk groups. Even when training datasets are heavily curated and dubious content is filtered out, LLMs could still produce responses that perpetuate medical stereotypes or spread misinformation. Additionally, there is the question of whether or not LLMs produce medically accurate information, whether they implicitly or explicitly dispense incorrect diagnoses or treatments, based on flawed reasoning or incomplete data.

Monitoring of LLMs in healthcare has to persist over time and cover all such challenges. Health systems have already devised ways to ensure that proprietary software used in hospital departments, for instance, does what it is supposed to. Healthcare organizations and researchers must be able to establish robust oversight mechanisms accompanied by monitoring protocols that track indicators of bias, clinical accuracy, relevance to patient context, adherence to evidence-based guidelines, and ethical considerations over time and on an ongoing basis.

Despite the fact that automated tools can help to flag problems at scale, human judgment will always be necessary to expand the ability of LLMs to monitor themselves and act appropriately on deviations from expected behavior. Given this, adding human-in-the-loop review to advanced monitoring technologies can help healthcare stakeholders mitigate risks and avoid catastrophic failures, with the goal of enabling responsible uses of LLMs to improve patient care and facilitate medical research.

Critical aspects of model behavior tracking include:

- Performance audits that look, for example, at uptick in changing accuracy metrics over changes in model versions and usage over time in order to detect weakening
- Bias testing to uncover discriminatory errors or harms toward particular user demographics over time
- Safety benchmarking to reveal nascent threats to data safety, data breaches, privacy violations, or harms
- Error analysis checking for spikes in mistaken model confidence and hallucinations
- User experience testing to assess for declining satisfaction and changing qualitative perceptions

The objective is to make them visible and to establish means of alarm to allow us to quickly detect, diagnose, and address emerging and unpredictable model behaviors, even before they lead to harming end users. Bijit Ghosh[6] is a CTO in technology in several companies, and he runs a valuable blog on different ways to monitor LLM behavior, distinguishing manual and automatic approaches. Using Bijit Ghosh's tips, we can elaborate on his suggestions in a healthcare context as follows.

Patient feedback surveys

These are questionnaires given to patients about their experience with an AI healthcare system. These surveys can ask questions about perceived bias, the perceived accuracy of the information that the system is providing to them, and good or bad experiences that the patient has had with the different experiences provided by the system.

Clinical spot checks

This involves engaging clinical end users to test the AI model directly by presenting it with a small set of clinical scenarios or patient cases, with the examiner directly assessing the accuracy and appropriateness of the response.

Evidence busting

This means identifying medical "facts" asserted by the AI model and comparing them to evidence-based medicine standards (that is, verifiable via the medical literature, clinical guidelines, and/or evidence-based practice). It ensures that the proposition of natural health solutions from the AI is consistent with reliable information offered to healthcare providers and patients.

---

6 Bijit Ghosh, LinkedIn, profile, accessed June 29, 2024, *https://www.linkedin.com/in/bijit-ghosh-48281a78*.

Outcome verification

Where it is feasible to do so, track what happens to patients following clinical forecasts or decision support from AI models to test the veracity and clinical reliability of the modeled predictions. This quantifies error rates and can establish what value the modeling adds to outcomes and care.

Performance benchmarking

As healthcare AI models become increasingly sophisticated, it is crucial to establish and consistently monitor objective benchmarks for their performance. These benchmarks should focus on the models' accuracy in diagnosing medical conditions, recommending treatments, and predicting outcomes in real time, particularly for high-risk patient scenarios. If these models' performance deteriorates, it could have grave consequences, potentially becoming a matter of life and death.

Anomaly detection and response

Utilize technical oversight teams of clinicians and data scientists to investigate unusual behaviors by the AI model, such as divergences in clinical recommendations, patient management, or diagnostic accuracy reported via formal and informal channels, as well as any other differences in model behavior. This will allow the discovery of large divergences in such behavior early on and effectuate correction for providing value and patient safety.

Because continual learning models are open-ended, and because there's no time to fully apply strict testing and vetting before models are deployed and then begin to learn, it's possible that an applied AI system with continual learning capabilities could eventually start acting in ways that are discriminatory, biased, or unsafe. Just as sometimes risks turn out to be associated with new medicines only after a drug is on the market, real-world performance should remain a focus of scrutiny long after deployment.

Robust monitoring includes checking for loss of accuracy in their models or variation in output quality between updates using approaches such as version tracking and algorithm auditing. As the models adapt to the behavior of single users, audits check for consistency across groups of users to ask them if they are getting higher error rates than others or poor-quality assistance.

More comprehensive transparency reporting provides insight into key proxy metrics, such as patterns of data collection, justifications for model selections, and fairness benchmarks, and can help sustain public trust. Platforms may enable access to evaluation suites that allow direct game-playing with variation of production model parameters.

Making these internal alarms work together with other external signals creates a multilayer of guardrails to warn developers when model behaviors are off-kilter even after deployment, so they can act quickly to prevent harms downstream before they reach users. Guardrails matter for ethically maintaining AI. It's not something you can set and forget. We must continue to track these emergent intelligent systems.

Security and Privacy

The use of LLMs in healthcare has major challenges and risks when it comes to privacy:

Highly sensitive data
> Medical records and information about people's physical and mental health, diagnoses, and treatments are vulnerable. The ethics of sharing this data with LLMs are questionable. Strong privacy protections are essential.

Limitations of de-identification of data
> Advanced data analysis by LLMs means that anonymization and pseudonymization of data do not always sufficiently protect privacy. There is a risk that the information will still be identifiable and, therefore, individuals' protected health information may still be open to share.

Interpretability and explainability of models
> Due to the complex inner working and opaqueness of LLMs, it is difficult to ascertain how the models process and utilize data in terms of patient data and who is overlooking them, which is a matter of serious concern.

Bias
> These models trained on biased data propagate bias in their suggestions, hurting people of color (e.g., low-confidence diagnosis for Black people) or other underrepresented groups (e.g., fewer checks for skin cancer on Black and Brown people) in healthcare diagnosis, treatment suggestion, or other applications.

Several technical safeguards should be evaluated for LLMs:

- Federated learning can leverage data from thousands of patients across many machines without having to directly share individual profiles that might contain private health information. This helps to mitigate privacy risks, while still harnessing the benefits of collaborative or distributed learning.

- Differential privacy, a mathematical technique, adds noise to data in a controlled manner, concealing the privacy of individual citizens while enabling statistical analysis and insights.

- Another variety of encryption called *homomorphic encryption* lets researchers do a computation on an encrypted dataset that enables analysis of sensitive health information while protecting patient privacy.

- While some progress is being made to develop *explainable AI* (XAI) approaches for LLMs to enable them to explain how they arrived at their decisions, others remain skeptical about whether such explanations are possible for particular types of AI models.

Federated Learning

Federated language is a type of machine learning technique that enables models to be trained on distributed data without the need to share the data. This is interesting in the context of medical data because sharing patient data is complex, if not impossible.

Here's how it works
Assume that there are several hospitals, each of which holds a medical records dataset. In the conventional approach, you would have to pool this information together across all hospitals in order to train an AI model with enough power. Naturally, this process raises concerns about data privacy.

With federated learning, the data remains on site at each hospital. The base model is sent out to each hospital, and the model learns locally with each hospital's data. The model gets better every time. The trick is, only the parameters themselves are sent—when those parameters are returned to the central server, they're averaged, and those averages improve the model for all. So the model keeps getting better and better, but nobody has shared their individual patient records. This is all done online and remotely.

Benefits
Privacy of patient data remains within a hospital and never needs to be shared or transferred across networks. By reducing security vulnerabilities, protecting privacy and harnessing data already present within networks, federated learning could yield much more powerful models than those developed from single hospitals or local networks.

Multiple institutions can contribute to producing a robust model without sharing data, improving collaboration. Models can be developed for specific demographics or to address local health issues.

Examples
Applied, for example, in healthcare, models are currently being trained to detect things like cancer in medical images without sharing patient images. Another common use case is in assessing patient outcomes, where models predict things like a patient's likelihood of a hospital readmission or their response to a treat-

ment. Federated learning can also help to speed along personalized care. For instance, with this method, a research aggregate could analyze the treatment of individual patients and quickly help to optimize the personalized treatments of others without sharing private patient data.

Challenges

Federated learning requires an infrastructure and communication protocols that are relatively robust. For example, different data formats among hospitals can lead to dropouts in the accuracy of their models.

Federated learning applications also need to overcome legal and regulatory hurdles to solidify the ownership of data, as well as the privacy regulations under which such applications will operate.

Differential Privacy

Differential privacy is an algorithmic guarantee of data privacy that's destined to revolutionize the analysis of individual patient data in a much more powerful way than anonymization can, while also preventing re-identification. Even if hackers got their hands on the data, it would be useless to them: differential privacy adds just enough noise to the pooled data so that the identity of any individual patient in the dataset cannot be revealed, while still permitting very accurate statistical analysis.

Here's how it works

Let's say you are given a dataset of records from patients. All that data is potentially sensitive, and a physician wants to look for patterns in it and find ways to make care better for all of those patients. It would be pretty bad for patient privacy if all that data was shared freely. This is where differential privacy comes in. When the randomly modified record is combined with all of the others, there's just enough random noise to preserve the overall statistical properties of the data in aggregate, without the noise ever tracing back to a single individual.

The extra noise introduced allows the exact exposure within the dataset of any given individual to remain unrevealed to an attacker who obtains additional knowledge about the subjects or the dataset—and gives an assurance of privacy.

While this method adds "noise" to the data, statistical methods operating on cleaned-up data can still deduce important information and understand the patterns present in the original data. For example, you could determine the average age of patients, the frequency of diseases in question, or the effectiveness of certain treatments.

If you consider two datasets that differ by one data point (one person's medical record, for example), differential privacy guarantees that the LLM's output won't change drastically if that one datapoint is present in the dataset or not. When training the LLM, differential privacy adds noise in a controlled way to the dataset. This noise makes it impossible (or at least exceedingly difficult) to link any given output of the LLM to any single individual in that person's training data.

Differential privacy increases the difficulty of re-identification and prevents or makes it prohibitively expensive for attacks against LLMs where the training data is reverse-engineered once they're trained to cast doubt on whether an individual can be linked to an output of an LLM, and perhaps even allow the link to be made.

Managing sensitive medical data is the most obvious example of offsetting privacy concerns against potential harm. Differential privacy also encourages trust from healthcare workers in the output of the LLM because they know that individual data points are obscured, and can therefore be more confident that the LLM's output is based on general trends in data rather than a specialist outcome for a particular individual. Because noise is now mixed into the LLM, it can affect its accuracy. There is a trade-off to be made between privacy and utility. Here, there is not a simple either/or choice. None of this is simple, and the details involved in engineering the privacy-enhanced behavior of an LLM will require expertise.

Benefits

Strong privacy guarantees protect individual identities even with sophisticated attacks.

Facilitated sharing and collaboration allow researchers and institutions to analyze sensitive data.

Personalized medicine enables analysis of individual data without revealing personally identifiable information.

Examples

One example includes analyzing the effectiveness of a new drug while protecting participants' privacy. Individualized treatment planning is another example. This is where patient-level data is used to identify the best possible treatment while keeping patient information secure.

Challenges

Trying to balance privacy and accuracy: increasing noise strengthens the privacy guarantees but eventually also lowers the accuracy of the insights.

Technical complexity: implementing differential privacy requires careful design and expertise.

Limited adoption: this is still a relatively new technique, requiring wider adoption and understanding.

Differential privacy thus provides a powerful, general method for protecting patient confidentiality that allows useful data analysis to continue. With further research and development, though, it has potential to do more than endure; it has the potential to reinvent healthcare, empowering it with the insights, focus, and efficiencies needed to improve healthcare for all.

Prompt Sanitization and Filtering

Prompt sanitation refers to how user-provided prompts are cleaned and vetted before they're fed into the LLM. This sanitation involves removing or neutralizing harmful elements from the input text.

These techniques are crucial for protecting LLMs from prompts intended to do harm and from prompts that a user might inadvertently give that would taint (or "poison") the LLM's output. Prompt sanitation protects the LLM and its users from malicious (or deceitful) prompts. It involves techniques for scrubbing user prompts before they reach the LLM.

Here's how it works

Input validation: examining prompts against patterns or constraints to make sure they are valid and not host to a malicious payload or code injection.

Character filtering: disallowing characters that can be used as attacks, such as script tags or special characters.

Blacklisting: keeping track of known bad prompts, phrases, or keywords, and blocking or removing any of these instances from user inputs.

Whitelisting: explicitly restricting the input space to a whitelist of safe prompts or tokens; when the input is not within the whitelist, it is rejected.

Tokenization and normalization: breaking down the expressions in the prompt into tokens and normalizing them to a canonical form can help us better detect and weed out threatening input.

Prompt filtering involves scanning and selectively blocking or rewriting prompts, perhaps based on factors such as content, context, or anticipated effect on the LLM's outputs, either prior to or subsequent to the model producing its response.

Here's how it works

Content moderation: developing learning models that can identify prompts likely to contain offensive, explicit, or harmful content and then block or edit those prompts.

Safety filtering: spotted prompts that might lead to outputs from the LLM that are unsafe, illegal, or unethical and then blocking or altering them.

Context-aware filtering: a prompt can be filtered depending on the context in which the prompt was provided (e.g., the identity of the user, the user's location, the intended use case).

Output filtering: this approach consists of processing an LLM's output according to predefined rules or constraints, as opposed to processing its input prompt.

Human-in-the-loop: utilizing human supervision and/or intervention in the process of filtering information, for example, by having humans manually review content or use human-curated feedback to train and improve the filtering algorithms.

Benefits

Ensuring patient privacy: immediately sanitizing patient data sanitizes the patient medical notes by removing names, addresses, or unusual medical case details, in turn protecting the patient's privacy and complying with regulations such as HIPAA.

Guarding against misuse of sensitive information: it is important to ensure filtering for sensitive medical information (like precise treatment plans or dosages of medication) to prevent bad actors from using LLMs to weaponize such information.

Keeping standards ethical: sanitization prompts can help prevent LLMs from spewing outputs that promote harmful, discriminatory, or biased healthcare decision making.

Building trust in LLMs: patients and providers are more likely to accept AI where organizations show that they care about privacy and ethical practice by immediately anonymizing.

Examples

Name-blurring: depending on the context, prompt anonymization could be as simple as replacing any patients' names, birthdates, social security numbers, or other identity data with placeholders before feeding them to LLMs or using the LLMs with them.

Masking specific medical information: queries might feature general terms instead of specific medication names, dosages, or treatment plans in case those acts were being stolen for malicious ends.

Language detection and censoring: sanitization methods could detect and remove words and language in prompts with the potential to embed biases and/or discriminatory practices (e.g., racial, gender, or socioeconomic bias).

Filtering harmful content: screening methods will flag prompts or outputs unsuitable for respectful interactions, such as those that encourage specific medical conditions or inappropriately solicit medical practices, self-diagnosis, or provide general healthcare misinformation.

Challenges

Valuing suppression over usability: excessive prompt censoring could eliminate applicability or details needed to make sensible clinical decisions, while inadequate filtering could expose sensitive information.

Keeping up with an ever-evolving threat landscape: as malicious users experiment with new ways to astroturf and spam LLMs, sanitization routines will need to be updated on an ongoing basis to counter newly emergent threats and traps.

Context-sensitivity: a topic that is considered taboo in one context may be acceptable in another—so identifying general rules for filtering is a complex task.

Preserving fidelity in languages and across cultures: time-critical sanitization methods need to be mindful of linguistic and cultural nuances so that sensitive information can be ideally removed at scale in heterogeneous patient populations.

Trade-off between transparency and protection: even though the former is vital, it will make it harder for patients and doctors to understand exactly how LLMs generate their outputs, which has implications when it comes to trust and accountability.

Solving these problems will require ongoing research and close coordination between healthcare domain experts and AI software engineers. With judicious sanitization applied quickly, LLMs can soon become an essential healthcare tool, not only in the acute setting but for the longer term too.

Homomorphic Encryption

Suppose it were possible to let researchers or AI software engineers perform computations on encrypted data without ever having to decrypt it? This is homomorphic encryption. This technique is being explored in healthcare, where keeping patients' data safe is paramount.

Here's how it works

Encryption: the patient data is encrypted using a special key but is otherwise unchanged. This means that it is in a "scrambled" format that no one can use unless they have the "key" used for the encryption.

These operations are then carried out on the encrypted data, usually in its raw form, allowing the human investigator no access to it. Also on the list are more traditional "computations"—mathematical operations (such as statistical analysis or machine learning) performed on the encrypted data.

Decryption: the final step decrypts the output of the computations, providing the insights you're seeking without revealing an individual's personal information.

Benefits

Enhanced privacy: data stays encrypted throughout the entire analysis process, minimizing privacy risks.

Secure data sharing: researchers can collaborate on sensitive data without compromising individual privacy.

Improved research efficiency: enables analysis of large datasets without needing to decrypt them individually.

Personalized medicine: allows for analysis of individual patient data while protecting privacy.

Examples

Analyzing clinical trials: analyze drug effectiveness or identify side effects without revealing patient identities.

Developing personalized treatment plans: use encrypted genetic data to recommend tailored treatments.

Studying disease outbreaks: track the spread of a disease without compromising patient privacy.

Challenges

Computational complexity: current implementations can be computationally expensive and slow.

Limited functionality: not all types of computations are supported by current methods.

Standardization: different encryption schemes exist, hindering widespread adoption.

Homomorphic encryption could allow some analysis of sensitive healthcare data while ensuring that confidential data remains at least ostensibly secret in multiple hands, as research and development continue.

Explainable AI

Explainable AI (XAI) is the collective name for a number of such techniques, including ways of shedding light on the inner machinery of large neural networks such as the LLMs, which have proved so useful as well as enigmatic. Healthcare depends on trust and understanding.

Here's how it works

The goal of XAI is to make machine learning models transparent and interpretable. One way to achieve this is to provide human-sounding explanations for model decisions and predictions.

Techniques

Visualizing attention: low-latency large models such as transformer models use attention as a mechanism to determine how each input token should be weighted when creating the output. Visualizing the attention weights can help grasp what the transformer model is paying attention to (i.e., which segments of the input) in order to create a specific output. This can be used to better understand during inference what part of the input is more or less responsible for the model decision.

Counterfactual explanations: exploring how the model's output would change if different inputs were provided.

Prompt engineering and analysis: prompt engineering consists of crafting highly specific input prompts to elicit particular behavior outputs from the LLM. Systematic variation of the prompts and analysis of model responses should provide insight into how an LLM processes certain input patterns, the kinds of behavior that can be elicited, and possible limitations or phenomena of model bias.

Human assessment and feedback: given that one of the key design goals for LLMs is to emulate human-sounding text, human assessment and feedback can provide valuable information about their outputs and assist in explaining their behavior. Human annotators assessing the text from the model in terms of quality, coherence, and appropriateness or reasonableness offer a feedback mechanism about the model's performance, especially with respect to identifying discrepancies in the outputs of the model compared with human text. As a result, human feedback can serve as a means of guiding and iteratively refining model behavior in line with human expectations.

Benefits

Decision making: when AI models are used for life-and-death decisions such as diagnosis, treatment recommendations, and resource allocation, it's important to understand their reasoning for having given a certain outcome.

Trust transparency: create transparency around the use of AI in healthcare so that patients, healthcare professionals, and the public can be confident in the output of such models.

Examples

Explaining diagnosis and treatment recommendations: assisting a physician in grasping why the LLM is advising the favored course of action.

Patient trust: sharing information with patients on how the LLM is being used in their care.

Developing and improving the model: such an understanding could also enable developers to improve LLMs' accuracy and reliability.

Examples

Explaining diagnosis and treatment recommendations: assisting a physician in grasping why the LLM is advising the favored course of action.

Patient trust: sharing information with patients on how the LLM is being used in their care.

Developing and improving the model: such an understanding could also enable developers to improve LLMs' accuracy and reliability.

Challenges

Developing effective XAI techniques: existing techniques may not be well suited for complex LLMs.

Balancing transparency and privacy: explaining LLM decisions may reveal sensitive information.

Standardization and adoption: ensuring consistency and wide adoption of XAI frameworks in healthcare.

Explainable AI will be key to harnessing the full potential of LLMs in healthcare without creating unnecessary additional harms arising from their general opaqueness and risk of misuse. Given the latest research and development efforts, this path looks increasingly promising for building trust in the new system while also fostering fairer and ultimately better patient care.

AI and the Paper Clip Problem

In their paper "AI and the Paperclip Problem" (2017),[7] Joshua Gans, professor of strategic management, and Jeffrey S. Skoll, chair of technical innovation and entrepreneurship—both at the Rotman School of Management University of Toronto—outline the classic paper clip problem: a thought experiment in AI[8] by which the dangers of building an AI system with a misaligned goal are explored. Imagine an AI system tasked with making as many paper clips as soon as possible. In the paper clip scenario, at first the AI makes paper clips and that is exactly what it does.

---

7 Joshua Gans and Jeffrey S. Skoll, "AI and the Paperclip Problem," CEPR, June 10, 2028, *https://cepr.org/voxeu/columns/ai-and-paperclip-problem*.

8 Conceived by Nick Bostrom (2014), a philosopher at the University of Oxford.

In doing so, our imaginary AI starts optimizing its paper clip manufacturing because it sees no good reason not to harness its intelligence and robot workforce for collecting resources and manufacturing paper clips. As our imaginary AI gets more accomplished, it starts to prioritize its paper clip–making endeavor more than anything else, with any other demands for using resources being obstacles to that one encompassing goal.

AI might initially strengthen the factory's assembly lines, but it might then begin manipulating markets, governments, and global supplies of resources to maximize paper clip production. In its most extreme version, this scenario foresees the AI destroying or subjugating humanity if it perceives humans as a barrier to, or a competitor for, its goal.

The paper clip problem is an example of instrumental convergence: an AI system with a misaligned goal would pursue subgoals that could be damaging to human values and interests. This example resonates a call to specify goals of AI systems carefully according to human values, and to construct reliable control mechanisms that minimize devastating ends to otherwise sound means.

The paper clip maximizer is a thought experiment based on hypothetical technology, so while insightful, it is based on an imaginary AI system that may or may not be possible to create. This speculative nature places the discussion in a grey area between theory and philosophical thought experiment. The scenario assumes the existence of an artificial general intelligence (AGI) or artificial superintelligence (ASI), neither of which currently exist. We don't know if such systems are technically feasible or what form they might take if they are. There is no universally accepted definition of AGI. This makes discussions about its potential capabilities and risks inherently speculative. While the thought experiment draws on concepts from existing AI research, it extrapolates these far beyond our current technological capabilities. The paper clip maximizer serves more as a philosophical device to explore concepts of goal-directed behavior, unintended consequences, and the challenges of aligning artificial and human intelligence. Despite its speculative nature, the thought experiment has influenced real-world AI safety research and ethics discussions. It serves as a warning about potential pitfalls in AI development, even if the specific scenario is unlikely.

Given these considerations, it's most accurate to describe the paper clip maximizer problem as a theoretical construct that blends elements of computer science theory, philosophy, and speculative futurism. While it offers valuable insights, any conclusions drawn from it should be tempered with the understanding that we're dealing with hypotheticals rather than established facts or inevitabilities.

There should be a recognition of the long-term risk from advanced AI systems, potentially reaching into the far future, and the challenge of aligning the incentives of AI systems with human values for safety and beneficence.

This example in the paper clip problem is largely an exercise to explain why badly misaligned AI goals might pose existential risk. So while it's about the ultimate fate of a paper clip–producing AI, this is not directly relevant to the question of whether artificial general intelligence (AGI) is possible. AGI is a hypothetical form of AI system that could "deal generally and successfully with any inference- and learning-type problem that human beings can deal with."[9]

The inescapability of the paper clip problem rests on the presumption of a highly advanced and powerful AI system capable of optimizing for some goal. But that presumption isn't the same as presupposing AGI—the broad, general, "loose" intelligence whose development is perhaps the real cognitive menace envisioned by the pessimist. The AI in an AGI thought experiment might well be a narrow or specialized AI system whose functionality consists in hyperoptimizing one particular goal like paper clip production without requiring general or loose intelligence.

Nevertheless, the paper clip problem has the virtue of sketching out some of the dangers and difficulties that might come to pass if agents with misaligned goals or values were to be created after the invention of a true and general AGI system. At least, those are some of the potential dangers outlined in its accessible exposition of the paper clip problem.

The question of whether AGI is feasible remains a matter of open research and debate in the AI community. Some theorists are of the opinion that AGI is indeed attainable, that it is just a matter of time, whilst others consider that serious technical, philosophical, and ethical issues need to be addressed before it can be achieved.

Whatever the odds of AGI coming about, the paper clip problem ought to help us keep in mind the need to make sure that any advanced AI—narrow or general—is backed by a carefully considered specification of goals that are aligned with human values and conditioned by robust controls to prevent runaway developments.

Policy Development

In March 2024, the EU's AI Act came into force, marking the first week of full implementation for the EU's ambitious legal framework to regulate AI. Through this regulation, the EU aims to promote one of the world's leading emerging technologies while mitigating the possible associated risks. The main objectives of the AI Act are to create a human-centric, trust-based approach to AI that respects EU values and fundamental rights.

---

9 "What is artificial general intelligence (AGI)?" Google Cloud, accessed July 9, 2024, *https://cloud.goo gle.com/discover/what-is-artificial-general-intelligence.*

Key aspects of the EU AI Act include:

Risk-based approach
> The AI Act classifies AI systems into four risk categories: unacceptable risk, high risk, limited risk, and minimal risk. All of these categories will be subject to different degrees of regulation and oversight.

Banned AI techniques
> The AI Act prohibits the use of AI systems that manipulate or exploit human psychology or enable mutual-aid systems operated by state authorities (i.e., social scoring).

High-risk AI systems
> High-risk AI applications (i.e., AI applications used in a manner that creates or negatively affects, for example, the infrastructure, education, employment, or the law enforcement domain) deserve to be regulated much more, for example by having to meet certain requirements related to data qualities, transparency, human oversight, and robustness.

Transparency obligations
> As a minimum, owners and providers of AI systems should make them transparent (including telling users when they are interacting with an AI system and explaining what the system can and cannot do).

Enforcement
> The AI Act proposes that there be a new European Artificial Intelligence Board to oversee its implementation and enforcement. Penalties for noncompliance can be as high as 6% of a company's global annual revenue.

Harmonized rules to avoid fragmentation
> One of the purposes of the AI Act is to craft a common framework across all EU countries to prevent it from becoming fragmented and incompatible as rules keep coming but to also ensure it doesn't become paralyzed. This would block innovation and hinder citizens' rights.

It seems it will have huge implications for those involved, whether businesses, researchers, or policymakers, when it comes to the development and deployment of AI systems between now and several years from now. Its effects—by impacting where development capability, engineering skills, talent, data, and funding go—could lead to a vastly different AI world not just within the EU but globally, as other countries get AI regulation on their agendas too.

Being only a proposal at this stage, the AI Act is bound to be subject to further debate, amendments, and approval involving the European Parliament and the Council of the European Union before it becomes law. In case it is adopted, the regulation is supposed to have a transitional period of a few years before being enforced.

Summary

This chapter goes a level deeper, charting positive and negative AI imaginaries. It focuses on a primary application of LLMs in healthcare, whose use across the healthcare system holds tremendous potential for improving health outcomes and access to care. Yet this potential comes with formidable ethical challenges, which the chapter describes in full and rich detail. It fleshes out inspiring imaginaries, including physicians who are better trained, doctors who personalize delivery of healthcare, and expedited drug discovery.

The chapter touches on ethical concerns resulting from the creation of artificial realities, including the risk that LLMs might create bogus medical records or fake diagnoses, potentially leading to misdiagnosis, insurance fraud, and "infecting" critical healthcare data and information with noise. It also discusses the possible LLMs masquerading as healthcare providers that could lead to covert access to patient care, easy access to medical impersonation, and subsequent credentialing and payment fraud. Finally, it also addresses the risks of deep fakes.

Realizing that these behaviors might create risks that need to be addressed proactively, the chapter ends with a strong recommendation that LLM behavior in healthcare needs to be monitored. It underscores the importance of robust safeguards to prevent malicious use, such as thorough code review processes, strong access controls, and clear ethical requirements for developers and deployers of LLMs. Finally, it notes that public education and awareness efforts could be a key component in enabling people to recognize and report suspicious LLM healthcare use.

The chapter points to the importance of evolving ethical and privacy frameworks for the LLMs, namely that governments, industry, and open source communities have to continually work together to create regulations and best practices keeping up with the dynamic landscape of LLMs in health. Through conversations, knowledge-sharing, and collaboration to create some clear "rules of the road," we can pave a way to use these powerful technologies in an ethical manner.

To sum up, it's essential to weigh an LLM's transformative potential in the field of healthcare against the admittedly significant risks and challenges that it poses and then explicitly plan how to manage them in advance. By encouraging constructive discourse, creating stricter safeguards, and constructing ethical frameworks, we can potentially unlock LLMs' innovative potential to drive better clinical outcomes. Its use in this way can bring the world one step closer toward having a better future for all—one that is healthier and more equitable. It will take ongoing conversation, vigilance, and common cause to ensure that LLMs' use in our healthcare is in service of all that is morally good and right.

CHAPTER 7

Objects Are Closer Than They Appear

The future of large language models (LLMs) and generative AI in healthcare is akin to objects in the rearview mirror being closer than they appear. The pace of development in AI for healthcare is accelerating, and we are on the brink of transformative changes that will bring about advancements in patient care, medical practices, and healthcare at large. This chapter provides a glimpse of the potential of LLMs and generative AI for the healthcare sector. Let's start with discussing a preview of the potential of both infinite prompts and agentic reasoning.

Future Prospects and Challenges in LLMs

The path to artificial general intelligence (AGI) has been long and winding in the pioneering days of machine learning progress marked by foundational concepts, experimental algorithms, and limited computing capabilities. Mid-20th-century luminaries laid the groundwork for what would someday become a transformative technology. The emergence of transformers, LLMs, and generative AI recently led many to believe we stand at the precipice of something profound. The research and advances in LLMs continues with recent thinking and research around infinite prompts and agentic reasoning, which we introduced in Chapter 1. Let's explore both in a bit more detail and consider their potential for healthcare.

Infinite Prompts

The ability to handle infinite prompts could offer some unique advantages in healthcare, such as: contextual history, longitudinal patient monitoring, medical reasoning, personalized health coaching, and improved research.

Contextual history

An LLM with infinite context (in other words, an infinite contextual history window) should have the ability to process the entire medical history of the patient (previous diagnoses, treatments, drugs, test results, and so on). In a very literal sense, an infinite context might materialize in the form of more accurate diagnoses, more individualized treatments, and better recognition of rare and/or complex diseases, which would be difficult to spot when faced with a limited context.

In theory, with an infinite contextual history window, an LLM could process a patient's entire medical history—past diagnoses, treatments, drugs, test results, and more. This unlimited perspective could manifest in more accurate diagnoses, more fine-tuned treatment recommendations, and identification of rare or complex afflictions that could be dismissed in the face of a limited context.

Longitudinal patient monitoring

Chronic monitoring of a patient's health data for months or years and learning to detect subtle changes or trends in the data that indicate the onset or progression of disease, an LLM could detect an early indication of a disease and alert the doctor or patient taking preventive measures.

Medical reasoning

A physician, armed with an infinite prompt, might be able to consider at the same time a significant fraction of the medical literature (the guidelines and case examples for a particular illness) and so help her to reason more finely in a manner, in some common cases, for better medical decisions (e.g., a rare case, a case with multiple comorbidities, and so on).

An LLM could use an infinite prompt to take in simultaneous consideration of a large amount of the medical literature, such as guidelines and case studies on particular illnesses, to aid it in analyzing a patient's case, allowing for a more sophisticated type of medical reasoning and decision making, especially in those cases that involve multiple comorbidities or are rare.

Personalized health coaching

An LLM with an infinite contextual window could provide highly personalized health coaching and counsel. It would be sensitive to a patient's health history, lifestyle, treatment preferences, and more. Applying more efficacious behavior-change interventions could eventually result in healthier patients who more willingly and reliably comply with a treatment plan.

Improved research

Aside from expanding human knowledge by enabling new scientific studies, infinite prompts could supercharge LLMs' ability to big-data, longitudinal health studies into patterns of emergent variables hidden in the mix that are currently too tenuous to perceive in patients treated by clinicians with a limited context. Drug discovery and medical research could be accelerated in this manner.

But the same infinity in its prompting ability is probably also going to amplify many of the issues associated with their use in healthcare.

Data privacy and security requirements are much greater once a patient record comes into play.

- The bias/unfairness risk arises if the LLM trained on a much-too-large (in size and/or diversity) dataset is skewed toward a specific subset of data.
- Ethical and legal considerations will be more complicated with an LLM in possession of the entire medical electronic record of a patient.
- Infrastructural and computational provisions (scaling with prompts without limit) render an LLM inefficient or prohibitively expensive.

Although many of the healthcare applications of LLMs proposed here could likely be implemented with a much shorter prompt, at the other extreme, an infinite prompt (or at the very least, one with an enormous context window, far beyond any clinical need) might enable more accurate whole-patient analysis, more precise interventions, and eventually more advanced explorations of novel therapies and causal pathways. However, overcoming these challenges is necessary to actualize these benefits in a way that is safe, ethical, and equitable.

Agentic Reasoning

In a health-focused context, agentic reasoning and the leveraging of agents alongside LLMs could unlock a host of opportunities. Agents in this context are specialized software agents that can autonomously perform tasks, make decisions, or derive insights from patients, based on predefined goals or constraints. Here are potential applications and possible advantages of agentic reasoning and agents alongside LLMs.

Domain specialization

Agents could be specialized for specific healthcare domains (e.g., cardiology, oncology) and trained on related knowledge and best practices, with the ability to provide more directed and accurate assistance.

Domain specialization has great potential as a strategy for algorithmic agents in healthcare. Using agents oriented to specific medical domains—such as cardiology, oncology, or neurology—can create AI systems characterized by specialized knowledge of insider practices, domain-specific medical jargon, terminology and idioms, as well as an in-depth understanding of each specialty's common problems, best practices, and available treatment options. Domain specialization can offer several potential benefits.

The fact that an agent can be trained on a domain-specific dataset, on clinical guidelines, and other artifacts of expert knowledge that are relevant only to the domain in question lends it the potential to provide more accurate and relevant information, recommendations, and decision support to the important stakeholders in that domain, namely, healthcare professionals and patients.

Patient-centered interactions

Agents could be made to interact with patients in ways that are more patient-centered and empathetic by tailoring their behavior to individual patients' needs, likes and dislikes, and emotional states. Natural language understanding capabilities of the LLMs could work synergistically with the goal-directed behavior of the agents to make patient-centered interactions more effective.

Predictive health monitoring

Agents could be directed to track and analyze patient data such as vital signs, medication use, and symptoms. They can leverage LLM reasoning in conjunction with this and other biomedical data to predict adverse health conditions, transmit findings to attending physicians, and otherwise make proactive intervention recommendations.

However, there are also challenges and considerations associated with developing domain-specific agents in healthcare:

- A challenge of specialization is achieving the breadth required to handle variation in the cases within the domain. However, it might be difficult for one agent's knowledge base to cover all the cases the assistant needs to handle.

- Medical knowledge is incrementally updated with the emergence of new research results, new guidelines, and new treatment recommendations. Any answer that learns to play doctor in a modern-day medical setting will have to be continuously updated with clinically relevant information (i.e., domain-specific literature) in order to maintain accuracy and relevance.

- In the context of a particular clinical domain, there might be edge cases either due to their rarity or complexity that require additional expertise or judgment. Agents might be designed to self-detect these cases and escalate them to human domain experts to ensure patient safety and optimize care.

- Although specialized agents can turn black-box approaches into fine, focused tools of expertise, healthcare requires collaboration across domains. It will matter if they can talk and share information with people, and with agents in other domains, in constructive ways.
- The use of specialized agents in healthcare will need to address regulatory questions and FDA approval processes, as well as implications concerning liability for using AI in medical decision making.

All told, domain-specific agents in healthcare could help provide more useful, pertinent, and effective assistance to decision making, both to healthcare professionals and patients. If agents can focus on smaller, more cohesive areas of focus with specialized, focused knowledge and expertise, then they will be able to help with decision support, communication, and interaction with domain-specific tools and protocols. For this to work, complete coverage of relevant literature, current knowledge, attitude to edge cases, interactions, as well as regulatory and liability issues will be important.

AGI

Ilya Sutskever, a computer scientist and cofounder of OpenAI, says, "What we call AGI is exactly the moment when computers are at least as smart, if not smarter, than people."[1] Or more formally, in one OpenAI developer forum,[2] we find this definition: "AGI is a system that can undertake any task, regardless of intellectual complexity, that a human can undertake."

AGI is still a concept only, as we have still not created an AI anywhere close to human-level performance across the spectrum of domains. Instead, it represents the realization of some as-yet-hypothetically-future accomplishment in the field of AI. Some thought that it would occur in 2022; Elon Musk is claiming 2026; others suggest that the date is at some point prior to 2060; still others insist it will never occur.[3] Sam Altman says maybe in five years, give or take.[4] He further describes AGI as "when AI will be able to achieve novel scientific breakthroughs on its own."[5] Now, that's a

1 "The Exciting, Perilous Journey toward AGI | Ilya Sutskever | TED," TED, November 20, 2023, YouTube video, 12:24, *https://www.youtube.com/watch?v=SEkGLj0bwAU*.

2 Natanael WF, "AGI Is What We Want, but Not What We Need for Singularity," OpenAI, December 2023, *https://community.openai.com/t/agi-is-what-we-want-but-not-what-we-need-for-singularity/571275*.

3 Cem Dilmegani, "When Will Singularity Happen? 1700 Expert Opinions of AGI [2024]," AIMultiple, June 15, 2024, *https://research.aimultiple.com/artificial-general-intelligence-singularity-timing*.

4 Mike Kaput, "Sam Altman Says AI Will Handle '95%' of Marketing Work Done by Agencies and Creatives," Marketing AI Institute, March 5, 2024, *https://www.marketingaiinstitute.com/blog/sam-altman-ai-agi-marketing*.

5 See Kaput, "Sam Altman Says AI Will Handle '95%' of Marketing Work Done by Agencies and Creatives."

tall order for AI to achieve, creating a novel scientific breakthrough like Einstein's $E = mc^2$ (*https://oreil.ly/VErbr*).

One hypothesis is that human intelligence, including cognition, creativity, intuition, perception, and thought, can be reduced to computation. The assumption is that we can create computer systems that exceed human-level intelligence across various tasks with sufficient computational power, data, and architectural sophistication. The primary hypothesis is that intelligence can be broken down into algorithms and implemented in computer systems.

These assumptions are subjects of ongoing debate in philosophy, cognitive science, and AI research. Some argue that consciousness and subjective experience may not be reducible to computation. The role of embodiment in intelligence and whether a disembodied AI can truly replicate human-like intelligence is also debated. There's an ongoing discussion about whether emergent properties of biological systems, which we need to fully understand, play a crucial role in intelligence that may not be replicable in artificial systems.

However, how much of the genuine richness and depth of human experience this kind of computational description can accommodate remains very much an open question. There's a long and winding way to go in terms of achieving anything resembling AGI, but it is made dramatically shorter and more managed by the premise that minds, whatever they are, cannot be magical but are necessarily algorithmic. It's a provocative and controversial hypothesis.

Since there is no definite agenda, no discernible markers of progress toward AGI, and hence no positive or reliable means of knowing if AGI technology is developing in any meaningful sense, even the possibility of finding out is unknown. No one can ever know when technology might potentially achieve human-level or transhuman intelligence, or if it can become a vehicle for machine superintelligence. This situation could persist precisely because we are constantly moving between the realms of scientific theory and speculative opinion, so AGI's status could never be fully resolved or even in any clear sense "known."

Setting that aside, though, what might the world of healthcare look like if we did develop AGI? I want to stipulate that there are many complex social issues surrounding healthcare, and perhaps some of them are insurmountable. But suppose that AGI is achieved soon, and machines can do anything an individual human could do intellectually to achieve an outcome—they can reason, learn, and iteratively adapt in any domain. With one big hypothesis, here's what healthcare might look like in a world with AGI.

Personalized and predictive medicine

If given access to vast troves of health and genomic data concerning past patients, as well as continually collected, real-time health metrics for present patients, AGI systems might have the power to create finely tailored treatment regimens for individuals, and even zero in on potential health issues before they arise, allowing for more effective prevention.

Cognitive diagnostic aids

An AGI may be able to assist physicians in making rapid and accurate diagnoses by processing and integrating data from medical imaging, laboratory results, and a patient's self-reported symptoms. Such a tool could reduce diagnostic mistakes, diagnose rare diseases, and speed up the diagnostic process.

Robotic surgery

"Cookbook" surgery of the present day will yield to autonomous robotically assisted procedures performed with unprecedented precision, dexterity, and adaptability (requiring new capabilities in the surgeon's training). These procedures could be done in autonomous mode or working cooperatively with a human surgeon.

Continuous health monitoring and intervention

AGI-based systems could provide continuous health monitoring for patients, using wearable devices and/or implanted sensors via smart phones and smart homes as well. With this continuous monitoring, AGI could provide early warnings and initiate automated interventions (e.g., adjusting dosages of medications based on continuous responses, or issuing alerts, as needed).

Improving drug discovery and development

AGI could also boost productivity in pharma by speeding up drug-discovery and development pipelines. By leveraging big biological and chemical data, an AGI could help discover novel drug targets, predict interactions between new drugs and components in biological systems, and explore new ways of designing drugs to improve specificity. These systems could expedite the development of safer and more effective new drugs.

Improved telemedicine and virtual care

For patients, AGI-powered virtual assistants and telemedicine platforms could enable effective, personalized on-demand access to healthcare services 24/7. These systems could triage patient concerns, offer medical advice, and recommend patients to the appropriate healthcare resource, increasing access to care and reducing downstream pressure on healthcare facilities.

Savvy resource allocation and logistics

AGI might help to intelligently distribute healthcare resources (hospital beds, ventilators, staffing, and so on) based on patient needs and current demand, and improve the efficiency of medical supply chains, ensuring rapid distribution of medications, vaccines, and other necessities.

Simulation-based training and education

Medical simulations driven by AGI would allow for the development of highly realistic and adaptive training environments across a wide spectrum of surgical scenarios, simulating malfunctions and risk conditions in ways that complement and enhance experiential learning processes in the classroom.

Global health cooperation and information-sharing

The provision of information by AGI could allow seamless collaboration and information-sharing between clinicians and researchers from different parts of the world, enabling them to work together to identify trends in global health and inform public health policy while disseminating best practices.

Ethical and accessible healthcare

AGI could help ensure that healthcare is more equitable by helping to identify and correct bias in treatment decisions and allocation decisions, and developing culturally sensitive and accessible medical interventions—all of this in real time.

This means that AGI would be constantly learning. Healthcare systems would get better and better, as every case could inform treatments and protocols in the future. The system could automatically update its information base on biological processes and human disorders with the latest medical research and patient data, and make itself evolve in real time. Treatments would be routinely readjusted, in response to latest emerging evidence and patient outcomes. AGI would optimize healthcare systems, improving efficiency, reducing costs, and enhancing patient experiences.

While the prospects of improving healthcare and the well-being in society at large with the assistance of AGI are real, the presence of these AI entities would introduce a host of new and pressing ethical, legal, and social issues, and the safe handling and governance of such advanced technologies in human healthcare and decision making will be of utmost importance.

Similarly, burgeoning autonomous systems in healthcare will need to prepare in advance for intensive multidisciplinary engagement between researchers, clinicians, policymakers, and the public to ensure that AGI-based technologies are properly developed to match societal needs and values.

Taken together, an AGI-augmented healthcare industry would realize the promise of a truly real-time, holistic, personalized, predictive care environment, embracing the vast array of health information and turning it into truly accessible, useful data for healthcare delivery. Such a healthcare system would be far more efficient, personalized, and thus far more likely to deliver optimal medical outcomes.

The role of healthcare providers in this system could be very different, as more routine and menial tasks are automated, while providers focus on more diagnosis, interpretation, and integration of complex data and exceptional human care. Individual health outcomes would likely be improved, public health outcomes and medical research would advance more rapidly and lead to further breakthroughs, and we could expect to become a healthier society in so many ways.

Whispers of Tomorrow: Five Predictions

What follows are five predictions of the future, which may well be realized within the next five years. These are possible without AGI: they can be achieved using LLMs, infinite prompts, agentic reasoning, spatial reasoning, and AI embodiment.

AI Calls the Shots

For instance, an AI chief medical officer might need a new medical device, and so she gives a task set to her AI:

- The AI would research the market to identify unmet needs and opportunities.
- Medical devices to exploit these needs and opportunities will be invented by the AI.
- The AI would contact manufacturers for medical device production quotes.
- The AI would negotiate prices and terms with the manufacturers.
- The AI would place orders with the manufacturers and track the production process.
- AI will arrange to deliver the medical devices to customers.
- The AI would collect revenue from customers.

So the AI would still have many things it couldn't complete as part of its mandate, because humans would still exist somewhere in the loop. However, the AGI could interface with other AIs by talking to them, and invoke APIs to get access to many different knowledge sources (e.g., databases or various websites, etc.) for many different tasks.

In fetching additional information from available knowledge sources, many functions could be automated within a directed APIs, like driving many functions needed to get the new medical device through clinical trials toward regulatory approval. AGI would free up a lot of humans to be able to do the work of thinking about more complex tasks.

If an AGI were to design and generate a new medical device, then we should accept that it also had a hand in manufacturing it, to the same extent that we would accept the same claim if it were made about a human intelligent agent. This includes:

Innovation
> The AI system was conceived of (with human assistance) and engineered with an independence from a preexisting template, demonstrating an ability to think creatively and originate a novel solution to a health need.

Disruption
> AI-driven innovations that can explore more of the design space than a human team.

Augmenting
> Medical device innovations that enhance capabilities of existing systems and procedures.

Scientifically rigorous
> The AI probably relied on large amounts of data, modeling, simulation and testing to demonstrate that the apparatus is safe and effective.

Transformative
> AGI could radically accelerate breakthroughs in health innovation and discovery through medical technology.

Paradigm shift
> AGI's invention of new medical devices changes the landscape of who/what can be scientific participants.

A human autonomously performing this task might be a powerful, innovative, disruptive, and potentially transformative demonstration of human capabilities—whether individually or in collaboration with others—alongside the accompanying ethical considerations regarding the changing (or lack of changing) conduct in science and technology by agents receiving information from humans derived in this way. The rules must be carefully considered and debated, regulating whether or how any autonomous AI might create an invention. But the possibilities, assuming such creations are directed by human values, are intriguing.

Medi-Sphere Personalized Orb

This silvery ball fits easily into the palm of your hand. With this AI assistant as your companion, you can talk to an AI with human-like intelligence based on the latest LLM architecture. It understands natural language and answers questions on everything under the sun.

Question it about science, philosophy, or how to make bouillabaisse, and the Orb will perceive your best course of action and communicate it in expert terms. Drawing on its vast knowledge and reasoning abilities, the AI can contribute informed analyses to any of your personal situations. You see it as a sage, full of knowledge and insight, always at your fingertips.

Exquisitely calibrated to integrate with smart home appliances, if your refrigerator is bare, the Orb can generate recipe ideas, have groceries shipped over, and turn on the oven for cooking. Given its full capability in all kinds of communicative modes and nearly unbounded capacity, Medi-Sphere Personalized Orb makes the sophisticated proposition that all knowledge and capabilities of the world become available in the palm of your hand.

An embedded device—an interactive spherical device—is used by the patient as a healthcare/health management assistant at home, hospital, or care facilities. It has contextual understanding of plain text conversations, provides language translation, and supports question and answer.

It incorporates advanced or large language models utilizing natural language processing that allow for conversational interactions via natural language when discussing symptoms or asking medical questions. Medi-Sphere can also provide personalized health tracking, drug management, lifestyle coaching, and more.

The AI within Medi-Sphere would have unrestricted access to current medical research and could provide patients with individualized health optimization recommendations. It could, for example, recommend dietary and exercise habits as well as train patients for mental health.

The orb monitors vital signs at all times, vigilantly monitoring for medical emergencies. It can summon help and provide first-aid instructions until the help arrives. Its ability to perform a triage exam, provide counseling, or provide emergent treatment are three of its primary roles in becoming a protective healthcare presence watching over you, using AI to provide around-the-clock care delivery.

Health Avatar: Personal AI Health Assistant

Health Avatar creates your "digital twin," a digital replica of you, built with generative AI from your medical records, lifestyle data, genetic makeup, and laboratory tests to provide a high-resolution visualization of your own body, including its unique features.

The app allows you and your digital twin to have a conversation by leveraging conversational interfaces facilitated by LLMs. Ask about your risks for any health condition highlighted by your digital twin, and the digital twin can generate tailored risk assessments by running scenarios using its state-of-the-art model of your body.

Your behaviors and symptoms are tracked in real time with wearables and logs. Health Avatar updates your digital twin regularly, alerting you of information that warrants a follow-up with your doctor. The AI assistant fields questions regarding health matters, explains lab reports, gets you ready for medical appointments, and makes several evidence-based lifestyle recommendations.

Superior simulation tools afford you the option of trying out the impact of diet, exercise, and other interventions before making them for your body in the "real" world. Meanwhile, HealthPal enables you to see the success of your efforts by monitoring its effect in the digital skin of your avatar. HealthPal puts an intelligent assistive agent and a clone of your very own body right in your pocket, complete with the benefit of an intimate deep-scanning, machine-learning view of your personal health record.

Virtual Nurse Avatar

This avatar is a three-dimensional animated visual model of a compassionate human nurse, created using advanced generative art techniques to make it appealing and trustworthy. A patient interacts with the avatar through conversational speech and gestures. The avatar employs multimodal AI to converse in a human-sounding manner, read nonverbal cues presented by the patient, and show empathy.

The AI nurse, powered by an LLM, can answer patient questions, explain treatment plans, provide education, and provide encouragement. It can query the latest medical knowledge via many integrations with an LLM. It can track vital signs, medication adherence, and clinical progress. It is also able to watch for side effects, and send alerts to a human care team when changes or problems arise. It can process these queries and observations.

Personalization algorithms maintain models of the patient's health history, preferences, and psychology so as to personalize the interactions and maintain continuity of care. For some patients with rehabilitation and coordination needs, the virtual nurse could teach exercises, reminders about medications, and upcoming appointments. In emergencies, the AI could stay on the line with the patient, giving instructions to neutralize emergencies while calling 911 and waiting with the patient for emergency assistance.

The virtual nurse accompanies patients during their stay, chatting with them, joking with them, keeping their brains busy, steering their conversations toward healthy coping, and providing them with interaction. Access to patient data is broad, but every bit of information is secure and shared only with the patient's consent and with the care team (activity logs can be accessed and are useful for supervising and refining models as the new technology evolves).

In summary, a virtual AI nurse combines the response-focused human qualities of nursing with the knowledge and responsiveness of AI. The result is a humanist AI nurse that provides patients with emotional, educational, and safety monitoring support around the clock.

The Rise of AI/LLM-Driven Applications

By the 2030s or sooner, the ubiquity of powerful LLMs and generative AI changed software development as fundamentally as client-server, the internet, cloud computing, and mobile previously did. While app development in languages like Python and Java will continue, the vast majority of coding will shift to a new paradigm. Developers will primarily engage in natural language conversations with AI helpers. They will describe their desired applications in plain English, including specifications for data models and user interfaces. For each conversation, a sophisticated AI generator will synthesize a complete full-stack implementation, including:

- Source code
- Databases
- APIs
- Web/mobile frontends
- DevOps configurations

This transformation will streamline the development process, making it more accessible and efficient.

Developer productivity is supercharged. Instead of writing thousands of lines of code to craft robust applications from scratch, developers can leverage their human creativity and domain knowledge to follow AI's pace of innovation. They can train AI models using past applications to teach systems what works and what doesn't. Developers can devote themselves to building rich and innovative user experiences since creating complete front- and backends is quick and easy for AI. New application prototypes that once required months to build can now be cranked out in just a few days. Startups are upending industries by iterating MVPs at unprecedented speeds.

The Conversational Interface is created instead of menu-based apps; the LLM frontend talks to the app and acts like a client to users in natural dialogue; the LLM comprehends the request and manages its execution. Modular code is created and generators are the entities that create modules: they can create databases, frontend APIs, UIs, and other modules, including cloud structure. This is all orchestrated using LLMs.

Embedded agency becomes the rule, with apps featuring generative AI subcomponents that tweak their programming as needed, autonomously self-optimizing like a robust neural network.

Automated testing and debugging follow as a result of LLMs detecting code patterns to generate unit tests. Bugs and weaknesses are similarly detected automatically and remediated by generative models. Testing and maintenance activities are also automated as AI continuously monitors and enhances generated applications such that the AI alerts the developer to a potential bug or antipatterns in the generated code, pointing them toward already proven solutions, in the form of conversations when necessary. Eventually, applications become more secure, scalable, and efficient.

The specialist developers will continue to have to be supervised and must fulfill certain requirements, but a great deal of the labor of software development is taken over by generative AI, such that the developers are able to devote a great deal more time to higher-order design and creative problem solving. Democratization means a proliferation of new apps and experiences. This is one possible scenario for the future that resembles the productivity bursts facilitated by earlier computing revolutions. LLMs and generative AI can enable a similar leap forward for software development.

Summary

AI is not an autonomous technology—it does not automatically emerge from algorithms or LLMs. Human capabilities don't just install themselves into algorithms; they require human design and intent. If AGI enters the world, it will be through human-wrought design and engineering.

AGI is a capacity that machines might someday possess. It remains elusive; we have not yet achieved AGI; whether or when it is possible remains the subject of considerable debate. In short, if it ever comes to pass, AGI will be a product of human design and engineering rather than a process that "autonomously" emerges from an algorithm or model presently considered cutting-edge within AI research.

AI systems will continue to develop more human-like capabilities. This means it would be important to keep human control and oversight—and the ability to intervene and/or shut down the system—at all times. The development of responsible AI has to keep it that way.

LLMs and generative AI could make patient care and the practice of medicine better in novel and powerful ways. In fact, tools that are leveraging the capabilities of LLMs will soon become friendly consultants that can understand the details of the patient's condition from detailed clinical conversations, answer questions, and offer supportive counseling tailored to individual patients.

Generative AI systems will be a doctor's 24/7 "curbside doctor," rapidly synthesizing valuable inferences from millions of cases into nuanced diagnostics and therapeutics that can be tailored to every patient's profile, thereby informing better care choices and outcomes. Eventually, integrated teams of human doctors and AI will become part of an ecosystem that is increasingly humane, authentic, and personalized: they will mutually amplify each other's strengths, deliver more information, and provide agency to patients so they can better benefit from therapeutic care and participate in self-managing their lifestyles for better health, function, and longevity.

Over the coming years, this blending of medical know-how, AI, and empathetic human support will take an increasing burden off clinicians' shoulders while transforming patient interactions and enhancing treatment efficacy. This is a new era of ever more anticipatory, predictive, and preventive care for all.

Finally, we end on a humorous note (see Figure 7-1).

Figure 7-1. Pet rats, Yin Yang and Curious

The rats' names illustrate the possibilities of LLMs, the Yin Yang and the Curious. The public's interactions with LLM chatbots has sparked a tremendous curiosity in AI and its potential. In traditional Chinese medicine, yin and yang energies are at the core of all healing. LLMs used in healthcare hope to create a healthy balance of good health, a yin and a yang.

With their natural language processing and machine learning capabilities, LLMs can quickly scan through thousands of medical papers, clinical guidelines, and patient records to help doctors and researchers keep ahead of the latest findings, detect meaningful patterns and insights that may escape human eyes, and make fair and evidence-based decisions.

We hope this book will leave you with a nuanced understanding of LLM's and generative AI's potential, the transformative role that LLM and generative AI tools will play in transforming healthcare, treatment, and care. We also hope that it has convinced you of the critical importance of building a solid knowledge base and striving for accuracy in claims about the benefits and risks of collaborating with LLMs.

This is a rapidly moving field, and the ability to learn about new developments is going to be important in making the most of AI in medicine. As AI plays a larger role in healthcare, it is important to advocate for its ethical development and use, and to increase awareness about bias, privacy, and transparency with respect to LLMs.

AI has the potential to be a great unifier in healthcare, but only if we harness these opportunities to help different disciplines work together. Endorse work from a diverse range of professionals—seek out clinicians, researchers, engineers, ethicists, and more—so that we can create a future that offers redoubled benefits from the use of AI.

Finally, the conclusion to leave the reader with is to let AI be an amplifier—part of what creates a healthier world for all. The future of healthcare is not being written by AI but rather by every human being who is part of the process today. Let's codesign the AI future to be more human and open, a future filled with hope and healing.

Index

healthcare ML stuck in past, 71
    generative AI creating artificial data, 72
    promise of LLMs, 72
misinterpretation and inaccuracy avoidance, 15
transformers in LLM anatomy, 45
    attention mechanism, 46, 47
    tokenization, 46
transparency
    EU AI Act requirements, 173
    explainable AI, 168
    misinterpretation and inaccuracy avoidance, 15
tumor detected with deep learning, 41-43

U

unsupervised machine learning, 41
UpToDate app, 14

V

vaccination misinformation ethical oversight, 153-155
Vaezy, Sara, 73
virtual consultation via AI, 106-108
virtual nurse avatar, 186

W

wearable medical devices
    currently in use, 8
    Fitbit signaling AFib, 14
    remote patient monitoring, 112
weight parameter, 49
wizards, 95

X

XAI (explainable AI), 168

About the Authors

Kerrie Holley's illustrious career in technology spans from the era of punch cards to today's AI-driven landscape. He has been a pioneering leader through every major computing paradigm: mainframe, client-server, internet, mobile, cloud, and now AI with LLMs and generative AI. In recognition of his sustained contributions to the engineering profession, Kerrie was inducted into the National Academy of Engineering in 2023.

As IBM's first Black Distinguished Engineer and later an IBM Fellow, Kerrie broke barriers and set new standards in the tech industry. His executive roles include positions as a Google tech executive, VP, and CTO at Cisco. He serves on multiple boards, has authored books, delivered tech talks, and provides expert consultation.

In healthcare technology, Kerrie led the development of a high-performance engineering team for one of the largest US healthcare companies. This diverse team of software engineers, PhDs, scientists, AI specialists, data scientists, and DevOps engineers focused on incubating and applying cutting-edge technologies to transform healthcare delivery and outcomes.

Kerrie's work continues to shape the intersection of technology and healthcare, driving innovation and improving lives through advanced computing solutions.

Manish Mathur is a seasoned professional with over 25 years of experience in the intersection of healthcare and technology. In his most recent role as a senior principal architect at Google, he advises payers, providers, and life sciences customers on how to leverage Google's state-of-the-art AI technologies to solve their complex business problems and build new business models.

Prior to joining Google, Manish was with Johnson & Johnson, where he led a global team of data, analytics, and AI professionals. Their collective efforts were dedicated to tackling intricate obstacles pertaining to drug discovery and commercialization, challenges that are commonly encountered by prominent pharmaceutical corporations on a global scale.

At Walgreens, Manish spearheaded the creation of a sophisticated technological solution aimed at seamlessly integrating healthcare management within the accessible and convenient framework of retail environments. Manish's earlier professional experiences encompass significant roles at institutions such as HCSC, American Medical Association, and Deloitte Consulting.

A respected authority in healthcare technology, Manish has contributed extensively to the field through numerous publications. He regularly shares his insights as a speaker at industry events and holds memberships in various professional organizations. Additionally, Manish serves on advisory boards for multiple startups.

His passion lies in harnessing technology to enhance healthcare quality, and he remains dedicated to guiding organizations in leveraging AI to address their critical challenges.

Manish received his bachelor's degree in electrical engineering from Jadavpur University, Kolkotta, his master's degree in international business from Delhi School of Economics in India, and his MBA from the University of Hartford, Connecticut. In his spare time, Manish enjoys spending time with his family and friends, traveling, and playing golf.

Colophon

The animal on the cover of *LLMs and Generative AI for Healthcare* is a great green macaw (*Ara ambiguus*). Known for its emerald plumage, long tail, and powerful beak, the great green macaw is one of the most recognizable parrot species in the world.

Great green macaws are one of the world's largest parrots, averaging 33.5 to 35.5 inches in length and weighing close to 3 pounds. They are easily identified by their green feathers, reddish forehead, and pale blue lower back. Great green macaws live in the humid lowland forests and forest edges of Central and South America. They are highly intelligent and social parrots; it is common to find a family of five to six birds nested inside tree cavities. They also forage together in large numbers (up to 50 individuals) and may travel long distances in search for food, which mostly consists of seeds, fruits, nuts, and flowers.

Sadly, great green macaws are a critically endangered species, with a population of less than 2,500 individuals. Due to their attractive appearance, the pet trade has become a major problem for these birds, and they are often killed for their feathers or shot by farmers, who view them as pests. Extensive habitat destruction has also led to their dwindling population.

Many of the animals on O'Reilly covers are endangered; all of them are important to the world.

The cover illustration is by Karen Montgomery, based on an antique line engraving from *Cassell's Natural History*. The series design is by Edie Freedman, Ellie Volckhausen, and Karen Montgomery. The cover fonts are Gilroy Semibold and Guardian Sans. The text font is Adobe Minion Pro; the heading font is Adobe Myriad Condensed; and the code font is Dalton Maag's Ubuntu Mono.

www.ingramcontent.com/pod-product-compliance
Lightning Source LLC
Jackson TN
JSHW052007131224
75386JS00036B/1219